D0199668

Letter to Pilgrims

The Seattle School
2510 Elliott Ave.
Seattle, WA 98121
theseattleschool.edu

WITHDRAWN

The Seattle School
10028417

Letter to Pilgrims

A COMMENTARY ON THE EPISTLE TO THE HEBREWS

ROBERT JEWETT

THE PILGRIM PRESS
NEW YORK

Copyright © 1981 The Pilgrim Press
All rights reserved

No part of this publication may be reproduced, stored in a retrieval system, or transmitted in any form or by any means, electronic, mechanical, photo-copying, recording, or otherwise (brief quotations used in magazines or news-paper reviews excepted), without the prior permission of the publisher.

Library of Congress Cataloging in Publication Data

Jewett, Robert.
    Letter to Pilgrims.

    Bibliography: p. 243
    1. Bible. N.T. Hebrews—Commentaries.   I. Title.
B32775.3.J48   227'.87077   80-28102
ISBN 0-8298-0425-0 (pbk.)

The author has translated the Epistle to the Hebrews from the Greek, and, beginning with chapter One, quotations from Hebrews, unless otherwise indicated, are from his translation. Other biblical quotations are, unless otherwise indicated, from the *Revised Standard Version of the Bible*, copyright 1946, 1952 and © 1971 by the Division of Christian Education, National Council of Churches and are used by permission. The excerpt from *The New English Bible*, is © The Delegates of the Oxford University Press and the Syndics of the Cambridge University Press, 1961, 1970. Reprinted by permission.

The Pilgrim Press, 132 West 31 Street, New York, New York 10001

To my parents, Walter and Elizabeth Jewett

Contents

Introduction

This commentary is the culmination of several decades of work on the Epistle to the Hebrews and the pilgrim theme in American culture. A University of Chicago dissertation on "The Conception of Worship in the Epistle to the Hebrews" was completed in 1958, and serious reflection on the idea of pilgrimage as a model for faith began around 1970. Carrol McLaughlin, a colleague who specializes in theology and American literature, has collaborated with me from the start in this exploration, and is joining me in writing two additional volumes on "The American Pilgrimage" and "The Planetary Pilgrimage," relating the provocative themes from Hebrews to literary works, studies of the anthropology of pilgrimage, and observations on civil religion. We are convinced that Hebrews' acceptance of adversity and rapid change, its conception of faith as a pilgrimage through insecurity, and its sense of dialogical fulfillment along the pilgrim path correspond with some of the most profound treatments of the American experience, and offer a significant resource for this era of planetary malaise.

In biblical thought, as well as in our cultural tradition, there are two basic forms of pilgrimage: one arrives at lasting cities and heavenly homelands, and the other confesses moment for moment, "Here we have no lasting city, but we seek one which is to come." The idea of pilgrimage that one finds in Chaucer's *Canterbury Tales* and in Twain's *Huckleberry Finn* stands close to that in Hebrews, because it never really arrives at its destination. Its fulfillment comes along the way in alehouses and on rafts, where fellowship is experienced and truth is shared. Abraham, the great model

1

of faith in Hebrews 11, remains a "sojourner" even after reaching the "promised land." Like Huck, who cannot remain in the secure confines of St. Petersburg, and Chaucer's pilgrims, who never reach the sacred shrine at Canterbury, the faithful pilgrim in Hebrews seeks "a better country" and finds "rest" in responding "today" to the word of God.

This commentary is written, therefore, with the conviction recently stated by William G. Johnsson, that "the recognition of the pilgrimage motif in Hebrews opens up a holistic view of the document." My goal is to set forth the relevance of the pilgrim faith for the original audience of the letter to the Hebrews, and thereby to suggest its possible bearing on the modern situation. I view Hebrews as a coherent and pentrating argument about the nature of the Christian journey through a threatening world. Despite the strange metaphors of priesthoods, cults, and angels, requiring leaps of imagination to discern their modern counterparts, the approach of Hebrews is well suited for our era. I hope to enable readers to assess this relevance for themselves. The translation I provide is designed for literal accuracy, which means that it is less elegant than the Greek original. So far as the exact sense of the text allows, I avoid the use of sexist language, rendering, for example, *anthropos* as "person" rather than as "man." The standard I seek to follow in my own exposition stands in tension at times with the task of faithful translation, but even here the pilgrim ethos encourages a movement to new standards, while remaining open to the "cloud of witnesses" who have used different terminology.

1. The dilemma of Hebrews and the promise of audience criticism. Although the Epistle to the Hebrews is ranked the most sophisticated writing in the New Testament in terms of literary style and organization, and although it contains many eloquent texts for sermonizing, its argument, as a whole, has never played a decisive role for the Christian community. A glance at representative commentaries reveals the difficulty in gaining an overview or even a sense of what the argument is all about. The dilemmas of interpreting this writing are formidable: its author is unknown, and its title stands a fair chance of being secondary; whether it is a homily or a letter is uncertain; historical references are skimpy and vague; its combination of apocalypticism and a mild form of Philonian philosophy seems contradictory; and its discussion of cultic ceremonies, Melchizedekian priest-hoods, eternal covenants, and the adoration of angels seems arcane.

All these puzzles would be solvable if we knew precisely what the historical situation was that called forth this writing. It is a fair assumption that each detail in a brilliantly written piece like this had a very precise significance for its original readers or hearers. But in view of the tenuous evidence and scholarly prudence, most com-mentaries on the Epistle to the Hebrews suggest a tentative solution to the audience question and then proceed with an exegesis that is largely untouched by it. Hugh Montefiore, for example, writes his commentary without specific reference to his audience and authorship hypothesis "in the hope that it may be of use to those for whom there is as yet no convincing solution to the difficult problems which this Epistle poses." This is a sane and fair-minded procedure, but it has a serious drawback: it results in exegetical generality. The thrust of Hebrews' argument is deflected and dulled, robbed of all specificity. In fact, it is safe to say that Hebrews commentaries, as a class, have one characteristic in common: they lack punch. Although they often contain solid scholarship, they rarely succeed in bringing the message of this mysterious letter to life.

The application of the method of audience criticism could break this impasse. If one were to select an audience hypothesis that seems most plausible and then take the imaginative leap of perceiving each verse as directly related to that situation, the fire of the argument might ignite, and the sparks could easily leap across time to the modern situation. This procedure is admittedly a risky one, because there is little likelihood of fully demonstrating ahead of time the plausibility of one's audience reconstruction. To a considerable degree the proof must lie in the verse-by-verse commentary, but this kind of proof is open to the charge of circularity: finding confirmed in the text what one has already inferred from it to reconstruct the audience hypothesis. I have come to the conclusion, however, that such risks are worth taking, and indeed, that they are inevitable if one wishes to penetrate the dialogue between an ancient writer and the writer's audience. If one has to make a case on the basis of hearing only one half of a telephone conversation, so to speak, then let it be done as extensively and accurately as possible, so that readers can assess whether the "other side" has been plausibly reconstructed on the basis of clues in the partner's voice.

This commentary presents an experimental approach to the author-audience relationship, which is rare enough in scholarly monographs and practically unheard of in popular ones. I summarize below the audience hypothesis that is presupposed throughout the commentary. The commentary can be viewed as an experimental testing ground for the audience reconstruction. Those interested in historical and methodological issues can make their judgment as to whether it results in a believable and coherent interpretation of the text. But a word of caution is needed for my readers who have less than a burning interest in such exegetical complexities. The audience hypothesis remains just that—a hypothesis. It should not be confused with historical fact, even though each chapter and verse of Hebrews is interpreted as if it were real. The detailed reconstruction of the lost half of the telephone conversation, so to speak, is necessary from an experimental perspective and is essential, in some form, for understanding what is going on in Hebrews. But you should take what follows with your natural caution: my audience theory may sound plausible, but it is certainly not the only one possible, and it may be dead wrong. Even here the spirit of pilgrimage ought to prevail: our task is open-ended and uncertain but engrossing and, I hope, productive.

2. *The audience and author hypothesis.* In searching for parallels to the argument and situation of Hebrews, the attention of scholars has occasionally been drawn to Paul's letter to the Colossians. Erich Grässer's account of the research reports that Perdelwitz, Weinel, and others from 1910 onward suggested that a Jewish Christian gnosticism similar to that reflected in Colossians is being countered in Hebrews. F.D.V. Narborough's commentary of 1930 tentatively related Hebrews to the area of the Lycus Valley where Colossal was located, and a few years later Günther Bornkamm noted the antignostic thrust of Hebrews' teaching about the angels, which seems similar to the thrust of Colossians 2:18. Then in 1949, T.W. Manson argued that in Colossians, as in Hebrews, a type of Jewish theosophic speculation was being countered. He noted the similarities in argument between Hebrews and Colossians, particularly in the matters of Christ's superiority to the angelic forces and the esoteric food regulations mentioned in Colossians 2:16 and Hebrews 13:9. His conclusion is that Hebrews is the "Epistle of Apollos to the churches of the Lycus Valley." Having worked with these details rather intensively, I have become convinced that at least the location and setting implied in this summary are the most plausible and fruitful alternatives to pursue.

The close parallels between Hebrews and Colossians that have been brought to light include a number of details that scholars reconstructing the Colossian situation consider crucial. In Colossians 2:16, for example, the author urges the Colossians not to let anyone criticize them in relation to foods. Hebrews 13:9 urges similarly that the audience not be "led away by diverse and strange teachings" about foods. In Colossians 2:20–23 there is a polemic against regulations concerning tasting and touching that were designed for the "self-abasement" of the body. In Hebrews 9:10 there is a similarly sarcastic reference to rules about "food and drink and various ablutions, regulations for the body" that are now outmoded. In Colossians 2:16 there is a warning about those who would "pass judgment on you" with regard to cultic festivals, while in Hebrews 9:1–28 there is an extensive discussion of cultic activities eliminated by Christ. Colossians 2:18 urges the congregation to "let no one disqualify" them by insisting on the "worship of angels," and Hebrews 1:4— 2:16 argues extensively that angels are inferior to Christ and that their purpose is to serve humankind rather than to be worshiped. Whereas Colossians 2:15 insists that Christ disarmed the angelic "principalities and powers," Hebrews 2:14 argues that Christ destroyed "the devil," and there are repeated references to cosmic "enemies" that have been placed under Christ's feet (1:13; 2:8).

Some of the most striking parallels relate to the position and role of Christ in relation to the rest of the created order. Colossians 1:15 celebrates Christ as the "image of the invisible God, the first-born of all creation." Similarly, Hebrews 1:3 claims Christ "bears the very stamp" of the divine nature and 1:6 refers to him as the "first-born." Colossians 1:16 insists that the entire created order, including cosmic powers, "were created through him and for him," while Hebrews 1:2 states that Christ created the aeons, that he is the one "for whom and by whom all things exist [2:10]." Colossians 1:17 claims that Christ is the principle of coherence in the universe, that "in him all things hold together," while Hebrews 1:3 celebrates him as the one who upholds "the universe by his word of power." Perhaps the most extensive parallel of all is to Colossians 1:18, that Christ is "preeminent" in everything. Hebrews 1:4—2:9 argues in detail that Christ is superior to the cosmic angels.

These parallels gain significance from the fact that the details in Colossians are important indications of a unique Jewish-Gnostic heresy prevalent in the Lycus Valley. Bornkamm made a case that the Colossian Gnostics urged obedience to the demands of the angelic powers in order that believers might participate in the divine power of the universe. He suggested that they identified these forces as portions of the gigantic body of Christ that makes up the universe, and that they hoped for apotheosis as divine aeons through esoteric practices and knowledge. Ernst Käsemann concluded that the Colossian heretics valued the angelic powers as guarantors of world order and as forces to be mollified in order to avoid evil destiny. Through ascetic practices and holy celebrations these demonic and angelic forces could be manipulated. He notes the importance of Colossians' argument about the sole rule of Christ, which serves to eliminate such a demonization of the universe. Hence the key argument in Colossians, as in Hebrews, is that Christ has overcome the elemental forces of the universe. Hans Martin Schenke insists that the Colossian Gnostics had a negative view of these forces, offering them ascetic worship because they hindered the ascent of believers through cosmic spheres to the spiritual homeland. Thus, the depotentializing of the cosmic forces through Christ is the key to Colossians' attack against this gnostic system. The recent commentary by Eduard Schweizer makes extensive use of such insights, interpreting Colossians as an answer to Christian speculation that borrowed philosophical concepts from the Pythagoreans and adapted esoteric ceremonies from the mystery religions and the Old Testament.

The parallels between Hebrews and Colossians raise the possibility that they were written by different authors to the same situation at approximately the same time. A series of articles by Charles P. Anderson brings other evidence to bear on this possibility, opening the way to one of the most intriguing breakthroughs in recent biblical scholarship. On the basis of the early inclusion of Hebrews into the collection of Pauline letters, Anderson showed that it was probably associated with the Pauline churches. In a second article, published in 1966, Anderson takes up the question of identifying the Laodicean letter mentioned in Colossians 4:16. He observes that Paul assumes this letter will arrive about the same time as the Colossian letter, and that it is assumed to be relevant to the Lycus Valley situation. Although Paul is certain enough of the contents to recommend it, it is apparent from his reference that he did not write the Laodicean letter. At this point Anderson makes a suggestion about the authorship of the letter which, in my judgment, is the most plausible yet made: The person who missionized the Lycus Valley, according to Colossians 1:6f. and 4:13, was Epaphras, who has apparently informed Paul about the situation there (Colossians 1:8). He is in prison with Paul (cf. Philemon 23), and thus is unable to fulfill his pastoral responsibilities to the troubled church except by means of a letter. The most likely author of the Laodicean letter would therefore be Epaphras.

In the following year, in his final article on the Lycus Valley problem, Anderson assembled the pieces of the puzzle, arguing that the lost Laodicean letter, written by Epaphras, is in fact what we call the Epistle to the Hebrews. His argument is that the early association of Hebrews with the other Pauline letters derived from the memory that it was written by Paul's circle and carried his authority. Anderson showed that the close association of Colossians and the Laodicean letter, as well as the reference to the latter in Colossians 4:14, make it likely that the church would have preserved both. The content of Hebrews is close enough to Colossians to fit the situation of the neighboring churches of Laodicea and Colossal in the Lycus Valley. Finally, the request in Hebrews 13:18f. for prayerful assistance in behalf of the author and his companions, combined with the hope that the author alone would be able to return to the congregation, correlates well with the situation of Epaphras imprisoned with Paul. Anderson's article does not develop what could be the strongest proof for his hypothesis, namely, detailed analysis of the similarities in argument and audience situation between Hebrews and Colossians.

One detail in Anderson's final article deserves to be developed more fully. The author of Colossians describes in 4:12 what the founding missionary, Epaphras, desires for the

Lycus Valley congregations: "Epaphras, who is one of your-
selves, a servant of Christ Jesus, greets you, always remem-
bering you earnestly in his prayers, that you may stand mature
and fully assured in all the will of God." Anderson observes
that Epaphras' desire seems similar to the exhortation in
Hebrews 10:23 that the congregation "hold fast the confession
of our hope without wavering." He concludes that "Epaphras is
described by Paul as being especially concerned that the Lycus
Valley Christians attain the maturity necessary to carry them
through their present crisis. How better can we characterize the
author of Hebrews?" I believe that Anderson's statement can be
decisively strengthened by observing that the two key terms
describing what Epaphras desires for his churches play a major
role in the argument of Hebrews.

"Maturity" is the first quality that Epaphras seeks, and
nothing could be more central as far as the argument of
Hebrews is concerned. The author of Hebrews develops an
elaborate doctrine of gaining perfection, or maturity (*teleios*,
teleioō), through Christ, using these terms in 2:10; 5:9; 7:19,
28; 9:9; 10:1, 14; 11:40; and 12:23. When the author breaks
into the discussion about the great high priest, with a personal
excursus relating to the situation of his congregation, this motif
comes to the fore:

> Hebrews 5:13: For every one who lives on milk is unskilled
> in the word of righteousness, for he is a child. ¹⁴But solid
> food is for the *mature*, for those who have their faculties
> trained by practice to distinguish good from evil. 6:1
> Therefore let us leave the elementary doctrines of Christ and
> go on to *maturity* [RSV].

As Otto Michel points out, the author of these verses views
himself as possessing the teaching that will make his
congregation mature, striving toward that goal in writing the
letter.

The second key term characterizing the hope of Epaphras
is "fully assured" (=*plērophoreō*). The same Greek root is used

in Hebrews 6:11 to describe what the author and his associates desire for the recipients of the letter: "And we desire each one of you to show the same earnestness in realizing *the full assurance* of hope until the end." The term is used again in the exhortation that climaxes the great central argument of Hebrews. Here in 10:22 the author exhorts his congregation: "Let us draw near with a true heart *in full assurance* of faith." The author of Hebrews, therefore, desires precisely the same things for his congregation as Epaphras, who is the most plausible author of the Laodicean letter. The statement of Epaphras' desire on behalf of the Lycus Valley congregations in Colossians 4:12 not only summarizes the intent of the author of Hebrews, but does so by use of the same terminology. The fact that these terms are used, with one exception (Luke 1:1), only in the Pauline letters and in Hebrews strengthens the impression that "full assurance" was a distinctive concept in the Pauline missionary circle, linking Epaphras with Hebrews.

When one compares the specificity of these links between Epaphras and Hebrews with the circumstantial evidence used to suggest authorship by Apollos, Luke, Priscilla, Barnabas, or some unknown leader in the second generation, it becomes clear that the Anderson hypothesis warrants serious consideration. When a firsthand witness, the author of Colossians, describes what his fellow prisoner desires for a congregation in terms that fit the anonymous letter to the Hebrews this exactly, it deserves notice. In fact, one would be hard pressed, even after more than a century of historical-critical research into the argument and purpose of Hebrews, to find a more succinct and accurate summary than in the ten words describing Epaphras' desire for his Lycus Valley congregations, in Colossians 4:10. The case is sufficiently strong to provide an audience and author hypothesis for this commentary: Hebrews was written by Epaphras to the Lycus Valley situation at approximately the same time as Colossians was sent, which would be the winter of A.D. 55–56, according to my chronology of Paul's life.

3. The bearing of the pilgrim faith on the Lycus Valley

controversy. Since this kind of commentary is not the place for a detailed reconstruction of the complex gnostic speculation in Colossal and in Laodicea that began in the 1950s, a brief overview will have to suffice. It appears that the Christian congregations in the Lycus Valley interpreted the intermittent harassment and persecution they had experienced as proof that hostile cosmic forces were still in control of history and nature. Although they had accepted the proclamation that Christ had triumphed over the principalities and powers, it is clear that some of the more speculative thinkers began to explain such adversity by a dualistic view of the creation. The evil angels and powers responsible for the disagreeable state of the world would have to be mollified by religious ceremonies that were prescribed by the Old Testament. If they could be controlled in this way, the elements of adversity would be eliminated and, even more importantly, a passage would be opened through these formerly hostile realms controlled by angels and aeons so that the spirits of the elect could arrive safely at the throne of God. There was a particular interest in the Melchizedek figure in this connection. As one can infer from the author's editing of a highly mythological Melchizedek hymn in Hebrews 7, Melchizedek was probably viewed as a friendly angelic being who could provide atonement for the elect and offer esoteric instruction in the sacramental meals and washings that would mollify other cosmic powers.

On the basis of references like Hebrews 9:23, the purpose of the esoteric cult being developed in the Lycus Valley was to provide "purification" of the evil elements in the world so that they would lose their threatening qualities. Salvation was therefore in part a matter of gaining power over the hostile cosmic forces. Another aspect is visible in the baptismal catechism cited in Hebrews 11:3-31, which was probably in use in the Lycus Valley, and which the author edits by insertions and additions in his distinctive style. The great models of faith, according to this catechism, gained righteousness, which consisted of spiritual perfection, perceiving of spiritual mysteries, and—like Enoch in the catechism (Hebrews

11:5-6)—being "taken up" into the heavenly realm. To become like these spiritual giants was to share in the power of God and thus, in a sense, to transcend the finite state. What Bornkamm summarized as the goal of the Colossian heresy appears to fit the desire countered by the Letter to Pilgrims: "apotheosis of the Gnostic into an Aeon," that is, transforming mere mortals into spiritual beings capable of coping with the evil angels.

It is clear that a form of pilgrimage was sought by the gnostic teachers in Laodicea and in Colossal. As Käsemann suggested in his untranslated classic, "The Wandering People of God," the author shared with his congregation a conception of the Christian life as a journey to a heavenly homeland. The difference was that they viewed this journey as beleaguered by hostile cosmic forces, whose appeasement would allow a safe arrival at the spiritual realm where adversity would be no more. Epaphras denied that cosmic powers were the cause of such adversity, and he insisted that no one, including the best of the Old Testament pilgrims, had ever "received" the promises. The meaning of the pilgrim journey is not in arrival, he argues, but rather in the encounter with God and God's word moment for moment along the pilgrim path. "Today, when you hear his voice" is when the heavenly city is reached, and that occurs not in the realm of cultic manipulation, but "outside the camp," in the secular realm of daily life. The pilgrim faith as described by Hebrews, therefore, contains a radical reinterpretation of adversity and a dialogical concept of fulfillment. Downplaying the cosmic powers—referred to as "angels," "aeons," and "heights"—Hebrews interprets adversity as an inevitable and unresolvable aspect of the created order as designed by God. Insecurity is built in, so to speak, as the "discipline" intended by the "Father" of all. There is no need, therefore, to offer obeisance to angels. To yearn for a troublefree life is to betray the relationship with Christ whose word encounters one "today," offering fulfillment in a dialogical sense but not release from the conditions of finitude.

The Christ of Hebrews is daringly reinterpreted as the one who redeems his pilgrim community by sharing the conditions of pilgrimage: insecurity, temptation, and death. He is the "pioneer" and the "leader" of a pilgrim band, striding before them through the secular realm of Golgotha, outside the walls of the holy city. His death is viewed as sharing the element of bodily vulnerability to the final degree, taking away its threat, and bringing a troubled band of pilgrims with him to the very throne of God. He is the great high priest whose activity eliminates the need for other cultic ceremonies, because he achieves what the best of cults intend but always fail to provide: atonement with God and transformation of humans into genuinely mature and humane persons. Rather than devoting their lives to gaining security through religious rituals, seeking to raise themselves above the plight of humankind, the followers of the great high priest find fellowship with fellow humans along the pilgrim way, serving and helping and exhorting one another to keep the pilgrim faith. A secular ethic with particular concern for outsiders, strangers, and prisoners thus emerges in the final chapter of Hebrews, integrating worship and service in the realm that Jesus made his own by suffering "outside the gate." The kind of "maturity" or "perfection" that Hebrews has to offer is to accept these relationships with those one meets along with Christ the pilgrim leader, to give up the illusion of escape from adversity, and to be sustained by the moments of fulfillment when the heavenly Jerusalem is encountered through God's word, so that one is able to keep moving responsibly in the direction of the realm of true justice and equality, the "city which is to come." To be "fully assured" is to accept such adversity without any fear that cosmic beings are coming therein to power, and to approach with boldness "the throne of grace" while on the daily march through the secular world that Christ has sanctified by his blood.

4. *Hebrews as the epistle for the twenty-first century.* When one grasps the thought of Hebrews in relation to its foil, the Lycus Valley heresy, it becomes apparent that a rich and provocative resource is at hand to grapple with the issues

of rapid change, planetary insecurity, and new forms of adversity that arise as a result of the application of technology. The increasing rates of industrialization, the dizzying trend toward the postindustrial era, and the threats of ecological imbalance will lead increasing numbers of people to despair about the manageability of life. There is a palpable increase in the appeal of a demonized, or magical, or fateful view of the universe, because so many people feel that things are out of control. Indeed, there is every prospect that the erosion of the concept of a universe—an orderly and sensible totality that is at least partially comprehensible—will continue. Specialists will continue to manipulate their discrete bodies of data and material, increasingly separated from one another and heedless of the impact of their "progress" upon the whole. Although the thought patterns are and will continue to be "scientific," the fearful sense of powerlessness in the face of mysteriously rising adversities links the mood of both the late twentieth and the twenty-first centuries rather closely with that of the first. This means that the argument of Hebrews about the coherent rule of Christ over the cosmic powers—the permanent, purposeful character of adversity—and the need to undertake a journey of faith from the known to the unknown becomes more and more relevant.

One of the most striking resources that Hebrews has to offer is its critique of human efforts to manipulate the cosmic powers in order to overcome adversity. All one has to do is substitute technological manipulation for cultic ceremonies, and the bearing of Epaphras' argument becomes apparent. He claims that manipulative ceremonies deepen rather than resolve the sense of human insecurity, bad conscience, and alienation. He shows how they eliminate the possibility of genuine dialogue, locking people into patterns of self-involution and illusion. Almost every problem that social critics have uncovered in the application of sophisticated technology to solve problems and to add security and happiness to life is touched on when one thinks through the implications of this argument in Hebrews. Yet there is not a single indication in this profound writing that humankind can opt out of the historical process, find security by going backward, or discover some final solution to its plight. Jesus himself shared the dilemma, says the Letter to Pilgrims, and strides before us to lead his followers to "endure" and to "give thanks" for their secure relationship with the God who "shakes" the earth and the heavens.

The message of Hebrews seems particularly suited to the dilemma of interpreting the American Civil Religion. With the shocks it has undergone in the last decades there is every prospect that the time verging toward the twenty-first century will find itself caught between reactionary efforts to restore the old myths of America as the Redeemer Nation on the one side, and nihilistic ventures that convey a loss of morale and of any sense of limits on the other. The old belief that America is a chosen nation, favored by God to avoid the wars and tyranny of the less enlightened breeds, will certainly continue to give way. Insofar as Americans have a view of their national experience that presumes its goal to be safe arrival in some happy and unproblematic realm they will continue to feel betrayed. But there is another side to the American pilgrimage—one that accepts insecurity as the norm and that assumes the meaning of the journey is to be found along the way. That is the side sustained by the Epistle to the Hebrews, encouraging the nation to think of itself as driven by what Herbert N. Schneidau calls "sacred discontent," a sense of the tension between the promises and the performance, between what we have already achieved and what we are yet called to accomplish.

Even more essential for our health and well-being in the long run, however, is the contribution the Letter to Pilgrims has to make in broadening our horizons to see that the entire planet is caught up in the same journey. There is a universal scope to the work of Christ in Hebrews, and the conditions of insecurity to which he submitted are essentially the same for everyone. When the pilgrim community experiences adversity and thereby finds its solidarity with other outsiders and victims, an ethic of shared vulnerability results. There are no safe refuges for any race or clan, and there is no possibility for any regime to secure itself against the onslaughts of God's word that works toward planetary reconciliation. The heavenly Jerusalem described in Hebrews 12:22–24, the spot where the pilgrim community is brought momentarily by the word of God, contains celebrants from every nation and realm of this world and the next. They praise Jesus, whose "sprinkled blood that speaks more graciously than the blood of Abel," offering reconciliation to sinners rather than vengeance for miscreants. It is this great universal company at the celebrative center of the universe that cheers the pilgrim band on its challenging way, as the author reminds them in the words "since we are surrounded by so great a cloud of witnesses, let us also . . . run with perseverance the race that is set before us, looking to Jesus the pioneer and perfecter of our faith [12:1–2]."

It is appropriate that this introduction comes to its end on the theme of the panegyric assembly, because pilgrimage, in the last analysis, is worship, even though its course and arena, according to Hebrews, is the secular world. The fierce realism of Hebrews—rejecting illusions of "lasting cities," shattering sophisticated schemes of cosmic manipulation, and insisting on the maintenance of genuine dialogue—is combined with celebration. The "flaming fire" who "shakes the earth and the heavens" gives itself in dialogue to the pilgrim band, conveying to them the "word of exhortation" and providing genuine "rest." It is God's throne they approach on their way to their daily tasks. Thus the pilgrim community can sustain its sharp realism without losing hope; it can endure without illusions; it can move on after every institution has been shaken and every finite surety destroyed. By including every one of its members and the fellow outsiders it meets along the way who wish to join in the celebration, this inclusive company of pilgrims keeps its morale intact as it moves resolutely toward the "city which is to come," seeking always to approximate that city in the locales it passes through. Its most effective "sacrifice of praise to God" is "to do good and to share" whatever it has with those in need. That too is worship, for, as Epaphras insists, "such sacrifices are pleasing to God [Heb. 13:15–16]."

To worship God in the secular realm is the surest approach to the ominous twenty-first century and beyond, until "the city which has foundations, whose builder and maker is God" shall arrive, in good time. In the meanwhile we turn to the question that concerned both the author of Hebrews and his audience: the method of God's rule over a seemingly discordant world. As we follow the argument, beginning with Hebrews 1:1, we find ourselves engrossed by a new sort of pilgrimage. Like the readers of Chaucer's *Canterbury Tales,* we are urged from the opening words to become "pilgrims" ourselves.

Chapter One

Christ's Rule of the World Through the Word (1:1-14)

1:1 **H**AVING multitudinously and multifariously spoken of old to our fathers by the prophets, God ²spoke to us in these last days by a Son, whom he appointed the heir of the universe, through whom he also created the aeons, ³who is the reflection of his glory and the exact representation of his reality, bearing the universe onward by his powerful word, (and) having made purification for sins, he took his ruling seat at the right hand of the Majesty in the heights, ⁴having become as much superior to angels as the name he has inherited is more excellent than theirs.

These opening lines are composed with great care for oral presentation, with the repetition of *poly* = "multi-" in the opening three words of Greek, the alliteration of *p* as the opening consonant five times in the first twelve Greek words, and the fine balance between dominant and subordinate clauses. Barclay notes that this "is the most sonorous piece of Greek in the whole New Testament. It is a passage that any classical Greek orator would have been proud to write." This design for oral impact is consistent with the dialogical interpretation of Christian existence set forth throughout Hebrews. The whole epistle is termed by the author a "word of exhortation" (13:22), and the Christian pilgrimage envisaged by the author moves from the "heavenly call" (3:1) that is heard "today" (3:7ff.) to the sanctuary where God's voice is directly encountered (12:24-26). So the significance of Christ in these opening verses is centered in the oral message from God,

19

which is therein addressed to the author's congregation: **God spoke to us in these last days by a Son.**

There is a remarkable directness of communication in this opening, characteristic of the letter as a whole. The author eliminates all mediation by the angelic forces, which fascinated his congregation in the Lycus Valley. The widespread feeling that angelic or demonic forces mediated the written word of the law to humankind is here countered by a straightforward affirmation that God has directly addressed human beings in various ways in the past and present. By this approach the author radically alters the focus of the religious life of the community he addresses. They are to concentrate not on the cultivation of the angelic forces of the universe through cultic observances, but rather on the dialogue they have been given with their divine covenant partner. This partner is pictured as one who has always been the initiator of such dialogue with humans, so any attempt to gain mastery over the word by pious theology or theories of inspiration is seen to be impossible. This approach would seem to eliminate the favored position of first-century Christian scholars, such as those in the "School of Matthew" who appear to have prided themselves as scribes "trained for the kingdom of heaven [Matt. 13:52]." It would undercut the position of the "divine-man" theologians who claimed to be uniquely enabled to peer directly into the hidden mysteries of God. And it would counter the pretensions of early Christian gnostic teachers who claimed sole possession of the divine wisdom, feeling that they were themselves divinely wise (1 Corinthians 1:20—3:16). Instead, the significance of the Christ event that forms the Christian community is grounded in the open, public, and direct speaking of God through that event. Although this word is contained in an exhortation, such as the Epistle to the Hebrews itself, its authenticity does not in any sense depend upon the writer or speaker. As Hebrews 2:3-4 indicates, it is a self-authenticating word in the sense that God bears witness to it. So the writer is content simply to affirm God's speaking, which climaxes in **these last days** with the Christ event. He provides no rational or moral justification for this vision. For in the last analysis, one can go no farther with the justification of one's ultimate premise than to show how it authenticates itself. A dialogue can have no other grounding than in its initiator.

Starting with 1:2b there is hymnic or confessional material in participial style, which, according to Otto Michel, may well stem from early Christian worship and antedate the writing of Hebrews. But this celebration of the role and status of the Son fits integrally into the argument against the false conception of Christian existence and of the universe that was current in the Lycus Valley. First-century hearers would have naturally associated sonship with inheritance, and in Psalm 8, cited in chapter 2, one finds this defined in terms of subjection of the universe to the Son. The polemic intention that Michel suspected at this point is therefore the insistence upon the domination by the Son over the whole universe, including the supposedly independent angelic or demonic forces. The word translated as "universe" in 1:2b and 3b (*pas, ta panta*) plays an important role in the Colossian heresy, and in the following citation from Colossians 1:15-20 the prominent inclusion of the angelic forces in this totality may be noted:

> He is the image of the invisible God, the first-born of *all* creation; for in him *all things* were created, in heaven and on earth, visible and invisible, whether thrones or dominions or principalities or authorities—*all things* were created through him and for him. He is before *all things,* and in him *all things* hold together. He is the head of the body, the church; he is the beginning, the first-born from the dead, that in *everything* he might be preeminent. For in him *all* the fullness of God was pleased to dwell, and through him to reconcile to himself *all things,* whether on earth or in heaven, making peace by the blood of his cross.

Thus, when the author of Hebrews affirms that the Son has been **appointed the heir of the universe,** the cosmic scope of his authority is being affirmed and the first step in the direction of the disenchantment of nature is taken. The universe is seen to consist not of independent and irrational forces vying for domination and inviting human manipulation of reality through magical practices, but rather of forces subject to the deliberate control by God through the agency God has chosen, namely, the Son.

This concern for the subordinate position of the cosmic forces is expressed in the wording of the succeeding clause: **through whom he also created the aeons.** The literal translation of *tous aiōnas* with **the aeons** lifts up the probable connotation of the term for the Lycus Valley controversy, namely, that of personified, superhuman forces which control the various cosmic spheres and time spans. Evidence pointing in this direction is the polemic statement in Colossians 1:26 that the mystery manifested to the Christian community had been "hidden from the [aeons] and from the generations"; one finds a similar deprecation of the rulers of the present aeon in 1 Corinthians 2:6-8, and in Ephesians 2:2 there is an explicit reference to the aeon ruling this evil world: "sins in which you once walked, following the *aeon* of this world, following the *ruler* of the power of the air, the spirit that is now at work in the sons of disobedience." This personified understanding of aeon is typical for the Hellenistic mystery religions, where a god by this name plays a substantial role. Günther Bornkamm has suggested that the Colossians believed these elemental forces, or aeons, were part of God, whose body makes up the universe, similar to the view presented in Iranian or Manichaean mythology. This would imply that the aeons are the uncreated primeval substance out of which the universe and its laws emerged. Our author cuts the nerve of such a conception by insisting that these aeons were created, not primeval; it follows, of course, that the aeons are anything but ultimate, and thus are not worthy of worship. The insistence that their creation was through the Son may well relate to the problem of alienation evoked by the aeon conception.

In Hellenistic gnosticism the aeons are either the closed power spheres that make up the labyrinthine and demonic world, or the endless series of ages that stand between the believer and the believer's desired redemption. In either case they mark the alienation and lostness of the soul. Hans Jonas has pointed to the feeling of separation evoked by the idea of the aeons, as the following gnostic excerpt makes plain: "You see, O child, through how many bodies, how many ranks of demons, how many concatenations and revolutions of stars, we have to work our way in order to hasten to the one and only God." [*Corpus Hermeticum* iv, 8] This feeling of powerlessness and alienation in the face of the cosmic forces is countered by the author of Hebrews through insistence that the aeons—whether in the sense of angelic forces or of time spans—were created by God **through him.** That is, the overcoming of alienation by the Son extends beyond the areas of death of the fear (2:14-18), human weakness (4:14-16), and sin (9:23-28) to infinity itself. The aeons, therefore, lose their threatening and demonic qualities and at the same time assume the character of an ordered universe instead of a collection of independent cosmic systems, each answerable to its own peculiar exigencies.

These motifs are carried on in 1:3, where the Son's task of overcoming alienation is depicted with the participial expression **having made purification for sins.** This motif is extensively developed in the body of the sermon to the Hebrews so that it will become clear how the purification allowing humankind to stand before God is accomplished. What strikes the hearer at this point is the complete finality of this task, as expressed by the choice of **purification** and the past participle. It implies that this matter is taken completely out of the sphere of the believers' religious efforts. What has already been accomplished needs no further painful striving. In eliminating such an effort on the part of believers, a bulwark against the practice of worshiping angels and aeons is established in order to reduce alienation. The scope of religious life is thrust outside the conventicle walls into the now disenchanted secular world. It is this world, indeed the whole universe with all its forces and spheres, for which the Son takes responsibility: **bearing the universe onward by his powerful word.** The rabbis spoke in a similar vein about God bearing the world in the sense of protecting it from destruction. In Hebrews the **bearing** has an active, dynamic sense, for as Brooke Foss Westcott noted, "the word *pherein* is not to be understood simply of the passive support of a burden. . . . It rather expresses that 'bearing' which includes movement, progress, towards an end." It is possible that the agency of **word** in the creation story (Genesis 1:1ff.) is alluded to here, but it is also possible that the author refers to the word addressed to humankind in the Christ event. This would seem to be more consistent with the opening two verses of Hebrews, as well as with the kerygmatic emphasis in the rest of the sermon. In this case God's word addressed to humans would be the means by which the universe is protected. The human race, set free from the demonic forces that were felt to dominate the universe, would thus be stimulated and empowered by the **word** to take up its due responsibility.

In affirming that the Son **is the reflection of his glory and the exact representation of his reality,** the author appears to be guarding against an attempt to differentiate between the external appearance (*doxa*=**glory**) of God and the reality of God. In Bornkamm's view, the Lycus Valley heretics held that Christ did not reflect the "whole fulness of deity" (Colossians 2:9), and it may be that the author of Hebrews wishes to counter such a thought. If the Son is both the glory and the reality of God, then the atonement he offers brings humans face to face with God; also, the universe God sustains is in no sense the product of some inferior forces. The word addressed to humans in the Christ event is in every sense of the term God's word. With this established, the author is ready for the affirmation that will carry the weight of the argument against angel worship throughout the rest of the chapter: **he took his ruling seat at the right hand of the majesty in the heights, having become as much superior to angels as the name he has inherited is more excellent than theirs.** The terms used to depict the rule of the Son are drawn from the traditional imagery of the divine throne room, with the messianic regent sitting at the right hand of God as the authorized agent of divine rule. Thus it is evident from the opening lines of Hebrews that the author is going to develop a theocratic perspective of some sort. First-century Judaism had several diverging viewpoints on theocracy, with the Sadducees advocating the status quo of priestly authority to exercise supreme power in cooperation with the Roman Empire, the Essenes advocating revolution to replace the present priesthood with themselves as agents of a messiah from Aaron who would be superior to the political messiah from David, and the Zealots advocating a similarly radical theocracy in which Yahweh would be the sole ruler. The theocratic assumptions shared by several of these groups were that messianic rule would take political form, that it would come after the destruction of evil, and that a new universal order would result in which chaotic and evil elements would be eliminated for the benefit of the elect. The Lycus Valley heretics apparently shared at least the last two assumptions, for they were deeply disappointed when the new age announced in the Christian kerygma failed to result in the destruction of the old age, with its evil manifestations of hostility and death. And they advocated worship of the angelic forces of the old age as a means of eliminating their threat to the elect. So as the first step in his radical transformation of the theocratic ideal, the author of Hebrews asserts that the divinely appointed rule has already begun. Despite the continuance of the old age, with all its evil manifestations, a new sort of theocratic era has been inaugurated. As 1:2 has already established, this new era has a dialogical character, being marked by God's speaking to humans by means of the Son. This emphasis is carried through in the phrasing of 1:4 and in the succeeding verses, because the authority of the Son is seen to rest solely on the name that God has enunciated. This basic conception of kerygmatic rule is carried throughout the sermon to the Hebrews, receiving detailed exposition in chapters 2 to 4 and reaching its summit in chapter 12. The affirmation in 1:3d-4 is assumed throughout the letter, namely, that this kerygmatic rule is already in effect.

A second step in the transformation of the theocratic ideal relates very directly to the Lycus Valley situation. The wording of 1:3d-4 seems designed to focus on the rule of the Son over the cosmic forces. The phrase **took his ruling seat at the right hand** is drawn from Psalm 110, in which the subordination of enemies is in view, and this motif is lifted up again in Hebrews 1:13. The expression **in the heights** seems to depict cosmic authority, and it would include the "thrones or dominions or principalities or authorities . . . in heaven and on earth" alluded to in Colossians 1:16. This term is of central importance for the Jewish-Gnostic sect of the Hypsistarians, which emerged somewhat later in the area of Asia Minor advocating worship of **the heights** as the source of cosmic force, and there may well be an antecedent to this movement in the Lycus Valley heresy. This dimension is explicitly lifted up in 1:4, where the rule of the Son is based on a status that is **superior to angels.** As the use of the comparative form of "powerful" makes plain, this status of the Son serves to reduce the power of the cosmic forces. It has often been noted that this superiority terminology is used thirteen times in Hebrews, while appearing only six times in the rest of the New Testament. The bearing of this distinctive and decisive argument becomes fully comprehensible against a background of honoring the cosmic forces as ultimate. If one can show that there is something superior in power to an angelic force that is being worshiped, its status claim is effectively undermined. It can no longer be viewed as an autonomous power sphere that continues to hold sway after the inauguration of the new age. If the author could dispel the feeling of awe his hearers instinctively felt toward the cosmic forces, then the effort to appease and control them through religious observances would drop aside.

At this point it is possible to focus more sharply on the subtle and strikingly modern type of idolatry that was prevalent in the Lycus Valley. At first glance it would seem illogical to ascribe ultimacy to angels, for they are presumably creatures of God that simply carry out certain tasks. Yet the argument in Hebrews and the reference to the worship of angels in Colossians 2:18 indicate that a sort of ultimacy was ascribed to them. It is quite different from the absolute infinity projected by primitive religions onto idols, because the word angel itself implies a function within an established order. It appears to be an ascription of functional ultimacy. The Lycus Valley congregations simply regarded the angels as ultimate within their functional limits. Each was thought to be sovereign in its particular area—the guardian angels over nations or individuals, the cosmic angels over the heavenly bodies, and still other angels over the forces of history and the natural world. This ascription of functional ultimacy to angels seems to offer a rather sophisticated way to avoid outright idolatry. It is similar to the modern ascription of ultimacy to the forces of economics or history, the institutions of government and business, or the methods of technological manipulation. In a similar manner Gabriel Marcel spoke of "pantechnicism," a tendency visible

> when technical knowledge begins to claim a sort of primacy in relation to modes of thinking . . . and in consequence to become the centre, the focus, of an obsessive cult. It is in this way that the abuse of technical knowledge and technical processes is in danger . . . of giving rise to an actual idolatry: an idolatry which, to be sure, is not recognized as such, its very nature excluding any such recognition.

The "worship" that technological moderns perform may be completely secularized, but the underlying idolatrous substance may well remain. Hebrews' argument about the superiority of Christ over the angels may offer an effective way to avoid an idolatrous attachment to the institutions and methods of a technological society.

1:5   **For to which of the angels did God ever say,**
      "You are my Son,
      today I have begotten you"?

And again,
> "I will be to him a father,
> and he will be to me a son"?

⁶But, when he again brings the first-born into the world, he says,
> "Let all the angels of God fall on their knees before him."

⁷But of the angels he says,
> "Who makes his angels winds,
> and his ministers a flame of fire."

⁸But of the Son he says,
> "God is your throne for an aeon of aeons,
> the scepter of uprightness is the scepter of your kingdom.
> ⁹You loved righteousness and hated lawlessness;
> therefore God, your God, has anointed you
> with the oil of gladness beyond your comrades."

¹⁰And
> "You, Lord, founded the earth in the beginning,
> and the heavens are the work of your hands;
> ¹¹they will perish, but you will remain;
> they will all grow obsolete like a garment,
> ¹²like a mantle you will roll them up,
> as a garment they shall be changed.
> But you are the same,
> and your years will never end."

¹³But to which of the angels has he ever said,
> "Take a ruling seat at my right hand,
> till I make your enemies
> a stool for your feet"?

¹⁴Are they not all ministering spirits sent forth into service for the sake of those who are going to inherit salvation?

The rest of Hebrews 1 is a series of citations from the Old Testament, cleverly chosen and organized to form a coherent argument about the superiority and character of the Son's rule.

In some cases the wording is slightly altered to make the citation fit the author's purpose, and in one instance the citation is a composite of several Old Testament sources. The hermeneutical principle that one must follow here is not what the passages meant in their original settings, but rather what they connote in their present setting. In other words, what do the phrases and ideas mean in relation to the Lycus Valley heresy and the author's argument as set forth in the work as a whole?

The citations from Psalm 2 and 2 Samuel 7 comprising 1:5 document the claim in the preceding verse that Christ inherited a superior name. That he is the Son is argued strictly on grounds of God's word. These citations, which the Jewish tradition associated with messianic enthronement, do not appear to be connected with incidents in the life of the historical Jesus, such as the baptism (Mark 1:11ff.) or transfiguration (Mark 9:7ff.). The author's intent is not so much to prove Jesus was the Son as to substantiate the claim that the Son has a superior position to that of the angels. It is interesting at this point that the author thereby disregards the biblical and apocalyptic tradition of the angels as "sons of God." Clearly, the principle of interpreting the Old Testament for this author is not to probe for the original significance of a text or to present a balanced picture of biblical usage, but rather to understand it in light of what he understands to be God's word in the Christ event. The premise for these citations is thus provided in 1:2: "God spoke to us . . . by a Son."

The contrast between the ruling Son and the angels is carried through the next verses, where the incarnation is greeted by angelic submission. The expression **when he again brings the first-born into the world** has occasioned a great deal of controversy. Syntactically, it appears necessary to connect the adverb **again** with the verb that immediately follows it in the Greek text, i.e., **brings.** At first glance this would seem to connote the Second Coming, but the aorist subjunctive of the verb can scarcely carry a future connotation when used in a sentence where the dominant verb **he says** is in the present tense. Some interpreters, such as Spicq and Moffatt, have found this Second Coming connotation so improbable in light of the argument elsewhere in Hebrews that the adverb is placed with the dominant verb to produce the translation "and again, when he brings. . . [RSV]." This has the advantage of bringing 1:6 into parallel with 1:5, but it seems rather strained grammatically. In light of the preexistent motif in 1:2-3 and the reference to Christ as the **first-born** of the creation in this verse, it seems likely that the author counts the creation of the Son as the first, and the life of the historical Jesus as the second bringing into the world. At any rate, as Michel has noted, the expression **brings . . . into the world** seems to be a Hebraism relating to parents bringing children into the world.

The term **first-born** relates very closely to the Lycus Valley situation, as the use in Colossians 1:15 and 18 indicates. There is a strand of the Jewish tradition that pictures the angels as being born on the first or second day of creation and then taking part in the creation of the universe, while speculative Hellenistic philosophy sometimes identified angels with the Logos, which again would suggest involvement of angels in creation. The Colossian heresy went even farther in viewing the aeons, or angels, as original parts of the body of the giant god-universe. The appellation **first-born** in this context, therefore, implies the creation of the Son before the angels and thus counters any notion of angelic preexistence or priority. In the citation that follows, the submission of the angels to the Son is explicitly stated. The author has constructed **let all the angels of God fall on their knees before him** out of Psalm 97:7 and Deuteronomy 32:43 (Septuagint), changing "sons of God" to **angels of God** in order to make his point. With this enthronement imagery the author suggests the acclamation of every creature in the realm to a newly crowned ruler. They cease playing the roles of independent forces and submit in an orderly fashion to the rule of the Son and heir of the universe. This verse therefore reiterates the stress on the disenchantment of nature that was detected in 1:2-3.

The climax in the campaign to disenchant nature is

reached in 1:7, where the author follows the Septuagint in turning the sense of Psalm 104:4 upside down. The original Hebrew text read, "who makest the winds thy messengers, fire and flame thy ministers [RSV]," implying that God takes the very forces of nature into divine service. Our author, whose interpretative intent becomes vividly clear in 1:14, uses this same text to prove that the cosmic **angels** and **ministers** are no more than fleeting winds and fire, and thus have no abiding ontological continuity. He draws at this point on the strand of Jewish tradition that denigrated the angels to momentary expressions of God. William Barclay notes that

> there was a rabbinic belief in some schools that "every day God creates a new company of angels who utter a song before Him and are gone." "The angels are renewed every morning and after they have praised God they return to the stream of fire from whence they came." 4 Esdras 8:21 speaks of the God "before whom the heavenly host stand in terror and at Thy word change to wind and fire." A rabbinic homily makes one of the angels say: "God changes us every hour. . . . Sometimes He makes us fire, at other times wind."

But Barclay does not draw the radical consequences that seem necessary: In an argument against angel worship in which their ontological preexistence has repeatedly been challenged, to **make his angels winds and his ministers a flame of fire** is to reduce them to a strictly finite level. This reduction is emphasized by the alteration of the Septuagint nominative "flame and fire" into an accusative with genetive **a flame of fire,** thus lifting up the transitory, flickeringly visible aspect of fire as that which corresponds to the cosmic forces. The magic and mystery of the angels is thereby diminished, with the result that the enchanted world is transformed into a universe in the full sense of the word, with the various laws and forces carrying out the rational purpose of the creator. To follow this audacious argument of the author to its logical conclusion would be completely to demythologize the angelic phenomenon. Translated into modern categories, this would mean that the laws and methods of politics, economics, and technology are not functionally ultimate, but rather serve the purposes of justice and order that the creator intends. This would have eliminated the last shred of support for the Lycus Valley worship of the cosmic forces.

If the cosmic forces do not exercise autonomous control over the world, then the rule of the Son must be set forth with more precision. The next citation, from Psalm 45:6–7, carries the author's reinterpretation of messianic theocracy past the first two steps outlined above. Having shown that this rule has already begun and that it is over the cosmic forces, the statement **God is your throne for an aeon of aeons** shows both the grounding and the duration of the Son's rule. This translation is preferable to the *Revised Standard Version*, "Thy throne, O God, is for ever and ever," because the psalm is addressed to the anointed king rather than to God. The *Revised Standard Version* shatters the parallelism and symmetry with 1:9, where the citation continues **therefore God, your God, has anointed you.** In light of the emphasis on the humanity of the Son throughout the later chapters of Hebrews, it seems unlikely that the author would here intend the Son to be addressed as God. Still, the expression **God is your throne** is difficult to conceptualize. The Hebrew text expresses the concept more clearly, namely, that "your throne is a throne of God." Here the righteousness and eternity of the heavenly throne (cf. Isaiah 6:1–5, 66:1) are transferred to the earthly throne of the Davidic ruler, as Otto Schmitz has shown. So in 1:8 it is probably best to understand the author's citation of the Septuagint as expressive of the Hebraic concept of the messianic throne that conveys the authority and benefits of the divine throne to earth. In the context of the argument of Hebrews, this serves to insist that the Son's rule is a valid extension of the divine theocracy, and also that it will outlast the aeons, which had seemed to offer the Lycus Valley religionists the avenue to the truly lasting city.

The citation goes on to specify the moral character of the Son's rule: **The scepter of uprightness is the scepter of your**

kingdom. You loved righteousness and hated lawlessness. Here are the traditional attributes of theocratic rule: **uprightness,** in the sense of open impartiality in the enforcement of law, and **righteousness,** in the sense of valuing the life of the oppressed. These are the ideals guiding each theocratic program in the first century, and the uniqueness of Hebrews' approach is not only its avoidance of political means, but also the strange inclusion of a fragmentary and perishing secular world within the divine plan.

The citation of Psalm 102 in the following verses serves to specify the character of the world the Son as lord has chosen both to create and to rule. It is an earth and heaven that **will perish . . . they will all grow obsolete like a garment, like a mantle you will roll them up, as a garment they shall be changed.** In the context of Hebrews, this citation gains a connotation that differs from the original intent of the psalm to celebrate the permanence of God in the midst of an uncertain world. The author uses the citation to define the character of the Son's theocratic rule: It is a rule that strives not to eliminate the changeable character of the world, but rather to offer humans **salvation** within it. Here the elements of chaos and obsolescence, which a theocratic hope such as the Revelation of John would seek to overcome, are instead affirmed as intrinsic to the creative plan of God from the beginning. Just as the cosmic angels are mere winds and flames that come and go, so the earth and the heavens are changing and deteriorating in a constant state of flux. In a world such as this there is no possibility of establishing theocratic "lasting cities." The threats of decay and entropy are unavoidable. The planned or unplanned obsolescence of all created objects is here affirmed to be what God has designed, and therefore "good." The rule of the Son is thrust out into the secular world, into the context of perennial rapid social change. The stage is set for Christian existence as a pilgrimage through a changing world, and the rule of Christ can now be defined in terms of such pilgrimage.

What, then, is permanent in such a world? If the very cosmic forces and principles are ephemeral and the entire universe subject to the laws of obsolescence, what remains as a basis for human security? Psalm 102 provides our author with the answer, which is developed through the book: **but you are the same, and your years will never end.** He puts it in his own words most clearly in 13:8, RSV: "Jesus Christ is the same yesterday and today and for ever." This affirmation counters the appalling threat of finitude and flux. It implies that the deterioration of the world is not caused by evil angels, so futile attempts to appease these forces are unnecessary. It shows that the chaotic, revolutionary character of world history cannot be blamed on the inciters and subversives of every ostensible "lasting city," and as a consequence the usual campaigns to purge and restore are pointless. Instead, the revolving obsolescence of life is seen to be grounded in the unchanging will of the creator and the creator's Son. The theocracy intended by God accepts this obsolescence as a premise, so that humans are led to live in praise of God in the merry-go-round of history. They are to give up their convulsive efforts to reconstitute the world and are to take up the acclamation of the angelic host in submitting to the rule of the Son. By basing their security on the archimedian point beyond the flux, men and women gain the capacity to live constructively within the secular world.

In verse 13 the opening lines of Psalm 110 are used to express the conviction that the theocracy of the Son will someday encompass even his enemies: **"Take a ruling seat at my right hand, till I make your enemies a stool for your feet."** This psalm connoted messianic rule and eschatological judgment for the hearers in the first century, picturing the rule as already established by God's command yet awaiting completion at the end of the age. In the context of a discussion about angels, the **enemies** in this citation would connote the hostile cosmic forces as depicted in Colossians 2:15 or 1 Corinthians 6:3. In Hebrews 2:14 the devil is depicted as such a hostile power. Just as in the early Christian hymn reflected in Philippians 2:6–11, it is these "dissenting deities," to use James A. Sanders' expression, that will ultimately come into submission to the Christ. This citation inserts a note of historical tension and moral seriousness into the theocratic ideal. The love of **righteousness** and the **hated lawlessness** mentioned in 1:9 receive here their due expression in a final triumph over evil. But it is a triumph that God alone provides, **till I make your enemies a stool.** Human crusading against evil is not called for. Nor is the effort of the Lycus Valley heretics to subdue the hostile forces by angelic worship an appropriate path of action, for as the author insists, the role of subduing these enemies has never been given to **the angels.**

The culmination of this argument is in verse 14, where the author breaks off his brilliant combination of citations and states the summary in his own terminology: **Are they not all ministering spirits sent forth into service for the sake of those who are going to inherit salvation?** This turns the relationship of humans and angels dramatically upside down. It is not human beings who are to minister to angels, but rather angels who are **ministering spirits** to human beings. The Lycus Valley "devotion and self-abasement" (Colossians 2:23) in honor of angels is here reversed by the angels being **sent forth into service for the sake of** humanity. At the same time the elimination of any form of ultimacy for angels is carried through to the end. They are no more than passing **spirits** that are **sent forth** momentarily by God. They function not for their own purposes, but rather for the sake of others. The demythologization is now complete; the disenchantment of nature is final; and the world with its mysterious laws and forces is shown to have been designed by the creator for the achievement of wholeness. The stage for accepting life as a pilgrimage of worship through the secular world is now set, and the exhortation may now be uttered.

Chapter Two

Response to the Gospel (2:1-4) Leads to Participation in Christ's Rule (2:5-18)

2:1 THEREFORE it is necessary to lay hold more firmly to the things we have heard, lest we drift away. ²For if the word declared by angels was validated, and every transgression and disobedience received a just retribution, ³how shall we escape if we neglect such a great salvation? It was first declared by the Lord, and it was validated to us by those who heard him, ⁴being simultaneously attested by God by signs and wonders and various powerful deeds and by apportionments of the Holy Spirit according to his will.

The exhortation that climaxes the argument of 1:1-14 focuses on the word, implying that holding fast to the Christian proclamation was the proper response to the salvation the Son offers. The opening word **therefore** refers back to the argument against the false conception of salvation in the Lycus Valley. If salvation is not the manipulation of the angelic forces through cultic practices, and if it is to be lived out in a perishing world, the logical necessity is to respond properly to the new relationship that the gospel establishes. In the **things we have heard**, God is addressing humans (cf. 1:1-2), thereby establishing a dialogue called **salvation** in the midst of this perishing world. Since this is the character of **salvation**, then it is fitting to **lay hold more firmly . . . lest we drift away.** The word translated here with **lay hold** *(prosechein)* can connote mooring a ship, so the contrast with **drift away** becomes quite striking. This term is frequently used in the New Testament to connote giving heed either to the gospel (Acts 8:6; 16:14; 1 Timothy 6:3; 2 Peter 1:19) or to heretical teachings (Acts 8:10-11; 1 Timothy 1:4; 4:1; Titus 1:14); it depicts the act of shifting one's attention to a particular matter rather than holding one's attention there. Later in the epistle the author uses *katechein* rather than *prosechein* to denote holding fast to what one has already received (3:6, 14; 10:23). The implication is that the congregation must turn vigorously—**more firmly**—from its drifting acquiescence in the speculation and manipulation of the angelic forces and **lay hold** as if for the first time to the relationship offered in the **things we have heard.** The real threat is not so much an explicit denial of the faith, but rather a slothful drifting away from the new relationship into a self-enclosed, complacent form of religiosity. The Lycus Valley worship of angels was undoubtedly intended to be nothing more than a humble addendum to the faith, and if it grew out of the enthusiastic piety produced by the gospel preaching, as was the case with similar groups in other Pauline congregations, its advocates felt it was perfectly consistent with what they had received. But with sharp discernment, the author points with **drift away** to the essentially slothful character of the Lycus Valley religiosity: it exchanged the active pilgrimage of faith through the secular world for a pious adulation of the supposed angelic powers within the confines of the sacred enclave; it exchanged responsibility in the world as it is for a theocratic dream of altering the world for the benefit of the elect; it perverted the character of religion from personal engagement in a new and transforming dialogue with the Son to impersonal manipulation of the divine through pious ceremonies. The author discerns here something similar to the sloth that Harvey Cox describes as the temptation in contemporary Christianity: "Sloth means being *less* than instead of *more* than man. Sloth describes our flaccid unwillingness to delight in the banquet of earth or to share the full measure of life's pain and responsibility. It means to abdicate in part or in whole the fulness of one's own humanity."

Verses 2 to 4 spell out why **it is necessary** to follow the exhortation. The **word declared by angels** refers to the agency of angels in the dispensing of the Old Testament cited in chapter 1 to delineate the character of Christ's rule. The reference here to the angels has clear polemical intent, because if the angels revered in the Lycus Valley declare a word that eliminates angel worship, the implications are apparent. The author goes on to insist that the angelic message was **validated** in the Christ event, as the argument in 3b-4 makes plain. The author's premise is that the good news **declared by the Lord** is consistent with and thus serves to substantiate the truth of what God has spoken through the prophets (1:1) and the angels from the beginning.

The principle of self-authentication noted in connection with 1:1-2 is spelled out here in more detail. God not only authenticates God's own word to human beings by means of the angels, the prophets, the Son who is **Lord,** and the apostles **who heard him,** but has also **simultaneously attested** to the word by the spiritual manifestations experienced in the Lycus Valley congregation. Like the other Christians in the first century, they had witnessed the **signs and wonders and various powerful deeds** of exorcisms, reconciliations, and dramatic conversions that accompanied the proclamation of the good news and gave evidence of the power of God. The author seems to draw here from the Pauline missionary rationale, because the same terms are used in 2 Corinthians 12:12: "The signs of a true apostle were performed among you in all patience, with signs and wonders and mighty works." The **apportionments of the Holy Spirit** appear to relate to the spiritual gifts of prophecy, speaking in tongues, healing, and so on, while the insistence that they are dispensed **according to his will** implies that they cannot be conjured up or manipulated by human effort. The miraculous amelioration of the human condition which the Lycus Valley religionists had hoped to achieve by worship of the angels is here treated as a gift that humans can never control, as a sign of God's transforming dialogue. Unlike the modern fundamentalist who tries to prove the existence of God and the validity of his or her own theology by a positivistic appraisal of these **signs,** our author seems interested solely in the validity of the dialogue thereby established. For the **salvation** in verse 3 is not the possession of fundamental truths by human beings or the possession of an effective means of manipulating the cosmic forces, but rather the dialogue itself.

This doctrine of the self-authenticating word seems to be rather close to what Norman O. Brown calls "Dionysian Christianity . . . in which the scripture is a dead letter to be made alive by spiritual . . . interpretations . . . in a continuous revelation; by fresh outpouring of the holy spirit. Meaning is made in a meeting between the holy spirit buried in the Christian and the holy spirit buried underneath the letter of scripture." In the case of Hebrews, the **salvation** referred to in verse 3 is participation in a transforming dialogue in which the ecstatic freeing of inner resources blends with communications of reality. It is a vital and open-ended process vastly different from the manipulation of cosmic forces or from the literal appraisal of the **signs** in order to prove the validity of one's theology. The implications of this **salvation** must be grasped and formulated ever and again as one clings to the dialogue. It can never be wrapped up in concise dogmas, reduced to cold facts, or objectified in final, literal terms.

In an impressive fashion, the author formulates the negative side of his exhortation to fit the situation of a dialogue inaugurated by the gospel: **every transgression and disobedience received a just retribution.** A **transgression** is a willful violation of a command by the divine covenant partner; **disobedience** is expressed here by the word *parakoē*, which denotes defiance of a command; and **neglect** is expressed by *amelein*, which carries the sense of disregarding or paying no attention to someone or something. The **just retribution** that follows spurned dialogue is spelled out by the author in chapter 3 through discussion of the desert generation's hardening of heart against the word and their resultant destruction. Operating within a strict framework of dialogue, the author cannot conceive of an ethic of a little more or a little less as a moralist might. He thinks in terms of either/or. One either responds to the covenant partner or refuses to respond, in which case one loses the new relationship and experiences **retribution.** The moral seriousness of Hebrews is not based on idealism, legalism, or moralism, but rather on the inexorable conditions of dialogue itself.

2:5 For it was not to angels that (God) subjected the world to come, of which we are speaking. ⁶But it has been testified somewhere,

> **"What is man that you are mindful of him,**
> **or the son of man, that you care for him?**
> **⁷You lowered him temporarily beneath the angels,**
> **you crowned him with glory and honor,**
> **⁸putting everything in subjection under his feet."**

Now in putting everything in subjection to him, he left nothing outside his control. But as it is, we do not yet see everything in subjection to him. ⁹But we see one who was lowered temporarily beneath the angels—Jesus—crowned with glory and honor because of the suffering of death, so that by the grace of God he might taste death for the sake of every one. ¹⁰For it was fitting for him, for whom everything exists and by whom everything exists, in leading many sons to glory—the pilgrim leader of their salvation!—to gain perfection through suffering. ¹¹For he who sanctifies and those who are sanctified are all from one, for which reason he is not ashamed to call them brethren, ¹²saying,

> **"I will proclaim your name to my brethren,**
> **in the midst of the congregation I will praise you."**

¹³And again,

> **"I will put my trust in him."**

And again,

> **"Here am I, and the children God has given me."**

¹⁴Since therefore the children share in blood and flesh, he himself participated in them, in order that through death he might abrogate him who has the power of death, that is, the

devil, ¹⁵and deliver those who, in fear of death, were all of their lives bound in slavery. ¹⁶For surely he doesn't help the angels, but he helps the seed of Abraham. ¹⁷Therefore he had to be made like the brethren in every respect, so that he might become a merciful and faithful high priest in the service of God, to make expiation for the sins of the people. ¹⁸For because he himself has suffered and been tempted, he is able to help those who are tempted.

In 2:5–18 the author sets forth the character and the grounding of the theocracy in which the Hebrews are to participate. The opening words take up the polemic against the Lycus Valley conception of angelic control of the universe: **it was not to angels that (God) subjected the world to come.** This cuts the nerve of angelic worship aimed at making use of their power to benefit the believer. It carries forward the author's campaign to disenchant the natural and historical world. The expression **world to come** is qualified by the phrase **of which we are speaking,** so that the attention of the hearer is drawn to "these last days" (1:2) whose power is now being manifested by the signs and wonders and gifts of the spirit (2:4). This new age was inaugurated by the Christ event, but in a conception similar to Paul's, this author sees the old age as continuing alongside the new (1:11–12; 2:8). If the angelic forces will not have control over the course of this **world to come,** who will take over their place as the regents of God? To answer this question, the author very daringly uses Psalm 8 to show that humans replace the angels as the ones to whom the world is subject.

The citation from Psalm 8 follows exactly the wording of the Septuagint, which offers a much more suitable basis for the author's argument about the angels than the Hebrew text, which reads "you have made him a little less than God." Yet the interpretation of the citation in verse 8 makes it clear that the author understands it quite differently from the original intent of the Septuagint. The psalm points to the high position of humankind, just "a little lower than the angels," enjoying the glorious and honorable dominion over the world in much the sense that Adam was thought to have dominion over the garden. The author of Hebrews, however, uses the phrase **putting everything in subjection to him** to prove that humankind has control even over the angelic forces. The term translated **everything** *(ta panta)* was used, as we have noted in 1:2b and 3b, and plays a decisive role in the Colossian heresy. The conclusion by the author is very sweeping: **he left nothing outside his control.** Here humans are placed fully in charge of the disenchanted world. But they are given to know that the chaotic forces of the old age still continue to affect the dawning **world to come.** The world, according to 1:11-12, was designed for deterioration, so this means that these chaotic forces are no longer to be considered the effects of evil angels. With this threat dismissed, Christians are able to face the fact that **as it is, we do not yet see everything in subjection to him.**

Here the author captures the dilemma that threatens the health of any secular stance: humans are given dominion over the world, yet there are constantly elements in that world which elude and resist that dominion. If the stance is based on a modern theory such as evolutionary progress, then the continuation of such resistance evokes either despair or fanaticism. But if the stance attempts to explain this resistance in terms of magical cosmic forces and to manipulate them through cultic observances—an approach followed not only in the Lycus Valley but also in the modern resurgence of the occult—then human independence and responsibility are destroyed. The author has developed a way to face this dilemma and to live creatively within it. It is the path of response to the Christian gospel that inaugurates a creative dialogue in the midst of the secular world and that evokes a due sense of finite responsibility for the created order. The grounding of this rationale is affirmed in verse 9, which is translated here with the emphasis on the word Jesus that the original word order suggests: **but we see one who was lowered temporarily beneath the angels—**

Jesus—crowned with glory and honor because of the suffering of death, so that by the grace of God he might taste death for the sake of every one.
This is a key verse in the development of the author's radically new approach to theocracy. What he sees in Jesus is the glory of finitude within a world subject to deterioration and death. He was **crowned with glory and honor** in his exaltation not by having gained control of the fallen world in a theocratic sense, but by suffering within that world on behalf of others. In sharing human limitations—not only in being **lowered temporarily beneath the angels,** but also in **the suffering of death—** Jesus overcame the alienation that had made finitude so threatening. He faced the same resistance that marks the life of every person in this hostile and deteriorating world. And he experienced the ultimate effects of such hostility against himself. The choice of the expression **he. . .tasted death** appears to denote a participation not only in death itself, but also in its bitter impact. The redemptive effect of this participation in finitude is alluded to by the traditional early Christian terminology for vicarious suffering: **for the sake of every one.** The author's view of redemption, however, is entirely lacking in the mystical or legalistic aura that later Christian theories of the atonement provide. There is no hint that Jesus paid the price in blood to appease an injured divine justice or that his obedience provides a perfect example for moral striving. Instead, the author concentrates on the redemptive power of participation itself. He lifts up the aspect of Jesus' ministry that had the most scandalous impact on first-century piety: "Behold, a glutton and a drunkard, a friend of tax collectors and sinners [Matt. 11:19]!" It was Jesus' participation in the life of the "people of the land" that gained him this unique reputation. He was known as one who took part in celebrations and funerals: he wept with those who wept and he laughed with those who laughed. And the gospels related something of the redemptive effect of this participation. People like Zacchaeus were transformed not by moralistic proddings, but by Jesus' sharing in celebrations in their homes. Mourners

felt comforted by his participation in their weeping. Similarly, the Christ of Hebrews is neither the successful organizer of piety nor the efficient promoter of virtuous projects, but one who redeems by sharing human suffering, temptation, and death.

The effect of this redemptive participation is spelled out in verses 10 to 18. What makes this method of redemption **fitting** for our author is (a) that Christ is the one **for whom everything exists and by whom everything exists.** If it is he rather than some angelic force who is responsible for the creation and sustenance of the universe, it follows that sharing in the deterioration and hostility of such a universe would take away the alienation. In achieving **perfection through suffering,** he takes this hostility upon himself and affirms the goodness of life within a broken, secular world. But the point that receives most immediate development is (b) that Jesus is **the pilgrim leader of their salvation,** meaning in light of the argument throughout Hebrews that he leads his people into the presence of God. The term *archēgos,* as Ernst Käsemann has argued, must be understood in light of 6:20 and 12:12 as depicting a leader who marches before followers through the cosmos into the holy of holies. I attempt to capture this nuance with the expression **pilgrim leader.** It is also possible that Käsemann is correct in suggesting a gnostic background for this term in light of the parallel in Colossians 1:18, whereby Christ becomes the one who spans the aeons and leads the enlightened into the sphere of perfection. This would be an effective affirmation of the triumph of Christ in the context of the Lycus Valley discussion. But it should be noted that the author of Hebrews goes much farther than any gnostic thinker would in affirming the historical dimension of the **leader's** and the congregation's path, as well as the full involvement in human suffering and death. Since the **leader** and the **sanctified** are all from God, sharing the common created status, he **is not ashamed to call them brethren.** The alienating shame of finitude is here dispelled by Jesus' sharing the status of his people.

The following citations lift up the dimension and result of

such sharing. In verse 12, Psalm 22:22 is used to indicate that Jesus' proclamation of the good news and his life of praise was to my brethren . . . in the midst of the congregation. As the following citation from Isaiah 8:17 makes clear, this participation in human life involves taking up the stance of trust, which, as Hebrews 11:1ff. shows, is the sole basis of security in the midst of a hostile world. But the climax is the citation from Isaiah 8:18, here am I, and the children God has given me. By sharing the life of the sisters and brothers, Jesus brings them with him into the presence of God. For here the pilgrim leader of their salvation announces their presence with him in the Holy of Holies, and if they are with him, then they are "atoned" with God. The alienation has been overcome and the basis for an open dialogue is established. The argument in the great middle section of Hebrews 4:14—10:31 rests entirely on this basis of atonement through participation. So in verses 17 and 18 the author prepares the ground for his later development of the high priestly doctrine by pointing to his hermeneutical principle: expiation for the sins of the people is brought by participation in the suffering and temptation of the brethren. It is by sharing finitude that Jesus overcomes the alienation of sin and leads humans into the new relationship with God in the midst of the secular world.

The most dramatic emphasis in chapter 2 is the abrogation of the devil that results from Jesus' participation in finitude, in verses 14 and 15. The term used in this connection, katargeō = abrogate, destroy, make powerless, goes much farther than the sort of demotion that the angels suffer in these first two chapters of Hebrews. Whereas they retain a fleeting existence as servants of God, the devil here loses both being and power because of the Christ event. This is the last step in the disenchantment of life, because the ultimate evil, namely death, is seen to result not from some cosmic force, but rather, by implication, from the deteriorating character of finitude itself. In sharing the death to which all blood and flesh fall prey, Jesus takes away the enchantment that produces the terror. This overcomes the fear of death, which holds persons in **slavery** throughout the course of life. The striking thing about this is that the victory of Christ over the devil is so entirely lacking in mythological overtones. Unlike the Christus Victor theories of the atonement, the Jesus of Hebrews does not engage the devil in a contest or take the devil into captivity through subterfuge. He simply shares life and death with his **brethren** and thus dispels the enchantment with its resultant terror. As verse 16 makes plain, the benefit of this does not accrue to the **angels.** They do not take over the rule of the cosmos after the defeat of the demonic, and thus it follows that any adulation of them as proposed in the Lycus Valley is excluded. The disenchantment of nature and history is complete, and the result is that humankind is offered participation in Christ's rule over the world. It is the **seed of Abraham,** defined by this context as the **brethren** of Jesus within the congregation addressed by our author, who are enabled to take up the proffered subjugation of the finite and deteriorating universe. It is to be a rule that operates within finitude, accepting death without fear, and willing to face the built-in resistance of a created order in which **we do not yet see everything in subjection to him.** The basis of this secular courage is the gift of a new relationship that ensues upon receiving the gospel about Christ's full participation in human life.

Chapter Three

Participation in the House of God (3:1–6) and in the Rest Along the Way (3:7—4:13) Through Response to the Word

3:1 THEREFORE, holy brethren, sharers of a heavenly calling, fix your attention on Jesus, the apostle and high priest of our confession. ²He was faithful to him who created him, as was Moses in God's house. ³For he was deemed worthy of more glory than Moses, inasmuch as the builder of a house has more honor than the house itself. ⁴For every house is built by someone, but the builder of everything is God. ⁵Now Moses was faithful in all his house as an attendant, to testify to the things that were later to be spoken, ⁶but Christ is over his house as a son, whose house we are if we keep fearless and proud of hope.

Having defined the scope of God's rule over the deteriorating and finite world, the author moves in 3:1–6 to show that participation in this rule is superior to that offered by faithful service in the tradition of Moses. The shape of this superiority is revealed in the opening words, **holy brethren.** Rather than striving to atone for their sins so as to be able to stand before God in the tradition of Moses, they are simply made **holy** by Christ's participation in human life. His overcoming of sinful alienation makes it possible for them to encounter the holy God, not as humble supplicants, but as **brethren** brought into the Holy of Holies by Christ. This new status, the result of unconditional grace, stands in stark contrast to the piety of the Lycus Valley. Yet, as the following expression, **sharers of a heavenly calling,** makes plain, the gift of this status through the Christ event does not establish a static form of existence. It is kerygmatic existence to which they are **called,** a matter of hearing and responding to God's word. The word God speaks through the Son **calls** them to share in a new relationship that is infinitely superior to the legalistic piosity to which the Lycus Valley religionists are tempted to turn. This superiority involves further the **heavenly** source of the word itself, for the one who addresses them as **the apostle** stands above the principalities and powers of the universe. The use of the word **apostle,** which in the rest of the New Testament depicts the role of early Christian missionaries or of other human messengers, appears to lift up the kerygmatic function of Jesus in speaking the genuine word to his congregation (Hebrews 1:2). Thus the combination of **apostle and high priest** brings into unity the Christology of Hebrews: as high priest he brings persons into the dialogue with the holy God and as apostle he initiates that dialogue by addressing them with the word. Since salvation is the dialogue itself, the fitting response is to **fix your attention** on the partner and to retain a rational grip on the **confession.** By responding in this way to God's word in the Christ event, the author feels the congregation has already experienced the superiority of their new life, which he goes on to spell out.

Verses 2 through 4 develop the motif of Christ as the agent of creation that we have encountered in 1:2, 10, and 2:10. By use of the Septuagint citation about Moses as **faithful . . . in God's house,** the author argues for the superiority of Christ on the grounds that he is the **builder** of this house. The analogy of the builder having more honor than the house itself has a significant impact, even though it is not carried through very coherently in verse 4. For it implies that Moses was nothing more than part of the **house** that Christ created. In this context, **house** is a "comprehensive term, including the father, the children, and the servants—indeed the whole spiritual community, with all its elements," according to Theodore H. Robinson. In the terms of this discussion, it depicts the theocratic realm—the kingdom of God—just as in the rabbinic and apocalyptic materials it refers to the realm where the Law is properly obeyed and where God is properly worshiped. If it is Christ who creates this theocratic house and offers it to his **brethren** who share the heavenly calling, it follows that Moses' position and the validity of the law he promulgated are radically diminished. Inasmuch as the Lycus Valley worship of angels included elements from the Mosaic law that were to be performed in order to actuate the theocratic realm, this argument is effective. But it is difficult to follow the logic through verse 4b, for why would the insistence that **the builder of everything is God** sustain the argument that Christ's superiority stems from his building the house? Some recent commentators appear to skip over this discrepancy, while others, such as Otto Michel and William Barclay, follow the ancient commentators in assuming that the author identifies Christ as God at this point. Perhaps it would be best to acknowledge the difficulty and to leave open the possibility that the author is logically inconsistent at this point.

Verses 5 and 6 move the discussion of Christ's superiority from the matter of creation to the arena of the new relationship. Moses was faithful as an **attendant**, which means he had a slavelike relationship to the head of the house. This term, which the author cites from the Septuagint version of Numbers 12:7, connoted in the Hellenistic world the slavelike service rendered by a worshiper to his or her god. This term relates closely to the abject "worship of angels" against which the author of Colossians polemizes in 2:18. That this negative connotation is intended by the author is indicated by the contrast with the position of the **son** in the house. At this point the author makes use of the Pauline contrast between the relationship of the slave and the relationship of the Son, whereby the law is seen as the enslaving force of Mosaic religion that had been abrogated by the Christ event (Galatians 4:1-7). Whereas the **attendant** is kept a respectful distance from the holy presence, the **son** can freely enter into relationship with his father. It is the openness and the freedom of this new relationship that are lifted up in the closing words of verse 6: **keep fearless and proud of hope.** *Parrēsia* (=fearlessness) depicts the boldness of a speaker standing before an awesome ruler and openly declaring his or her case without fear of the consequences. Heinrich Schlier notes the importance of this term for the author of Hebrews (cf. 4:16; 10:19, 35), lifting up the freedom, the capability, and the openness of the Christian standing before God. Schlier also notes that this term was used in Colossians 2:15 in a unique fashion to depict the bold and public triumph of Christ over the cosmic forces. It seems quite in contrast to the "self-abasement" characteristic of the Lycus Valley piety (Colossians 2:18, 23). In a similar vein the author uses the word pride as characteristic of the relationship inaugurated by the **son.** Whereas Paul often uses this term in a negative sense, the author emphasizes hereby the sense of boasting in a new relationship, similar to the joyous boasting in the eschatological fulfillment that one occasionally finds in the Old Testament (Zechariah 10:12; Psalm 149:5; 1 Chronicles 16:33). Again, this attitude seems much more robust than the "self-abasement" in the Lycus Valley, based as it was on a feeling of inferiority before the cosmic forces of the universe.

The source of this robust feeling of fearlessness and pride is the astounding fact alluded to in verse 6: **whose house we are.** Here the congregation is flatly identified with the theocratic realm over which Christ rules as the **son.** They replace Israel—the **house** in which Moses served as an **attendant.** It is the same antithesis as found in the Pauline letters, which contrast the "Jerusalem above" with the "present Jerusalem" (Galatians 4:21–31). In other passages one finds the claim that the Christian congregation is the "temple of God" (1 Corinthians 3:16; 6:19; Ephesians 2:19–22) or the "spiritual house" in which God dwells (1 Peter 2:5). It is noteworthy that this motif was very popular in gnosticism, with the soul seeking to return to the spiritual house from whence it was alienated by having descended into the constraining material world. Philo individualized this concept so that the enlightened soul became the divine house: "Hurry therefore, my soul, to become God's house, a holy sanctuary, the loveliest resting place [Som. I, 149]." On the basis of this widespread usage, Ernst Käsemann has suggested that the author of Hebrews takes over the gnostic conception of salvation as restoration of heavenly particles to their rightful heavenly house. If this is so, then it is essential to note the radical departures from the gnostic viewpoint that are implicit in the author's argument. In contrast to the doctrine that one regains one's position in the divine house by esoteric ceremonies designed to appease the aeons, the author claims this status as a pure gift on grounds that the **son** has brought his **brethren** with him into the Holy Place (2:13; 3:1). And in contrast to static gnostic possession of spiritual identity, the author inserts a dynamic sort of historical tension into the idea: **whose house we are if we keep fearless and proud of hope.** Since being God's **house** means taking part in a new relationship, it must constantly be renewed. It can be lost if one grows too fearful and abject to engage the partner once again in the enlivening dialogue. And there is a future dimension of **hope** that the dialogue will be continued tomorrow and will finally be consummated "when all things are put under his feet." Thus the author's claim that the congregation constitutes the intimate sphere of the theocratic realm has the result of thrusting Christian existence out into the arena of secular history. Whereas the Gnostics and their Lycus Valley counterparts encouraged retreat to a spiritual enclave, and offered methods to secure this enclave against the threats of the supposedly evil secular world, the author understands the Christian's **heavenly calling** as evoking a mature, bold sense of responsibility to the creator out in the secular sphere where **hope** alone gives meaning to life.

3:7 **Therefore as the Holy Spirit says,**
   "Today, when you hear his voice,
   [8]harden not your hearts as in the rebellion,
   on the day of testing in the wilderness,

⁹where your fathers put me to the test
and saw my works for forty years.
¹⁰Therefore I was provoked with this generation,
and I said, 'They always go astray in their hearts;
they would not know my ways.'
¹¹So I swore in my wrath,
'They shall never enter into my rest.'"

¹²Take care, brethren, lest there be in any of you an evil, unfaithful heart, standing in apostasy from the living God. ¹³But exhort one another every day, as long as today is called out, that none of you be hardened by the deceitfulness of sin. ¹⁴For we are participants with Christ provided that we keep firm to the end the assurance with which we started, ¹⁵this word ever sounding in our ears,

"Today when you hear his voice,
harden not your hearts as in the rebellion."

¹⁶For which hearers were they that rebelled? Was it not all those who fled from Egypt under Moses? ¹⁷And with whom was he provoked for forty years? Was it not with those who sinned, whose bodies fell in the wilderness? ¹⁸And to whom did he swear that they should never enter his rest, but to those who were disobedient? ¹⁹So we see that they were unable to enter because of unfaithfulness.

In the next twenty-six verses the author sets forth the conditions of present participation in the eschatological fulfillment. Countering the anxiety and complacency of the Lycus Valley religionists, he emphasizes both the present enjoyment of the theocratic rest and the stern requirements of its dialogical character. In 3:7-19 it is the latter that are under discussion.

The case rests on an interpretation of Psalm 95:7-11, cited here from the Septuagint except for two alterations that relate the text more closely to the addressees. In verse 10 the original "that generation" is changed to this generation, thus making the connection with the Lycus Valley congregation more explicit and sharpening the seriousness of the warning. The second alteration is necessitated by the first, for the Septuagint "your fathers tested me; they put me to the test and saw my works; for forty years I was provoked with that generation" would imply that God will be provoked with the Lycus Valley congregations for forty years. By changing this to seeing **my works for forty years** the difficulty is partially alleviated, and it is interesting to note that when the author later specifies the desert generation as those who experienced God's wrath, he follows the Septuagint precisely. These alterations clearly express the hermeneutical intent of the author, because he wishes to warn his congregation about the requirements of dialogue without contributing to their anxiety that the **rest** is barred by divine wrath.

The **rest,** the concept that dominates 3:17—4:13, connoted the eschatological fulfillment in first-century Judaism and Christianity. In the context of Psalm 95, of course, it connotes the promised land, i.e., the theocratic kingdom fully freed from its enemies and fully provided with God's bounty and thus at peace. These theocratic connotations are clearly visible in the way **rest** is used in the Old Testament. Deuteronomy 12:9-10 is a good example: "You have not as yet come to the *rest* and to the inheritance which the Lord your God gives you. But when you go over the Jordan, and live in the land which the Lord your God gives you to inherit, and when he gives you *rest* from all your enemies round about, so that you live in safety. . . ." The idea of the theocratic realm protected from God's enemies is visible in Deuteronomy 25:19: "Therefore when the Lord your God has given you *rest* from all your enemies round about, in the land which the Lord your God gives you for an inheritance to possess, you shall blot out the remembrance of Amalek." When one examines the Septuagint usage of this term, it depicts the promised land itself, or the peace of the promised land; otherwise it connotes the sabbath or cessation of work and other activities; and in a less technical sense, the verb can depict completing a task or laying something down. In light of the experiences of the author's congregation at the hands of their enemies (10:32-34), it seems probable that **rest** for them would include something of this theocratic conception of a divinely defended territory. But as Käsemann has shown, the author's definition of this **rest** in terms of the seventh day in 4:4ff. relates it to the speculations about the sabbath as the highest aeon in Jewish and gnostic writings. In Pirke de Rabbi Eliezer 18, a late Jewish version of this speculation is described as follows: "Seven aeons has God created, and of them all he prefers the seventh; six are there for coming and going and one is entirely a Sabbath and quiet in eternal life." In gnostic writings like the Acts of Philip (148), the Odes of Solomon (38:4; 25:11f.; 26:11f.; 2:5), and the Acts of Thomas (10), the *rest* is depicted as the goal of the ascent through the cosmic spheres.

In contrast to Käsemann, however, it appears more appropriate to assume the presence of gnostic speculation about the **rest** in the Lycus Valley than on the part of the author himself. He consistently treats this **rest** as the present reality in which the congregation participates through dialogue with the gospel, retaining a very ungnostic emphasis on the possibility of losing it through unfaithfulness. Given the worship of the cosmic aeons and the emphasis on the sabbath in the Lycus Valley (Colossians 2:16-18), however, there is good reason to believe that they would desire permanent ascent to this blessed aeon of sabbath ease. They would have thought of it as the realm that transcended the threatening power of the lower aeons, and that the way to ascend to it was through appeasing these lower forces by cultic observances. In this way the Old Testament concept of the **rest** as the theocratic kingdom at peace from its enemies was taken up into the gnostic religiosity in the Lycus Valley, and a new method of entering this realm was promulgated.

With this background in mind, the author's argument in verses 7 to 19 stands forth in its antignostic thrust. Participating in the **rest** is not a matter of possessing the gnostic mind or self-knowledge that incorporates one in the divine, but rather of having a **heart** that **stands** in relation with the **living God**. The term **heart** implies an understanding of human nature as a unity of thought, emotion, and body in a way that is antithetical to gnosticism. This Judaic usage views humans not in terms of their knowledge or their divine origin, but rather in terms of their covenant loyalty, their will to stand faithfully in relation to God. Thus in his warning, the author defines **evil** in the sense of **unfaithful**ness to the covenant partner, of **apostasy** or breach of relationship with the **living God.** The Lycus Valley piety would clearly constitute **apostasy** in this sense, because it ascribed ultimacy to the cosmic forces and urged a worshipful relationship to them in order to free the self for ascent to the **rest.** To fall prey to this set of pious illusions would constitute, in the author's opinion, being **hardened by the deceitfulness of sin.** The deceit lies in the false premises and promises of this cosmic foolishness, for the angels are not ultimate and the **rest** cannot be gained by pious manipulation. Yet there is a terrible moral realism in the author's discernment of a **hardening** that ensues from a false religion of this sort. There is a fanatical, ossified texture to any religion based on the manipulation of the world to the advantage of the elect, because its motivation is anxiety rather than faith. It lacks that openness and resilience of faith standing within a deteriorating, secular world in relationship with **the living God.** It lacks the readiness and present-mindedness of those who respond **today.** Those who are obsessed with schemes to manipulate tomorrow receive a peculiar form of **harden**ing: they lose the capacity to enjoy and to respond **today;** they allow the enlivening dialogue to slip away and be lost.

In light of this danger, the author calls upon the members of the congregation to take up the task of mutual exhortation: **exhort one another every day, as long as today is called out.** This task is given not simply to the evangelists, such as the author who pens this "word of exhortation" (13:22), but to every member of the pilgrim community. The laity is not relegated to the field of diaconic service, while the clergy carries on a more exalted task of proclaiming God's word. In a radical democratization of the church's function, the Epistle to the Hebrews places the proclamation of the gospel on the shoulders of each member. As the wording of the passage makes clear, each member participates in the work of the Holy Spirit. For in and through this mutual exhortation, the congregation is to hear the **Holy Spirit** when the Script says, "**Today** . . ." The power and the effectiveness of the exhortation is therefore not due to the training and the skill of the exhorter, but to God's spirit. By speaking to people in this way, God carries out dialogue with covenant partners. The theme of God's speaking, which opened the Epistle to the Hebrews, comes here to its effective channeling, not so much in the cult of the pious enclave, but in the mutual exhortation that takes place **every day** in the life of the pilgrim community.

Yet the content of this mutual exhortation must be acknowledged to differ from the usual pious admonitions of religious communities from the Lycus Valley to the corner of Fifth and Main. The Epistle to the Hebrews itself, as a "word of exhortation," provides a fitting pattern for evaluation. It eschews the rules for self-improvement, the guidelines to conform to petty morality, and the castigations of the secular world that have so vitiated the substance of Christian preaching. It avoids that laming sense of religious distinction between exhorter and exhorted, because it remains conscious that God "has spoken to us [all] by a Son [Heb. 1:2, RSV]," and that to **exhort one another** requires exchanging roles day by day. It lacks that desperate tone that marks every effort to shore up the crumbling walls of would-be "lasting cities," and it retains the freshness of a word that relates the Christ event to **today** rather than to the so-called perennial problems of humankind. Furthermore, it is an exhortation that is, at the same time, encouragement or comfort. The word *paraklēsis* (=exhort) connotes both warning and comfort, and nowhere in Hebrews is this double connotation more clearly in view than here: the congregation that is offered the possibility of entering the eschatological **rest** in the midst of its daily pilgrimage is urged to take seriously the exigencies of such a fulfillment defined as dialogue with the **living God**. That which holds the warning and the comfort together is the relational character of Christian existence. So with magnificent consistency and clarity the author's exhortation fits the pattern of the pilgrim community's life before God, thus providing a fitting model for daily mutual exhortation.

The claim that provides the title for this chapter is found in verse 14: **for we are participants with Christ.** A quick glance at a concordance indicates the unique importance of "participation" in the argument of Hebrews. The verb *metechō* is found in 2:14; 5:13; and 7:13, and elsewhere in the New Testament only in 1 Corinthians. The noun participant—*metochos*—occurs in Hebrews 1:9; 3:1, 14; 6:4; and 12:8, and otherwise only in Luke 5:7. The shape of Hebrews' radical reinterpretation of these terms is discernible when one recalls the Platonic usage that came to be widely used in Hellenistic literature. One spoke of the object "participating" in the eternal idea, the lower in the higher, the earthly in the heavenly; under the assumption that humans have something of the divine in them, one spoke of their having "participation" with the gods, just as church leaders like Irenaeus and Origen came to speak of a virtual apotheosis of Christians, making "participation" with God or Christ possible. This Platonic legacy was related to the gnostic conception of the self that finds redemption by its knowledge of union with the divine. Günther Bornkamm uncovered this conception in relation to the Colossian heresy and thereby offers a basis for reconstructing what the Lycus Valley religionists would have envisioned with the expression **participants with Christ.** Their natural tendency would be to understand this in terms of being united in the highest aeon—the **rest**—with the divine Christ. This was what they sought to attain by appeasing the cosmic forces so as to make an ascent to the blessed realm possible. In contrast, Hebrews eliminates all qualifications and mystical precautions in the flat claim **we are participants with Christ.**

The basis for this striking claim is not the divine nature of the gnostic-self, but rather Christ's participation in the limited human nature of flesh and blood. This basis is not only provided by the argument of 2:10–17, but also by the use of the noun *metochos*, "comrade, participant," in 1:9 and the verb *metechō*, "participate," in 2:14. In this regard the author of Hebrews is much more radical than the Lycus Valley Gnostics in his claims for the present status of believers. He can claim present participation with Christ, because participation for him means relationship, not divinization. Thus a three-faceted qualification of this new relationship is provided as a defense against gnostic misunderstandings.

First, the participation requires **keeping firm . . . the assurance** in the sense of 3:6, being bold enough to enter into dialogue with the awesome covenant partner. It is Christ's participation in our human plight that dispels its alienation and makes such **assurance** possible within the limitations of finitude. Threats are not overcome, as in gnosticism, by claiming to transcend finitude, but rather by being offered a new and sustaining relationship within finitude.

Second, the participation with Christ has a historical horizon, because the relationship **with which we started** is to be kept **firm to the end**. There is a strong sense of the exigencies of time in this expression, for the relationship enjoyed today must be renewed tomorrow or be lost. This is a point where the author must challenge the Lycus Valley assumptions, for they yearn for a participation that unites divine souls with a divine source in an eternal union, and thus they cannot envisage the loss of such union through the sort of unfaithfulness the author sees in Psalm 95. They assume an ellipse between the *archē* (=starting point, beginning) and the *telos* (=end) in which redemption constitutes restoration to one's original divine status.

Third, **participants with Christ** have God's word **ever sounding in** their **ears, "Today, when you hear his voice, harden not your hearts as in the rebellion."** Participation is here defined in terms of dialogue. Their salvation was inaugurated by the gospel (1:1-2; 2:3-4), and now they are to recognize that it addresses them day by day, in the mutual exhortation of the pilgrim community and in the words of the scripture. And in the situation of the Lycus Valley congregations, a particular word of warning is encountering them. It shatters their illusions about any security achievable through cultic adoration of the angelic forces. For if participation with Christ is dialogical, then it enters under the exigencies of history and must be faithfully maintained.

In verses 16 to 19 the author specifies the condition under which entrance into the rest can be barred, making clear that the ancient Hebrews had disqualified themselves. They, like the Christian congregation addressed by this epistle, were **hearers** of God's word. But they were **disobedient** to this word, resulting in a denial of access to the rest on account of **unfaithfulness.** The author abstracts this single point from Old Testament accounts of the incident at Rephidim (Exodus 17:1-7; Numbers 20:1-13), where the people expressed their discontent with their desert situation and Moses irritably struck the rock to provide water, although there are many tempting points of comparison with the situation of the Christian congregation. His attention is focused on just one thing: the requirement of dialogical existence to respond faithfully to the partner. This and this alone led to the dreadful consequences of provocation **for forty years,** collapse **in the wilderness,** and the utterance of the curse that **they should never enter his rest.** In avoiding any discussion of disposition or conformity to moral codes, the author insists that response to the gospel is the sole requirement for entering the theocratic rest.

4:1 **Therefore, while the promise of entering his rest remains, let us be afraid lest any of you be judged to have remained behind.** **²For we are gospel recipients similar to them, but the auditory word did not benefit them, because it was not blended by faith with the hearers. ³For we enter into the rest as persons of faith, as he said,**

"So I swore in my wrath,
'They shall never enter into my rest,'"
and yet the works were finished from the foundation of the
world. ⁴For somewhere he has spoken about the seventh day as
follows: "And God rested on the seventh day from all his
works." ⁵And again in the same place, "They shall never enter
into my rest." ⁶Since then it remains for some to enter because
of disobedience, ⁷again he sets a certain day—today—saying
through David after so long a time, as was said earlier,
"Today, when you hear his voice,
harden not your hearts."
⁸For if Jesus had given them rest, he would not speak later
about another day. ⁹So then, there remains a sabbath rest for
the people of God. ¹⁰And the one entering into this rest is the
very one who rests from his works, just as God rests from his.

The affirmative, comforting thrust of these ten verses is
epitomized by the opening words **while the promise of entering
his rest remains.** I noted in connection with the author's
alteration of Psalm 95 that he was concerned to warn the
congregation, without contributing to their anxiety, that the
path to the rest was barred for them. While they feared that the
path to the heavenly homeland could only be opened by appeasing the cosmic forces, he insists that it is in a very simple
and radical sense wide open in the present moment. This theme
receives its development in 4:1-10, whereby the time and the
place of the rest are defined in a way that differs markedly from
either the Lycus Valley assumptions or traditional Christian
viewpoints. An important feature about the opening lines of
this argument is that the promise provides the basis for the
demand. The indicative precedes the imperative, for the rest
lies open in an unconditional fashion, not requiring the
fulfillment of a demand before entering into it. Instead, the
demand rises out of the unconditional openness itself. Since the
way is open, **let us be afraid lest any of you be judged to have
remained behind.** The requirement rises out of the nature of
dialogue within history. The dialogue, once opened up, must

be entered into ever and again, for it can never be possessed in a static fashion. It moves irresistibly toward the future, from today toward the next today. The author captures this sense of movement with the verb *eiserchomai* (= enter into) in 3:11, 18; 4:1, 3, 5-6, and 10-11. In this term the sense of pilgrimage and the sense of entering into the holy sanctuary are combined. The image of being left behind also connotes a result of motion.

The author goes on to explain this requirement in evangelical terms. The ancient Hebrews and the Lycus Valley Christians are all gospel recipients. The participial form is difficult to render in English, but it shifts the emphasis to paraphrase the thought with something like "good news came to us just as to them (RSV)." The author is interested in defining the structure of Christian existence, favoring participial expressions like "hearers" (2:3; 3:16; 4:2), "men of faith" (4:3), "inheritors" (6:12), "sanctified ones" (2:11; 10:10, 14), and now kerygma or gospel recipients (4:2, 6). He communicates the thought that the gospel fundamentally conditions the structure of their existence. From the moment it encounters them, their present and future are determined by their response to it. To turn away from it is to forfeit life in the wilderness, but to accept it in faith is to enter his rest. The auditory word, or word of hearing, is a technical expression for the early Christian proclamation (cf. 1 Thessalonians 2:12). As the use of this expression in Romans 10:16ff. and Galatians 3:2 reveals, the assumption was that faith was made possible by hearing the gospel. With this conception, the author explains the tragedy of the desert generation in a sharp and memorable expression: the word did not benefit them because it was not blended by faith with the hearers. The word translated blended was often used to depict the blending of paints, the tempering of metals, and the joining of friends, or the implication of a person in a conspiracy. The idea here is that the kerygma, when received by faith, blends in and alters the person. Just as two tints join together to produce a third, so the person is changed when the gospel is received. If persons refuse this transformation, the word does not benefit them, and they are lost. The author's assumption here is that a person is determined by the reality in which he or she places faith; this reality gives shape to one's self-understanding and a sense of direction to one's life. To refuse to place one's faith in the promises of God is to retain one's faith in oneself or in human institutions, and either choice produces distinct and fundamental changes in the person. A faith in the human capacity to manipulate the cosmic forces leads to an anxious, involuted perspective, while faith in God's word leads to openness and courage in face of a threatening world. Thus, one choice leads to a **rest** and the other choice leads to destruction in the wilderness.

In verses 3 to 5 the author attempts to draw the dichotomy of **faith** versus **works** out of his text concerning the **rest**. His disjointed method of argument at this point leads most interpreters to skip over the verses without clarifying them. The use of the conjunction *kaitoi* (=**and yet**) in verse 3 makes it plain that the point about **works** is in some sort of tension with the citation about entering **my rest**. Of course, it is confusing that the word **works** is cited in verse 3, before the statement in Genesis 2:2 is adduced in the following verse. Further confusion is caused by the author's failing to develop his premise that **rest** in the sense of Genesis 2:2 implies cessation of **works**. He appears to feel this is self-evident, and it seems that he presupposes the Pauline tradition of faith versus self-justifying activity under the law to supply the required negative connotation for **works**. At any rate, I could reconstruct his argument as follows: (a) Since rest implies cessation of works, and (b) works are finished now that God founded the world, it follows that (c) we enter the rest not by works, but by faith. The negative implication concerning the plight of those barred from the rest is that (d) they attempted to enter not by faith, but by works. That something like this is intended by the author is indicated by his conclusion: **the one entering into this rest is the very one who rests from his work, just as God rests from his.** It is also consistent with the author's statement of the "elementary doctrines" in 6:1, "repentance from dead works and of faith toward God" (RSV), as well as with his negative use of the term in 9:14, RSV, "purify your conscience from dead works."

If this interpretation is correct, then there is a sharp polemic thrust in the thesis sentence: **we enter into the rest as persons of faith.** For **faith** would thereby have not only the positive sense of acceptance of the gospel, but also the negative sense of giving up **works.** It is this negative sense that counters the Lycus Valley heresy most directly and brings the disbarring of the desert generation into correlation with the present. The worship of angels, particularly if based on Mosaic regulations concerning proper foods and festival days, would constitute an extreme form of works-oriented religion. Its premise was that ascent to the divine sphere was possible only by performing the works demanded by the hostile aeons. It was a religion in which salvation depended not on grace, but on human effort. Thus the author completely reversed the claim of the Lycus Valley religionists. Despite the pretentious appeal of esoteric ceremonies, their **works** of pious manipulation could not provide access to the **rest,** because it could only be entered through **faith** in the gospel.

In verses 6 to 10 the author argues that the **rest** is presently open to the believing community. Those who were first invited to enter failed **because of disobedience,** preferring to set their faith in their own abilities or in the fleshpots of Egypt, and so remaining in a religion of *"works."* Thus the promise to enter remained for someone to take it up, and the author notes that the psalmist—David—writes long after the period of the desert wandering about the promise of the entrance into the rest. The translation of verse 8 is somewhat problematic in this connection, for at first glance *Iēsous* would seem to refer to Joshua, the leader of the desert community. Commentaries and translations all appear to render it with this assumption. But if Joshua is the subject of the first clause (verse 8a), then it must also be supplied as the subject for the verb in the second clause (8b)—which is patently absurd. How could Joshua be thought to "speak later of another day" in Psalm 95? The author seems to assume, as Paul did in his interpretation of the desert generation (1 Corinthians 10:1ff.), that Christ was present there, acting in and through the symbols and the persons in the story. So it is actually Christ himself who speaks **later about another day** in the exhortation "**Today, when you hear his voice, harden not your hearts.**" The result is that the rest may be entered right at the present moment by the Christian community: **So then, there remains a sabbath rest for the people of God.** Using the present tense of the verb in verses 9 and 6 makes it perfectly plain that the author does not have some future entrance into heaven in mind. Commentators such as Charles Erdman, thinking of this in terms of "the heavenly rest which awaits the followers of Christ," seem to miss the point of the argument.

This thesis had radical implications for the Lycus Valley situation. If entrance into the **sabbath rest** is a present possibility for the **people of God,** then the elaborate manipulations of the cosmic forces to open up the ascent to such a rest are entirely unnecessary. There is no necessity to perform the tedious works of the cult in order to guarantee one's future. This would seem to apply equally to the modern forms of guaranteeing access to blessedness, whether they be the fulfillment of institutional obligations or conforming to the standards of consumer culture. Rather than providing access to the **sabbath rest,** these forms of religious and secular piety lead humans to a self-dependence that stands in opposition to faith. They bar one from the **rest.** Furthermore, to take another tack, if the relationship called rest is now open to the **persons of faith,** then the Lycus Valley effort to avoid the challenge of **today** is shown up for what it really was. Their assumption was that enjoyment of the **rest** was impossible **today** because of the threats and uncertainties of life in a deteriorating secular world. Thus they devised the method of appeasing the cosmic forces so that the present dilemma could be overcome by recapturing the past, for the uniting of the gnostic self with the divine sphere was thought of as a restoration of the original divinity of the self. The nostalgic premise of this gnostic theology is countered by the author's repeated emphasis on today . . . today . . . today, which lifts up the possibility of fulfillment right in the midst of secular history, right in the path of one's worldly pilgrimage. If one enters into the rest today, then the point of the pilgrimage is not to arrive at some predetermined goal or to achieve some predetermined virtue in the end. Rather it is to be encountered by Christ, who addresses us in the kerygma, and in responding by faith, to carry on the enlivening dialogue. The author would agree with Martin Buber's dictum that all real living is meeting. With this reinterpretation of the rest, the author inserts dynamic activism into what has traditionally been a rather passive concept. It is no longer the promised land secured from its enemies, but rather a possibility in the midst of battle. It is no longer the sabbath when one's work is done, but rather entrance into dialogue in the midst of one's work. It is no longer an image of heaven, when the golden slippers replace the harsh struggle of pilgrimage, but rather an entrance into the relationship with God, which is called faith.

In light of these implications and of the author's polemic definition of works, the closing verse serves as a fitting climax: And the one entering into this rest is the very one who rests from his works, just as God rests from his. This does not imply that entrance into the rest produces cessation from all activity or that it brings the pilgrimage to a halt. The works he has in mind are the self-justifying activities of religious persons, specifically the sort of frantic effort to manipulate life that was being advocated in the Lycus Valley. It is such anxiety-driven works that corrode the capacity to achieve fullness. They isolate people from God and from one another, and drive them in upon themselves in a futile ellipse. They make life-giving dialogue impossible, for they pit persons against their peers, and even against God, in the drive for status. Therefore, to enter into the rest, which is dialogue with God, is to cease from one's works to manipulate life. It is also to cease dealing with another person as an "it." And perhaps this is the sense in which the author speaks of God resting from his works which, as stated in verse 3, were finished from the foundation of the

world. Does he feel that God no longer relates to God's creatures as **works,** i.e., as objects, but rather as subjects to be personally addressed by the word? The following verses (4:11-13) seem to have something like this in view. Another possibility is that the point of comparison between the person of faith who **rests from his works** and God who **rests from his** is simply in the term rest and not that from which they rest.

This matter of **resting from his works** relates closely to a major problem in the contemporary psyche. The **works** of both business and charity, which some moderns feel impelled to do, clog their leisure hours and their conscience, destroying the possibility of **rest.** The conscience today is plagued not so much by the memory of evil deeds as of unaccomplished deeds. The paragons of virtue in modern society, whether secular or religious, are kept awake nights worrying not about their sins of commission, but those of omission. Not only are we oppressed with the **works** that never end, but we are torn between a multiplicity of equally good causes. It is not just that we cannot make up our mind as to which work should get priority, but that we feel guilty when we cannot accomplish them all. The unfinished work rises as a specter out of our conscience, driving us to sleep that is sufficiently drugged and entertainment that is sufficiently absorbing to offer **rest.** The motivations which produce these **works** are difficult to untangle, but it would appear that desires for human betterment and improvement of personal status play important roles. There is an assumption operating here, differing only in its implementation from the Lycus Valley religiosity, that persons and institutions can be manipulated to produce salvation. There is also an assumption, deeply grounded in the American mentality, that status is grounded in quantitative achievement. For the effort to justify oneself by **works** has shifted from doing what is right or legal to simply doing much. The highest accolade is to be acknowledged as hard working and ceaselessly active in behalf of one's projects: the person active in five organizations has superior status over someone active in only four. But whether it derives from the desire to manipulate the world for human betterment or for personal status, this propensity to endless **works** has become one of the major burdens for the American psyche. The redemption that such a person requires, therefore, is not so much forgiveness of sins as **rest . . . from his works.**

4:11   **Let us therefore strive to enter into that rest, that no one fall by the same sort of disobedience.**
12For the word of God is living,
    active, and more cutting than any two-edged sword,
    piercing to the division of soul and spirit, of
    joints and marrow, and scrutinizing the desires
    and thoughts of the heart.
13And no creature is hidden before him, but all lie naked and vulnerable before the eyes of him, before whom our word stands in dialogue.

With the exhortation to **enter into that rest** and the hymnic praise of God's word in verses 12 to 13, the argument begun in 1:1 is brought to conclusion. If Christ's rule over the world is kerygmatic; if response to the gospel leads to participation by the humans in that rule; and if participation in the divine house and rest is possible through such response—then it is appropriate to conclude by exhorting the hearers to a proper sort of **striving**. Hitherto, the Lycus Valley congregations had been striving to manipulate the cosmic powers so as to make entrance into the blessed aeon of **rest** possible, but now this sort of striving has fallen under the judgment of "works" and has been classified as the sort of disobedience that actually bars one from God's presence. So the sort of **striving** required by the gospel is the striving of dialogue, a matter of seeking and holding fast a new relationship that one has been given. Even though such dialogue offered by the word of God is a matter of unconditional grace, the most vigorous kind of response is required. The word *spoudazō* (=**strive**) depicts both haste and zealous engagement. The choice of this term counters the assumption that the **rest** can be maintained permanently in sloth. Just as the Lycus Valley Gnostics sought that rejoining of the self with the divine aeon from whence it could never be endangered again, yearning for a "lasting city" that was secure from threat and alarm, so religious persons in every period have sought a resting place where striving is no longer necessary. The heavenly Jerusalem! The final refuge! The City of God! The last best hope on earth! The bastion of freedom! These are some of the religious and secular equivalents of the "lasting city," and there is a slothful premise to each one of them. They appear to offer a life in which zealous engagement and personal transformation are no longer required. This complacent yearning is taking new forms in the modern world. As Emil Fackenheim has noted, a new form of slothful, self-idolatry is emerging in modern drama: the person who scoffs at all ideals and exhortations to take up her or his human responsibility. "A type of idolator currently at large in the secular city wants simply to *be*." Against this perennial human effort to leave the slothful self unchanged while demanding the alteration of others and of the world for the sake of one's own comfort, the author of Hebrews posits a vigorous life of transforming dialogue in the midst of the secular world. It is a life that increases rather than abates the threats against the self, for to **fall** as the desert generation fell is a constant possibility. It is not that human beings are afflicted by weakness or any inherent tendency to fall out of dialogue; the great threat in the opinion of the author is to exchange the relationship with a living God for a manipulation of God and the divinely created forces for the sake of the self as the Lycus Valley Gnostics have done. Despite the deceitful lure of such manipulation, the author's point is that it constitutes a reversal of true faith and leads irrevocably to a **fall.** It is a form of "cheap grace," presuming in face of the sovereign demands of God that life can be received without attendant responsibilities. It fails to take account of the fearsome power of God who encounters humankind in the gospel. So it is on this motif that the first great section in the argument of Hebrews closes.

The paean to the living **word of God** in verses 12 and 13 is marked by solemn cadence in participial style that Eduard Norden showed was typical for Hellenistic hymnic materials. The terminology is unique for the New Testament, and there is little doubt that the closest parallels are in Hellenistic literature such as Philo (de Cherub. 28; quis rer. div. her. 130ff.) and the Wisdom of Solomon (7:22-24; 18:15-17). The suggestion has been made by Hans Windisch and Ernst Käsemann that the author modifies a traditional hymn at this point, but since no really precise citations have been documented and since the rhetorical flow in both verses is even and coherent, it is difficult to discern where or if the author's modification ends and the original material begins. When one takes account of the close relationship of these two verses to the argument of the preceding chapters in Hebrews, it seems more probable that the author has shaped the traditional Hellenistic materials quite freely and freshly for his own purpose.

Verse 12 lifts up the dynamic character of God's word. It is **living** in the sense that it **acts, cuts,** and **pierces** to the core of the person, **scrutinizing the desires and thoughts of the heart.** The **heart,** here as in chapter 3 used as the unified source of emotions and ideas, is pictured as the target of this attacking **word.** That which each person shields from view—the inner source of deeds whether religious or secular—is here under judgment. And there is no escaping it. The **word** is sharper than **any two-edged sword** used by the soldier or executioner, and it thrusts through to the mysterious structures of both the inner and the outer person. The author speaks here in the same breath of the **spirit** that the Gnostic adored as an irreproachable portion of the divine, the **soul** that the Gnostic despised as earthbound, and the **joints and marrow** that are the integral structure of the body that the Gnostic viewed as the source of evil. All are on an equal plane before the scrutiny of this **word,** and none can be thought of as exempt because of intrinsic virtue or evil. So humankind is held accountable by the **word of God,** called away from its artful excuses into the realm of responsibility.

The following verse completes this picture of persons laid

71

bare by the **word. No creature is hidden before God** who is the author and ruler of the entire universe. There are no independent powers behind which humans may contrive a refuge, no matter how effective their appeasement of the aeons or how sophisticated their cybernetics. Every effort to manipulate life so as to produce some "lasting city" is doomed by the finitude of the **creature** and the power of God's **word.** Far from being capable of protecting themselves from mortal threats, humans cannot even shield their own nakedness from that penetrating and scrutinizing vision. One meaning of the word translated **vulnerable,** as Michel has shown, is bending back the throat of the sacrificial animal for the death-dealing knife. In the context of the **eyes** of God, both **naked and vulnerable** depict exposure and openness. They indicate an enforced frankness and honesty on the part of the faithful pilgrims. Their facades of superior virtue and pretentious knowledge are all destroyed, and they are forced to live with raw nerve endings and without defenses in the midst of a deteriorating world. The crooked hypocrisy of the religious and the covert deviousness of the secular are unveiled. The images that we so carefully construct about ourselves and our institutions are torn asunder by this penetrating glance. And as a result, we are brought face to face with reality. Under the impact of God's **word** we are driven to see ourselves as we are and the world as it is. Such a person evolves into a "man come of age," mature in the full sense of the word.

The author's vision of the awesome power of God's word stands as much in judgment of modern poses as it does of the Lycus Valley piety. The yearning today is for a word that is "relevant" to present needs, as if it would redeem humans from their deadly inversion to hear another word that pleases them. This yearning is largely motivated by a conception of religion as fulfilling basic human needs. The result is that religion ends up as simply the embodiment of human projections, an expression of the desire for security and for answers to questions. Such a religion deserves the condemnation of Feuerback, Marx, Freud, Fromm, and its other notable modern critics. But it receives a much more telling condemnation in the face of God's word, because as the author discerns, that word never leaves humans alone with their defenses, illusions, and projections.

In light of verses 12 and 13 it would appear that the path to a revitalization of kerygmatic activity in the modern church is to relate that word in such a way as to expose hiding places. This need not be done with the self-assurance that has marked some of the moralizing evangelists of our time. If God's word is **living** and **active**, then it can simply be allowed to play its searching light on the pretensions and the escape mechanisms of modern humans in the full awareness that it lays the proclaimers as bare as it does the listeners. Furthermore, it is interesting to note that the author does not speak of the **word** being "entertaining." It is part of the slothful syndrome of a consumer culture that we demand to be entertained in church. We desire the **word** to be "interesting." It must titillate and keep our attention, but it dare not disturb. The typical modern exhorter, whether in the pulpit or on the secular daises of the mass media, clothes his or her moralizing with delightfully entertaining episodes and illustrations. One senses an underlying anxiety that the **word** cannot stand on its own power and do its own work unless it first entertains. Hebrews rejects the slothful premise of this anxiety, because God's word does not leave the consumer complacent as entertainment inevitably does. It shakes people out of their lethargy and shatters their illusions so that they get off their couches, turn off the entertaining images, and enter the arena of real life.

It is in this way that the dynamic work of God's word provides the indispensable basis for valid secularism. It drives humans to see that they cannot assume that God, the world, and the neighbor are simply extensions of themselves, to be manipulated by sophisticated means. In this sense, it was ridiculous for secular theologians of the sixties to imply that it was the modern world that first overcame the notion of God as an answer to unanswerable questions and the provider for unfilled appetites. Genuine biblical faith has always countered this idolatrous conception, and "man come of age" is not a human being without further "need" of God but rather a human being with a proper faith in God. Persons on the secular pilgrimage envisioned by Hebrews are disabused of any notion that they are manipulating the world to their advantage, because they are conscious of being constantly under attack by God's word, which encounters them on the course of this pilgrimage and invites them into the **rest** in which illusions and pretensions are put aside.

Thus it is appropriate for the author to close his first portion of the argument on the term *logos* (=Word). As Franz Joseph Schierse has noted, the entire first portion of Hebrews is dominated by the imagery of speaking. The verb *lalein* (=speak) occurs in 1:1, 2; 2:3; 3:5; and 4:8; the term *logos* is used in 2:2 and 4:2, as well as in our present verse; the term calling is used in 3:1; the verb listen is used in 2:1; 3:7, 15; and 4:2, 7; and the term "to proclaim" is found in 4:2, 6. The translation of the last five words in this section, which I render with **before whom our word stands in dialogue**, is very much under debate. Michel translates this with "before whom we speak," which comes about as close as any commentator to taking the phrase as it stands. For Michel, it expresses the responsibility of the speaker before God. However, Spicq charges quite properly that such a translation is simply banal, preferring to follow the route of most English commentators. Theodore H. Robinson, for example, argues that *logos* here is used in a radically different sense than elsewhere in the argument of Hebrews, rendering the expression as "with whom we have to reckon." None of the advocates of this translation seem to be able to explain the peculiar use of the preposition *pros* (=to, with reference to, before), the dative *hemin* (=to us, in relation to us), or the emphatic position of *logos* at the end of the sentence that closes the entire first three and a half chapters of an argument centering on the concept of the **word**. It goes without saying that it is difficult to make a plausible case that *logos* is used in a different sense in verse 13 than in verse 12. The clue that led to the translation suggested here is the use of the preposition *pros*. Bauer's *Lexicon* lists under *pros* with the accusative the category of use in connection with terms like "saying or speaking." The Hebraic expression of speaking face to face is *stoma pros stoma*. The phrase *pros hon* thus means "toward whom" or in the context of the eyes of God, "before whom." I would prefer to retain the sense for *logos* that has dominated the argument of Hebrews up to this point, i.e., a spoken proclamation. Finally, it must be admitted that the dative *hemin* (= to us) is only imperfectly rendered by attaching it to *logos* as "our word." The author appears to feel that the word resonates between the speakers and God, and the translation **before whom our word stands in dialogue** is an imperfect effort to express this thought.

Chapter Four

The Exhortation to Approach God's Presence (4:14–16) Through Christ's Atoning Humanity (5:1–10)

4:14 **H**AVING therefore a great high priest who has passed through the heavens, Jesus, the Son of God, let us hold fast to the confession. ¹⁵For we do not have a priest who is incapable of sympathizing with our weaknesses, but one who has been tempted the same as we without sins. ¹⁶Let us therefore with boldness approach the throne of grace, that we may receive mercy and find grace, to help in time of need.

These verses mark the beginning of the great middle section of the argument in Hebrews concerning the ministry performed by Christ the high priest and by the participating community. They form, as Franz Joseph Schierse has noted, an exhortative bracket corresponding to 10:19–31, so that the intention of the speculative, theological argument in this middle section is clarified. The author wishes to call his congregations to take up their rightful share in the ministry Christ the high priest performs, entering into God's presence in the course of their daily pilgrimage. His ministry makes their ministry possible; his worshipful approach to God breaks a pathway for their worshipful approach; his liturgy of suffering and participation in the secular world make it possible for them to offer a similar liturgy to God. This interlacing of the indicative and the imperative that marks the argument of 4:14—

10:31 as a whole also comes to expression in the wording of the exhortative brackets themselves. The urge to participate in the heavenly liturgy flows from the assurance that the great high priest has opened up access to the divine throne. The result is that the author avoids the moralizing tone that frequently infects the exhortative mode of discourse.

The exhortation in 4:14-16 is twofold: **hold fast to the confession** and **approach the throne of grace.** The terminology used here is both vigorous and technical. *Krateō* (= **hold fast**) is derived from the term power, and it often depicts seizure of power or taking something under control. The vigor of the term is visible in the usage elsewhere in the New Testament. Mark uses it to depict John the Baptist's seizure by Herod (Mark 6:16), the desires of the high priest to seize Jesus (Mark 12:12; 14:1), and the final episode in the garden. Judas says, "The one I shall kiss is the man; seize him [Mark 14:44, 46, 49, 51]." Acts reports the charge against Paul laid before Felix: "He even tried to profane the temple, but we seized him [Acts 24:6]." The same term is used in Revelation to describe the violent demise of the dragon: "An angel . . . seized the dragon . . . and bound him for a thousand years, and threw him into the pit [Rev. 20:1-3]." That which is to be forcibly held in Hebrews' exhortation is the **confession.** As one can see from the use of this noun in 3:1 and 10:23, as well as the corresponding verb in 11:13 and 13:15, what is to be confessed is not one's sins or merely a traditional set of dogmas. The term has something of a liturgical sense in Hebrews, depicting the response of the believing congregation to its covenant partner. It is an aspect of communal dialogue, and the content of the confession is derived from the worshipers' sense of the meaning of the salvation offered by the partner. Just as the patriarchs "confessed" out of their experience that "they were strangers and exiles on the earth" (11:13, RSV), so the Christians confess that the **great high priest** defines the meaning of their existence. Thus to **hold fast to the confession** is vigorously to engage in the dialogue with the divine covenant partner, responding to the gift of salvation by stating its meaning in a public setting.

The second part of the exhortation is to **approach the throne of grace.** The verb *proserchomai* is used seven times in the epistle, each time in terms of approach to God. This regularity of usage suggests it is a technical cultic term for the author. The fact that he twice uses the verb in its absolute sense (10:1, 22), the object understood as being God, adds credence to this suggestion. The word is used always to describe the response of the community to the perfect worship performed by Christ, and never in description of Christ's worship. Walter Bauer states that the basic meaning of *proserchomai* is "to come, go, or to approach." His lexicon divides the occurrences into two large classes: literal and figurative. It is under the second rubric that he groups the numerous occurrences of cultic approach to God or altar. He also notes several absolute usages. The older Cremer *Lexicon* noted that the word has a technical cultic meaning in the Epistle to the Hebrews but doubted that it was taken as such from the Septuagint. It notes that the absolute usage of **approach** means "approach to God." Of the 117 references to *proserchomai* in the Hatch and Redpath Concordance to the Septuagint, thirty-four are in connection with approach to God either directly or indirectly in worship. Here are some examples:

Exodus 12:48	And he shall approach to sacrifice it
Exodus 16:9	Say to all the congregation of Israel, Come near before God
Leviticus 9:5	And all the congregation drew nigh, and they stood before the Lord
Numbers 16:40	No stranger might draw nigh to offer incense before the Lord
Deuteronomy 4:11	You drew nigh and stood under the mountain
Joshua 5:13	Joshua drew near
I Samuel	Let us draw hither to God
Sirach 1:2	Do not approach him with a divided heart
Jeremiah 7:16	Pray not for this people . . . approach me not for them.

Even more striking are the absolute usages in the Septuagint. For example, in Leviticus 9:5: "And all the congregation drew near and stood before the Lord." It is risky to make too much of this, especially since the object of the verb is always made clear from the context. But there are nine such absolute occurrences out of the thirty-four listed in Hatch and Redpath. This confirms the judgment that the author derives the technical use of **approach** from the Septuagint. But it is still an open question as to whether the author has in mind the cult practiced in the early Christian liturgy, as Schierse would suggest, or the cult to be performed at the end of time in heaven, or some other alternative.

The answer depends in part on the definition of **throne of grace.** This phrase does not occur anywhere else in the New Testament or the Septuagint, and it has not been found in other Jewish writings. Apocalyptic and mystical Judaism had a definite interest in the "throne of glory" as the primeval source of the divine mysteries and the place of refuge for martyrs. When one reflects on the Jewish mystics' concept of the gigantic throne situated in the seventh heaven analyzed by Gershom Scholem, one wonders if the uniqueness of Hebrews' expression may not relate in some way to the Lycus Valley speculations. If the throne speculation were alive there—and there are many indications of its widespread popularity in the first century—the divine throne would be viewed as the goal of one's ascent through the cosmic spheres. In achieving union with this throne, one would share the "glory" of God's rule of the universe and would have access to the divine knowledge. But if the usual throne speculation would correlate well with the Lycus Valley desires for apotheosis, the expression **throne of grace** would be quite obtrusive. For **grace** is a quality of relationship. It is mortals who stand in need of **grace** in order to relate to the living God, so if one's goal is apotheosis, the usual expression "throne of glory" would express much more clearly what one hoped to achieve, namely, a share in the divine glory. If these reflections are sound, it follows that the **throne of grace** is the symbol of God's presence as merciful ruler. God's rule is inherent in the concept of the divine throne, and mercy is expressed by the word **grace**. The expression as a whole implies that access to God's presence is an immediate possibility for the pilgrim community, evoked by the grace manifested in the great high priest. Coming as this passage does on the heels of the insistence upon entering "today," it would appear that the present tense of the verbs in verses 14 to 16 should be taken at face value. The exhortation, therefore, is to approach the **throne of grace** day by day on the secular pilgrimage.

The radical implications of this double exhortation for the Lycus Valley situation should be lifted up. If the way to the **throne** is now open, then the entire effort to prepare the way by appeasing the cosmic forces would appear to be superfluous. And once one has come before this **throne**, absorption into the divine does not follow, for one receives instead the **grace** to maintain relationship as a finite creature with the divine covenant partner. One continues to have the obligation to respond with the creaturely **confession** in which one lifts up the meaning of the relationship one has been given. In short, the goal of Christian existence is seen to be dialogue now rather than absorption later.

With this starting point, the other details in the exhortation fit into the Lycus Valley situation quite coherently. The statement that Christ **has passed through the heavens** alludes to power and authority in the context of a gnostic theology in which redemption is thought of as ascent through the hostile cosmic spheres to the spiritual homeland. A gnostic type of redeemer must show superiority over these spheres by passing through them to earth and back again. Thus the author's expression reiterates the claim of 1:2ff. concerning the superiority of Christ over the cosmic angels, utilizing terminology that would be readily accepted in the Lycus Valley. But the author's exhortation concerning this Christ differs sharply from gnostic guidelines. The Lycus Valley Gnostics would have enthusiastically agreed that Christ **has passed through the heavens,** but they felt that the malevolent heavenly aeons would still bar the passage of the individual believers, as Hans

Martin Schenke has shown. They did not think of Christ as a **great high priest** who instituted access to the Holy of Holies for all those he represents, and thus they could not feel **bold enough** to **approach the throne of grace.** They assumed that access was possible only through divine power and that as long as one was beset with finite **weaknesses,** the situation was hopeless. So the author is contradicting each of these assumptions when he pictures the effectiveness of the **great high priest** in terms of **sympathizing with our weaknesses.** This implies that access to God is established not by divinizing mortals, but by reconciling them to their creaturely status. By sharing this mortality, even to the point of being **tempted the same as we,** Christ takes away the alienation of finitude and leads those he has reconciled into the dialogue with God.

This insistence upon the possibility of access to God in the midst of finite daily existence is also visible in the closing clause of the exhortation: **that we may receive mercy and find grace to help in time of need.** The Lycus Valley religionists were interpreting their present **time of need** as evidence of the malevolence of the cosmic powers. The author reverses this: the **need** does not bar humans from God's presence, but instead, access helps to sustain them in face of the **need.** The pilgrimage of faith that approaches the throne of grace day by day does not, therefore, release mortals from the threats of the secular world. Rather, it dispels the alienation of **weakness** and sustains in face of **need.**

This opening exhortation, moreover, announces the themes of the chapters to come and reveals the practical significance of the theological arguments. Here we have the themes of 5:1-10—the participation of the high priest in human **weaknesses;** of 6:13—7:28—the atoning divinity of **Jesus, the Son of God;** of 8:1—10:18—the purifying effect of the **high priest . . . without sins;** and of 10:32—12:17—the **grace** that sustains a pilgrim community. It is to the first of these great themes that the author turns at the conclusion of his exhortation.

5:1 For every priest chosen from humans who is appointed to act on behalf of humans in relation to God, offering gifts and sacrifices for sins, ²is able to empathize with the ignorant and wayward, since he himself is beset with weakness, ³and because of this he is bound to offer sacrifice for his own sins as well as for those of the people. ⁴And one does not seize the honor for himself, but he is called by God, just as Aaron was. ⁵So also Christ did not glorify himself to be made a high priest, but he was appointed by him who said to him,

"You are my Son,
today I have begotten you";
⁶just as he says in another place,
"You are a priest for the aeon,
after the order of Melchizedek."

⁷He, in the days of his flesh, offered prayers and supplications with loud cries and tears to him who was able to save him from death, and he was heard for his piety. ⁸Although he was a Son, he learned obedience through all he suffered; ⁹and being made perfect he became a source of salvation for an aeon to all who obey him, ¹⁰being designated by God a high priest after the order of Melchizedek.

The form of argument in these ten verses is chiastic, as Otto Michel and others have shown: (a) a high priest must empathize (verses 1 to 3); (b) a high priest must be divinely appointed (verse 4); (b) Jesus was divinely appointed (verses 5 and 6); (a) Jesus can empathize (verses 7 and 8); (c) therefore, Jesus is the perfect source of atonement (verses 9 and 10). This form of argument communicates the unique emphasis of the author on both the suffering humanity and the divinely appointed authority of Jesus the great high priest. From the perspective of the tradition of the high priest in Judaism and the tendencies of the Lycus Valley Gnostics, this combination is strikingly distinct. The Gnostics were primarily concerned with the divine power of Christ and the Jewish priestly traditions aimed at retaining a high level of cultic purity that required separation from common sinful humanity. So the author strikes an independent hermeneutical path in his reading of the biblical precedents, uniting the tradition of priestly appointment with a new emphasis on priestly humanity in order to do justice to the Christ event. By so doing, he develops a doctrine of atonement that is consistent with his starting point in 2:9–18, i.e., atonement through participation.

In generalizing about high priesthood, the author lifts up the motif of intercessorship. The **high priest** acts **on behalf of humans in relation to God.** The terminology used here is drawn from the Septuagint discussions about priestly service. The goal of this intercession is atonement: **gifts and sacrifices for sins.** The author thus begins with the assumption that the cult was an effective means to overcome the alienation caused by human transgressions. But while traditional Jewish theology concerned itself with the purity of the priest, the necessity of repentance, and the precise fulfillment of divine ordinance, Hebrews lifts up the fact that the priest participates in human weakness. There are, to be sure, analogies to this idea in the actual wording of the high priestly ritual on the Day of Atonement. Theodore H. Robinson provides the following example from Yoma iii, 8: "O Lord, I and my house have committed iniquity, transgressed, and sinned in Thy sight. O Lord, pardon, I beseech Thee, the iniquities, the transgressions, and the sins, which I and my house have committed in thy sight." This background provides the basis for the author's observation that **he is bound to offer sacrifice.** But nowhere in the tradition is the effectiveness of the priestly service based on the fact of human weakness as in this argument of Hebrews. The uniqueness of this focus may be measured in the line **is able to empathize.** The term *metriopathein* is used by the Stoics to depict the "measured" response between passion and indifference, while Philo uses it in connection with Aaron as one who "moderates his passion," since he could not entirely control it (Leg. All. iii, 129). But Spicq makes a good case that the author is using this term in the sense of Plutarch (De frater amore 18), i.e., of condescension, indulgence, and natural sympathy. The standard by which the sympathy is "measured," therefore, is the human weakness of the priest himself. **Since he himself is beset with weakness,** he is able to put himself in the place of those for whom he intercedes. The translation **empathize** would seem to convey this thought. The author's emphasis, therefore, is that the priest is an effective intercessor not because he was raised above human weaknesses by his ritual purity, but because he shared so completely in those weaknesses. It is a scandalous argument from the point of view of Jewish orthodoxy.

The train of thought is carried through in verse 3. While the expression **he is bound** would seem to point to the legal necessity imposed by Jewish law, the author chooses to ground it in the need to atone **for his own sins,** thus relating back to the argument concerning **weakness** in the preceding verse. By starting verse 3 with **and because of this,** i.e., the fact that the high priest himself was afflicted with **weakness,** a priestly rationale is developed that departs radically from the traditional ideals of ritual purity and sinlessness. Rather than a priest gaining his effectiveness by differentiating himself from secular existence through particular religious observances—a procedure favored not only by Judaism but also in a sense by the Lycus Valley religionists—Hebrews insists upon the efficacy of involvement in secular existence. The high priest is effective not because he transcends the human plight through cultic holiness, but because he fully shares that plight. The author's goal in violating the premise of both the Jewish tradition and the Lycus Valley religion is to provide a basis for his new interpretation of the atoning work of Jesus, the great high priest. In contrast to the atonement theories featuring victorious battle with the devil, successful placation of divine wrath, balancing out of divine justice, or provision of an uplifting moral example, Hebrews has in mind a dispelling of the alienation of secular existence through participation. But before moving on to the elaboration of this new concept in verses 7 to 10, it would be well to note the historical realism of the author's view of the high priesthood. Although he rejects the key premise of priestly theory, he is certainly on solid ground in discerning the human fallibility of the typical high priest. The judgment that **he himself is beset with weakness** and must **offer sacrifice for his own sins as well as for those of the people** was as accurate for the corrupt holders of the priestly office in Jerusalem during the period of the Herodian temple as it would be for other priestly classes down through the centuries. The clear-eyed realism of the author's viewpoint is a rather impressive, though perhaps incidental, aspect of his secular approach to high priestly activity.

The second element of the argument is laid down in verse 4: **and one does not seize the honor for himself, but he is called by God.** It may be that the reference to taking the honorable position upon oneself, though a traditional negative motif in connection with the priesthood, alludes to the various instances of seizure or intended seizure of the priestly office in the first century. But the antithesis serves chiefly to affirm that the priest is **called by God,** that is, that his authenticity rested strictly on a direct, divine appointment. It is this motif that is picked up immediately in the chiastic phase of the argument beginning with verse 5. The author claims that Christ corresponded to the requirement of divine appointment and personal abnegation. That **Christ did not glorify himself** is consistent with Hebrews' insistence that he participated fully in the humiliating human condition, and also with the evidence about the historical Jesus in the Synoptic Gospels. But the emphasis in verse 5 is clearly upon the fact that Jesus **was appointed by him who said to him.** Hebrews' idea of the divinely self-authenticating word, developed in connection with the opening lines of the letter, is at the forefront here. The content of this word is spelled out in the following two citations from the psalms.

As can be seen elsewhere in Hebrews, the significance of the citations like these in 5b and 6 is not so accessible when taken individually as when one discovers why they are combined and fit into this particular spot in the argument. As James Moffatt has noted, "there is something vital, for the writer's mind, in the connexion of . . . [priest and son], implying that the position of divine Son carries with it, in some sense, the role of [priest]." The connection is particularly striking in light of the fact that other materials such as the Dead Sea Scrolls explicitly separated the roles of messianic sonship and high priesthood. The task, therefore, is to discern the author's intent in combining these two disparate citations, that is, the sense in which sonship bears priesthood. It may well relate to Hebrews' concept of atonement through participation. Sonship is a relational concept, and in fact, it is precisely this which stands in the forefront of this particular citation: **"You are my Son, today I have begotten you."** In this case, the relationship is established by God who is seen to utilize the traditional formula for adoption. Without regard to previous status or natural alienation, a relationship of trust and responsibility is inaugurated here by the statement of adoption. And when one reflects on the use of the "Abba, Father" materials elsewhere in the New Testament, it would appear that the gift of such a relationship implies open, intimate, and secure access to God. This is precisely what Hebrews feels was accomplished by the priestly activity of Christ. It would be appropriate to conclude, therefore, that the intent in combining these two citations was to lay out the basis for interpreting the **priest**hood of Christ in terms of providing a new relationship as children of God. As 2:13 has already indicated, the "children" are brought with Jesus the **Son** into the very presence of God to indicate that at-one-ment has been achieved.

This hypothesis can be corroborated by the final stages of the chiastic argument in verses 7 to 10. The emphasis in this section is that the redemptive, priestly work of Christ was carried out by his relationship as a **Son**. The author pictures this as being marked by the full agony of earthly sonship. It may be that verse 7 alludes to the struggle in Gethsemane on the eve of the crucifixion, with the **prayers and supplications** being directed **to the one who was able to save him from death.** Commentators have frequently noted the parallel with Jesus' prayer "Take this cup from me" in Mark 14. The author, however, heightens the agony motif by alluding to **loud cries and tears,** which are not reported elsewhere in the gospel tradition. Whether he has authentic historical reminiscenses at this point, or perhaps utilizes the tradition of the suffering of the righteous in the Old Testament, as Egon Brandenburger has suggested, it is at least clear that total involvement in mortality is communicated. Jesus qualifies as a high priest because he shared fully in the human **weakness** described in verses 2 to 4. This is an essential element in the new doctrine of atonement the author is developing: in order to dispel the alienation of finitude, Jesus had to participate in it fully. Not only does his sharing of the human plight serve to dispel the sense of abandonment and gloom of those who suffer under it, but also he provides a powerful dialogical example. In the midst of impending doom, he cried out for help and **was heard.**

The phrasing of this line is intriguing: **he was heard for his piety.** On the one hand, it is clear that Jesus was not **heard** in the sense that he was released from the threat of death. The cup did not pass from him in Gethsemane, for in the end he rose to meet his captors and his doom. Nor was Jesus' **piety** able to earn him the reward of happy release from his plight. Hebrews concentrates the attention here solely on the element of dialogue. It is the calling out and the being heard that Jesus exemplifies as savior of the human condition. This results in a radical reinterpretation of **piety.** For the Lycus Valley as for religion in general, **piety** was a matter of performing the required ritual. It had a religious connotation. For Hebrews, **piety** is a thoroughly secular term. Jesus is pictured as having **piety** because he participated fully in the human condition, yet retained the redeeming dialogue. It is a matter of holding to the covenant partner through all adversity, being sustained by the fact that one is being **heard.** Furthermore, for modern as well as for ancient piety, the major interest is in the reward. The Lycus Valley religionists offered apotheosis as the reward of piety, and the modern religionist is apt to offer success and happiness, both in this life and in the life to come. But all Hebrews offers is to be **heard.** One wonders if the viewpoint of the poetic writer of Job is not reasserting itself here once again. It is not the release from the sores that redeems, but rather awareness of having been directly encountered by the divine covenant, so that Job can exclaim: "I had heard of thee by the hearing of the ear, but now my eye sees thee [42:5]." Such dialogue is redeeming, because it dispels the alienation that so frequently accompanies suffering. It reveals that tribulation is not due to divine wrath or, as the Lycus Valley congregations seemed to fear, to the malevolent cosmic forces. It sustains because the dialogue partner is none other than Christ, the **Son** and **high priest** who shared human tribulation to its fullest extent.

This dialogical model is fully integrated into the **Son** concept in verse 8. Whereas the term **Son** had a divine connotation, not only in the earlier chapters of Hebrews, but also in Hellenistic gnosticism with its interest in the first-born as a spiritual redeemer, the author emphasizes his **obedience** as a sign of subordination to the will of God. If the Son **learned obedience through all he suffered,** he not only shared finitude in the sense of having to learn, but also in the sense of submitting himself to the dominant covenant partner. This verse has caused problems for defenders of Christological orthodoxy, but the author's intent is very clear. It is the fact that Jesus shared so completely in the human condition that makes him **a source of salvation.** The author's theory of atonement through participation is what makes this scandalous description of the **Son** possible. It also leads to the rather unusual definition of **perfect** as used in verse 9. Given the discussion in this section, Jesus could not be perfect at the point of knowledge, and he certainly was not perfect in the sense of being above the **loud cries and tears** of the creature in face of his doom. **Perfect** in this context is defined strictly in a dialogical sense, namely, being obedient to the will of the partner. Yet even here, the author has a unique twist in his wording. In using the passive **being made perfect,** he avoids the implication that the learning of obedience through suffering was a cumulative process of self-improvement that led to salvation. He is operating on a premise visible elsewhere in his discussion of dialogue and salvation, namely, that in holding fast to the partner, something redemptive happens to people that is beyond what they can do for themselves.

The **salvation** offered by the **Son** is pictured in verse 9 as being available **to all who obey him,** thus carrying through with the dialogical mode of thought. Just as Jesus stood in obedient dialogue, so also those who receive the salvation he offers stand in obedient relationship to him. The connection between sonship and priesthood, inferred from the combination of the two citations in verses 5b and 6, is here carried through to its logical conclusion. The inauguration of obedient dialogue is set forth as the essence of high priestly office in verse 10. With this, the basis of a new doctrine of atonement is developed, and the radical reinterpretation of priesthood, sacrifice, atonement, and perfection in the succeeding chapters of Hebrews can proceed logically from this starting point. So concerned is the author to ensure this common point of departure that he drops the argument about the **high priest after the order of Melchizedek**—to be picked up again in 7:1ff.—and turns to a negative exhortation concerning the requirements of dialogue.

Chapter Five

The Warning About the Maturity (5:11—6:2) Required to Avoid Apostasy (6:3-8) and to Approach God's Promised Presence (6:9-20)

5:11 **A**BOUT this the word has much to say to you that is hard to explain, since you have grown sluggish in hearing. [12]For though by this time you ought to be teachers, you need someone to teach you again the fundamental principles of God's words. You are in need of milk, not of solid food. [13]For everyone who lives on milk is unskilled in the word of righteousness, for he is a child. [14]But solid food is for the mature (=perfect), for those who have their faculties trained by exercise to discern good and evil.

6:1 Therefore, leaving the fundamentals of the word of Christ, let us go on to maturity (=perfection), not laying the foundation over again of repentance from dead works and faith in God, [2]with instruction about baptisms, laying on of hands, resurrection of the dead, and eternal judgment.

The characteristic interlacing of exhortation and theological argument in Hebrews is particularly evident in this section, which breaks in upon the discussion of the great high priest. If this section were deleted, chapter 7 would follow very smoothly after 5:10. The purpose of this striking exhortative insertion is hinted in verse 11: **About this the word has much to** say to you that is hard to explain. A certain level of maturity on the part of the listener is required if the doctrine about the great high priest is to be understood. But as one reads on in this section it becomes apparent that a maturity of a very specialized sort is in view. It could be defined as "dialogical maturity," because responding to the word, accepting dialogical principles, and refraining from apostasy are the dominant themes in this section. The author is not merely concerned, therefore, with conceptual maturity, a mastery of fundamental ideas before moving on to the subtle complexities of an abstract theory. He insists rather upon the necessity for personal maturity. The matter of holding fast to dialogue is viewed as the prerequisite for comprehending the dialogical service of the great high priest. The assumption is that one cannot really understand dialogical reality unless one participates in it. Only those engaged in the pilgrimage marked by the encountering **word** are capable of grasping its significance for their existence. For this **word** has more than intellectual content and impact; it inaugurates a relationship that leads to personal maturity. This seems to correlate with the fact lifted up by Otto Michel, that in no other section of the letter does the word-oriented character of the argument stand out more clearly: **the word has much to say to you**, in 5:11; the **teachers** deal with **God's words**, in 5:12; the **fundamentals of the word of Christ** are mentioned in 6:1; tasting the "goodness of the word of God" is referred to in 6:5; and the chapter ends with a discussion of the divine promises in 6:13–20.

The first of three major hindrances to grasping fully the dialogical doctrine is that **you have grown sluggish in hearing**. The fact that this term **sluggish** is not used elsewhere in the New Testament indicates the fresh approach of Hebrews to the dialogical aspects of Christian existence. To be **sluggish** is to fail to respond to the partner's **word**, and given the use of the term elsewhere in the Hellenistic world, the connotation of laziness or carelessness would be implied. But why would mere **sluggish**ness be the first sign pointing to the disastrous apostasy described in 6:3–8? It is comprehensible if one keeps the dialogical model in mind. If one is **sluggish** before the **word** of the partner, this indicates that one does not rest his or her life on the relationship. Since one hears what one wants to hear, selective nonlistening shows misplaced interest. It shows that the source of one's faith and self-identity is no longer the partner but something else. If one is **sluggish** before God's **word** and alive before some other word, this reveals what one really worships. In the case of the Lycus Valley, the real interest had shifted to worshipful manipulation of the cosmic forces for the advantage of the self. With this slothful syndrome, a yawning **sluggishness** in face of the disturbing and transforming **word** was a natural result.

The second major hindrance to true dialogical comprehension is forgetting **the fundamental principles of God's words.** Before analyzing the content of these **principles**, it would be well to note the ironic juxtaposing of **teachers** vs. those needing instruction, **milk** vs. **solid food**, and of **mature** vs. **child.** The full irony of this argument becomes visible when one takes account of the gnostic background of the terminology as it relates to the Lycus Valley situation. As Ernst Käsemann has shown, the Gnostics distinguished sharply between **milk** and **fundamental principles** of their catechism and the esoteric knowledge available only to the **mature.** Gnostic leaders prided themselves in being **teachers** of this spiritual wisdom, and Hebrews refers to such esoteric "teachings" in 13:9. The author uses this gnostic terminology without a qualm, even using the expression **someone to teach you,** which may relate to the gnostic claim to be taught directly by God. Yet from beginning to end, the author inverts this terminology, suggesting that it is precisely the gnostic teachers in the Lycus Valley who are lacking the **fundamental principles** and need to be fed **milk** again. Verse 13 goes on to add insult to irony, for what could more completely shock a gnostic pride than to be told that one who still needs milk **is unskilled in the word of righteousness, for he is a child.** If they are incapable of digesting **solid food,** then they are not **the mature,** the "perfect ones" Gnostics frequently claimed to be. This effective use of gnostic terminology against the Lycus Valley Gnostics is based on a single starting point: their slipping away from the **fundamental principles of God's words.**

To assess the validity of the author's allegation, it is necessary to analyze what he considered the **fundamentals of the word of Christ . . . i.e., the foundation . . . of (a) repentance from dead works and (b) faith in God.** These two items are the first in a series of six listed by the author, but their grammatical connection with **foundation** and the connection of the latter four with **instruction** forces one to distinguish between them rather sharply, as James Moffatt has argued. Only **repentance** and **faith** are classified as **fundamentals** in the sense of a **foundation** upon which more advanced doctrine could be erected. But how could the Lycus Valley religionists properly be charged with forgetting these two **principles?** We can safely assume that it was more than simple oversight, for one is unlikely to forget what is truly vital to one's life. Rollo May has suggested in this connection that "memory is a function of intentionality. Memory is like perception in this regard; the patient cannot remember something until he is ready to take some stand toward it." If the Lycus Valley congregation had forgotten the first principles, this was a sure sign that their piety rested on some quite different foundations. How would the Lycus Valley religion relate to **repentance from dead works and faith in God?**

The expression **dead works** is unique to Hebrews, being used again in 9:14 in a decisive passage that relates Jesus' sacrifice to the individual's conscience. It probably is derived from the Pauline polemic against "works of the law" which ostensibly lead to life but in reality lead to death. Just as pre-Christians were led astray by the law, so that "the very commandment which promised life proved to be death to me [Rom. 7:10]," so Hebrews views the self-justifying **works** as inextricably bound up with death. To turn away **from dead works** is thus to cease the hopeless task of justifying oneself through the performance of presumed religious duties. But this is precisely the principle the Lycus Valley religionists have discarded, for their performance of cultic duties aimed at securing the self against the threats of the cosmic powers. Whereas they assume these **works** could guarantee their life, Hebrews denotes them as essentially **dead**. It is precisely these **works** that must be discarded in the **repentance** marking the fundamental step into Christian existence.

Both expressions, **repentance from dead works and faith in God,** fit into the dialogical framework of Hebrews. To base one's life on **works** is to turn in upon the self and away from the rightful and divine covenant partner. The word **faith** itself implies relationship, and the idea of directedness toward a partner is neatly expressed with **faith in God,** which stands as the dialogical antithesis to the first **fundamental principle.** One might even say that **repentance from dead works** and **faith in God** depict a single dialogical act of turning from self-involution toward the divine partner. But again, this is precisely what the Lycus Valley religion repudiated. Rather than setting **faith in God,** which involves trusting a covenant partner who cannot be controlled, they set about to manipulate the cosmic forces by ritual observances. The cleavage is profound, with Hebrews advocating dialogue with a transcendent partner beyond the reach of human manipulations, and the Lycus Valley religionists seeking to control the ultimate by ceremonies that contribute to the security of the oppressed.

It is a strange quirk in the history of exegesis that the Epistle to the Hebrews, which holds so strongly to the Pauline heritage of justification by faith alone, should have been despised by Luther and others because it seemed to lack this doctrine. The widely respected studies by Erich Grässer, in particular, advance this erroneous opinion. The confusion is perhaps due in part to the fact that the **fundamental principles** are simply listed, as if the readers should know precisely what was involved. The principles themselves are not extensively expounded in the letter, which may have led exegetes to overlook their centrality. For the author appears to be completely serious when he insists that the comprehension of the mystery of the great high priest is impossible unless these fundamentals of the word of Christ are incorporated in the daily life of the Christian pilgrims.

The third thing that the author feels can make the word . . . hard to explain is immaturity. The antithesis between child and mature (or perfect) was typical for gnostic theology, and the author is, of course, using it against those in the Lycus Valley who falsely prided themselves in possessing spiritual perfection. But he develops a definition of immaturity that relates closely to his own theological perspective. It consists of being unskilled in the word of righteousness and not being trained by exercise to discern good and evil. Käsemann suggested that the former was esoteric doctrine suitable for mature Gnostics. Michel views it simply as "rightful speaking." But in light of Hebrews' use of righteousnèss in 7:2 and 11:7, it would appear to denote the fundamentals of righteousness through faith rather than works. The mark of the truly mature is becoming skilled in leading one's life on this premise and, moreover, to move from this premise to practice critical discernment between good and evil. Maturity therefore is a life firmly based on the reality of the covenant partner, deriving its critical discernment from faith in God and repentance from dead works. It is a pilgrim existence, a leaving behind and a going on to maturity. As the following chapters make plain, the path follows the great high priest into the very presence of God, so not only the basis but also the goal of maturity is dialogue. This distinctive definition of maturity stands out in marked contrast when compared to the Lycus Valley ideology. It is not a matter of gaining knowledge and learning ceremonies regarding the cosmic forces, as the Gnostics would feel. It is quite separate from the areas of intellectual capacity or social adjustment that play such an important role in other conceptions of maturity. Here is a form of maturity accessible to all people who respond to the gospel that shatters their pride in their works and inaugurates a relationship with God.

The final verse in this section lists four instructions that obviously comprised part of the early Christian catechism, and that appear to be of particular significance for the Lycus Valley controversy. The first two relate to cultic practices. The use of **baptisms** in the plural has always been felt to be odd, because Christian baptism was not repetitive and other ablutions were not widely used in the early church. G.R. Beasley-Murray concludes from this reference "that the writer implies a *contrast* between Christian baptism and other religious washings." Günther Bornkamm inferred a similar antithesis between an orthodox Christian sacrament and repeated gnostic washings from details in Colossians. It appears likely that this reminder concerning previous instruction about **baptisms** would call to mind the fact that the Lycus Valley Christians had been taught the efficacy of a single baptism into the death of Christ that made all other cultic washings unnecessary.

It is harder to reconstruct what the problem with **laying on of hands** might have been. In contrast to the probable content of the catechism in Pauline churches, there were branches in early Christianity that appear to have linked the gift of the spirit (Acts 8:17; 19:6) and ordination (Acts 6:6; 1 Timothy 4:14; 5:22; 2 Timothy 1:16) to a sacrament of laying on hands. If the Lycus Valley religionists were developing such ceremonies, possibly to ensure the passage of the gnostic elect through the threatening aeons to the spiritual throne, it is likely that the author of Hebrews—who had been involved in their early instruction—would have felt such innovations were inappropriate. At any rate, in the later chapters of Hebrews, he sets forth a devastating critique of such cultic regulations whose roots were in the Old Testament tradition.

The catechetical instruction about **resurrection of the dead,** as can be reconstructed for the Pauline congregations from 1 Thessalonians 4:13–18 and 1 Corinthians 15:1–58, concentrated on the miraculous causation of bodily resurrection at the parousia, the reunion of the living and the dead, and the eternal assembly "with the Lord." If the Lycus Valley religionists were speculating on the preparations required for a mystical ascent, with the body specially purified by cultic ablutions, this traditional teaching may have seemed too abrupt, too completely in divine control, too somatic, and too indiscriminate. As the parallels to the Corinthian situation indicate, the resurrection doctrine stood as a bulwark against gnostic elitism, sacramentalism, and spiritualism.

Finally, the expression **eternal judgment** would refer to the traditional apocalyptic scheme of the divine court scene at the time of the parousia, and thus would stand in contrast to the Gnostic's illusion of being beyond moral evaluation in the mystical ascent to the divine. It would also counter any teaching about the role of malevolent cosmic forces in rendering judgment on the elect or hindering their passage to the heavenly assembly.

In conclusion, these three factors—**sluggish hearing,** forgetting **fundamental principles,** and lack of **maturity**—not only mitigate against the comprehension of the dialogical mystery of the great high priest, but also indicate a trend toward apostasy. They reflect a denial of dialogue at the present moment, being replaced by a false faith and a false worship oriented to the self rather than to the partner. And unless the Lycus Valley Christians were willing to rely on the **fundamentals,** disregarding the esoteric gnostic **instructions,** and advancing to dialogical **maturity,** the consequences would be serious. The next section moves on to show how dialogue, once received, can be lost.

6:3   **And this we shall do if God permits. ⁴For it is impossible in the case of those who have once been enlightened, having tasted the heavenly gift, and become sharers of the Holy Spirit, ⁵having tasted the goodness of the word of God and the powers of the coming aeon, ⁶and having fallen away, to again restore them to repentance, since they crucify the Son of God again for themselves and hold him up to contempt. ⁷For land which drinks the rain that often falls upon it, and bears plants that are useful to those for whom it is tilled, receives a blessing from God. ⁸But if it bears thorns and thistles, it is unworthy and on the verge of the curse; its end is to be burned.**

The sentence with which this section opens is sometimes

viewed as a parenthetical remark to the effect that the author would go over these elementary teachings at a later time, perhaps when he visited the congregation (13:23), or that the explanation about the more advanced doctrine of the great high priest could only be done with divine permission. But the first person plural (**and this we shall do**) appears to refer instead to the exhortation in 6:1, "let us go on to maturity," as James Moffatt suggests. It is thus a transitional statement that relates the material about apostasy in verses 4 to 8 to the concept of dialogical maturity in verse 1. It follows that the proviso **if God permits** is more than pious rhetoric. Despite the efforts required from the individual to maintain dialogue, it still remains a matter of pure grace that **God** condescends to enter into relationship. Unless **God permits,** how could anyone engage in the life-giving dialogue that makes comprehension of the mystery of the great high priest possible? By using the word **permits,** the author stresses the fact that such dialogue is neither automatic nor manipulatable. The Lycus Valley religionists had falsely assumed that they could control their relationship by cultic ceremonies, thereby dispelling the risks of finitude. But in so doing they tried to make ultimate reality into something it is not. They lost sight of the freedom of **God,** who alone **permits** humans to "approach the throne of grace" (4:16). It was similar to the modern presumption that grace is always there for the asking, that if God is love, forgiveness is always automatic and restoration is easy. Dietrich Bonhoeffer described it as

> cheap grace . . . sold on the market like cheapjack's wares. The sacraments, the forgiveness of sin, and the consolations of religion are thrown away at cut prices. . . . Grace without price; grace without cost! The essence of grace, we suppose, is that the account has been paid in advance; and, because it has been paid, everything can be had for nothing. Since the cost was infinite, the possibilities of using and spending it are infinite. What would grace be if it were not cheap?

To relate this to Hebrews' viewpoint, cheap grace is desiring a dialogical salvation without paying the price of dialogue. The Lycus Valley religionists and their modern counterparts refuse to accede to the partner a precedence as one who alone **permits** relationship. So they refuse to respond vigorously to the partner. They are "sluggish in hearing," shrugging off the responsibility of dialogue. They forget the "fundamental principles of God's words," exchanging these for some nonsense about how to manipulate ultimate reality. The criterion by which **God permits** dialogue is therefore anything but arbitrary; it is a matter of permitting dialogue solely on a dialogical basis.

The negative aspect of this fundamental requirement is set forth in verses 4ff.: **for it is impossible . . . to restore them to repentance.** It is this statement that evoked the denunciation of Luther and the other Protestant interpreters as a denial of the grace of God. Erasmus sought to soften the word **impossible** to "difficult," and Bengel insisted the **impossib**ility pertained only to a human's incapacity to evoke repentance in another, while leaving the boundless grace of God out of account. William Barclay describes their views and suggests that the radicality is due to the persecution situation facing the author's congregation, insisting that the passage "was never meant to be erected into a doctrine and a theology, that there is no forgiveness for postbaptismal sin. Who is any man to say that any other man is beyond the forgiveness of God?" One could go on with many examples in this vein, but it is questionable whether such special pleading would be necessary if the dialogical basis of Hebrews' position is kept in mind. To begin with, it is important to measure the connotation of the active verb "to restore" in relation to the closest parallels in the New Testament. Paul uses a similar term in 2 Corinthians 4:16 and Colossians 3:10, but in both cases the voice is passive, "to be renewed," which is consistent with the usual theological stress on the priority of divine power in human transformation. But Hebrews' use of the active voice implies that no outside agency can **restore** a person who refuses dialogical salvation. Neither the church nor even God can give the **repentance** that turns away from self-enclosure toward dialogical commitment, and if people refuse it, they should not delude themselves about the consequences. And it is precisely such delusions that the author wishes to dispel. That grace is cheap, that salvation can be granted without repentance, or that dialogue can be had on a nondialogical basis are delusions that require the prophetic shattering by one who dares to say **for it is impossible.** Thus in a sense, Barclay and others are correct in insisting that Hebrews does not deny the grace of God. It does not put the verb in the passive, implying that the recalcitrant cannot be received if they repent. But the effort to retain cheap grace could easily lead to blunting the moral realism of the author's point. For divine grace, though boundless, cannot be presumed upon, and it cannot be received by anyone who refuses to turn toward the graceful partner. This moral realism stands as a bulwark against human religiosity, which always tends to debase the grace of proffered relationship into coinage to operate the machinery of human comfort and security.

The dialogical character of the salvation Hebrews has in mind is clearly described in the remarkable wording of verses 4 and 5. Here the author uses terminology typical for gnosticism to describe a nongnostic type of personal salvation. **Those who have once been enlightened** is an expression used both for early Christianity and gnosticism, but the qualifying word **once** points away from the typical successive stages of gnostic enlightenment and toward an unrepeatable moment of transformation such as that associated with Christian conversion and baptism. The content of this single **enlightenment** is therefore what the author described in 6:1, "repentance from dead works and faith in God." Rather than the gaining of esoteric knowledge, it is a matter of turning away from self-dependency and toward a valid relationship with the living God. The complete personal engagement implied by such a salvation is expressed by the author's double use of "tasting": **having tasted the heavenly gift . . . having tasted the goodness of the word of God and the powers of the coming aeon.** In this context, "to taste" is personally to experience, as Michel suggests. Yet "to taste," like personal encounter, is a momentary thing, a matter that cannot be possessed in any static sense. The salvation the Lycus Valley Christians had already received was dynamic, and its overwhelming abundance was expressed in the multiplicity of expressions. The first of the four expressions is the **heavenly gift**, presumably salvation itself. Like the "heavenly calling" in 3:1 and the "heavenly Jerusalem" in 12:22, this is the eschatological reality that has already encountered them in the Christ event. The third expression relates to the **word of God** whose **goodness** they had **tasted** or experienced when they encountered it day by day on their pilgrimage. The author has already developed the quality of **goodness** in relation to the **word** in chapters 3 and 4 with the idea of the "promise of entering his rest" (4:1, RSV) to those who respond to the word that sounds forth, "Today . . . Today, when you hear his voice." The fourth expression, **having tasted . . . the powers of the coming aeon,** probably relates to the "signs and wonders and various powerful deeds" (2:4) that marked their conversion and that became activated within each one of them by the gospel. Inserted into this series of three dialogical gifts that they had **tasted** is the expression which points unmistakably to the intent of the author: **become sharers of the Holy Spirit.** To **share** is to become a partner, a full participant in a relationship. This is the same term as was used in 1:9 and 3:1, 14 for the "comrades" or the "partners with Christ." The combination of this term with **Holy Spirit** ensures that it is not to be understood as some magical gift or some power within people themselves, but rather as a relationship that they share as active partners. All four expressions, therefore, point to dialogue as the essence of the salvation the congregation had received.

Given this description of salvation, to **fall away** means to fall out of relationship. This is quite different from the usual definitions of apostasy, in which **falling away** is defined as deviation from some orthodox standard of belief or behavior. It is therefore a matter that cannot be judged or evaluated by a third party. The specter of church heresy trials, with their bloody, sordid history, should not be conjured up at this point, except to indicate the radical differences from Hebrews' perspective. For Hebrews, apostasy is strictly a matter of rejecting relationship with the partner, so that both evaluation and punishment are intrinsically limited to the partners involved. In this connection, the remarkably personal aspects of verse 6c should be noted. To **crucify the Son of God again for themselves** is to turn against the potential covenant partner with the fiercest enmity. To be sure, this may not have been the conscious goal of the Lycus Valley religionists or their modern counterparts. But the cross event reveals the depraved depths of religiosity, bringing to light its deeply buried enmity and its propensity to violence. For when humans lose the sense of transcendent limits presented by a lively covenant partner and fall into a manipulative type of religious exercise designed to promote their comfort and security, they become capable of viciously lashing out against whatever threatens the castle of sand. In fact, Hebrews goes beyond the mere description of capability; as far as this author is concerned, to **fall away** from proper relationship is at the same time to **crucify the Son of God again.** It is to turn against Jesus with the disdain and cruelty that were expressed on Golgotha. This is a shocking charge to level against the well-meaning religiosity of the ancient or the modern world. For a characteristic mark of religious people is that they feel sure they are doing God's will. When their system and prestige are challenged, they feel justified to react with a vengeance. The cry, "Crucify him!" fits in rather smoothly with the religious mentality of every generation and culture, unless the Epistle to the Hebrews is exaggerating. At the very least, the wording of this passage places a bulwark against an anti-Semitic theology, which assumed that killing the Christ was due to some unusual perversion in the Jewish culture. It is rather a potential of all human religiosity, especially theologically and organizationally sophisticated versions like the Lycus Valley heresy. The really crucial word in the author's formulation is therefore **again:** they kill Jesus **again for themselves.** This means that the cross event is not limited to past history. Crucifying the **Son of God** is repeated whenever humans turn away from valid relationships into manipulative religiosity.

The second expression for spurned personal relationship is equally shocking: those who fall away **hold him up to contempt.** Once again, the present tense of the participle is used, implying that this is more than a faint possibility for those who reject true dialogue. Whether the person is conscious of it or not, to turn away is to treat the partner with derision. It is to enter into the spirit of those who derided Jesus on Golgotha, "wagging their heads and saying, . . . If you are the Son of God, come down from the cross [Matt. 27:39-40].'" So there is no neutrality in the realm of dialogue. The author does not concede that it is possible to enter into a little innocent religiosity, to appease the cosmic forces through harmless ceremonies, and still to honor Christ. He shatters the complacency of those who would prefer the shelter of the cult instead of the rigors of personal relationship. There appears to be no middle ground and, on this decisive point at least, no room for compromise. The radical alternatives are rooted in the structure of relationship itself.

The last two verses in this section describe the reward and the punishment as the inexorable results of the fruits produced. The **rain that often falls upon** the land is analogous to the rich gifts of the new age that the congregation has "tasted" and "shared." They are the gifts of a new relationship, and their purpose is to free humans from the idolatrous attachments that hinder their creativity, and thereby to release their creative powers. The result is that God, like the **land** in Hebrews' analogy, **bears plants that are useful to those for whom it is tilled.** The point here is that the dialogical life is a productive life, and that this may be tasted in its results for the pilgrim community as a whole and for the secular world it serves along the path. If pilgrims are unproductive, bearing **thorns and thistles** that harm others rather than help them, then something very significant is revealed about the form of life they are living. Still turned inward toward the idols of the self, they have not been freed for true relationship either to God or to the neighbor. Thus the fruits are an accurate indication of the use to which a person has put the gifts of the new age. And the ultimate results in either case are commensurate with what is actually produced. To **receive a blessing from God** implies that the ground is to be augmented in its productivity. To be pronounced **unworthy and on the verge of the curse** is the appropriate result of producing useless or harmful fruits. What else is to be done with **thorns and thistles** than to **burn** them? But to make the analogy complete, Hebrews suggests that it is the unproductive land itself whose **end is a burning.** The image may not be particularly apt, but the point is quite clear: each person is held responsible for the productivity of her or his own life.

There is a serious and, for the modern world, a distressing moral realism in this section of Hebrews. A relativistic age tends to lack the author's sense of horror at apostasy, to assume that a little sluggishness in hearing, a little wavering in the direction of works—righteousness, and a little immaturity are harmless. But the author sees these as signs of misplaced loyalty and perverted relationship. They make participation in Christ's high priestly worship impossible, not because Christ does not desire it, but because they bespeak a slothful, manipulative disinterest on the part of the pilgrim. Hebrews is very concerned to point out that there is a point of no return, that if one continues long in this false worship, all can be lost. For as long as these seemingly insignificant indications are present, one is on that path and nothing can retrieve one except one's own will to repent. None other can restore one. To this end, the author wishes to shock his hearers into an awareness of the seriousness of the symptoms. He does not define the moment along this slothful path when the point of no return is reached, and he does not yet presume to utter the final, annihilating curse that only divine judgment can reveal. He sees only that the person on this path is on **the verge of the curse,** because it is a path which leads away from a productive life as worship.

6:9 But we are convinced concerning you, beloved, of things that are better and belong to salvation, even though we speak like this. [10]For God is not unjust to overlook your work and the love that you demonstrated for his name, having ministered to the saints and continuing to minister. [11]And we desire each of you to demonstrate the same striving for the full assurance of hope until the end, [12]so that you not be sluggish, but imitators of them who through faith and patient endurance inherit the promises. [13]For in making a promise to Abraham, God (since he had no one greater by whom to swear) swore by himself, [14]saying, "Surely blessing I will bless you and multiplying I will multiply you." [15]And so having patiently endured, he obtained what was promised. [16]For humans swear by what is greater than themselves, and the end of their disputes is the oath for confirmation. [17]So when God willed to show even more clearly to the heirs of the promise the unchangeability of his purpose, he guaranteed by means of an oath, [18]so that through two unchangeable things, in which it is impossible for God to lie, we pilgrims might have powerful exhortation to seize the hope set before us, [19]which (hope) we have as an anchor of the soul, safe and firm, and entering into the inner side of the veil, [20]where Jesus entered as leader for us, having become a high priest for the aeon after the order of Melchizedek.

After the dreadful warnings of the preceding section, the author assures his congregation of his confidence that they had not yet succumbed to the Lycus Valley heresy. The address, **beloved**, indicates the motivation of these preceding warnings as well as the deep personal commitment of the exhorter to his people. Indeed, it is this love that sustains the moral realism in 6:3-8, a matter which is more fully developed in 12:5-11. But love does not soften the content of the proclamation, as is so often the case in popular preaching. There are still only two alternatives, and the author sees evidence of **things that are better and belong to salvation** in the life they have led. Their **work and love** are indications that they have been standing in faithful covenant with their divine partner. These are the natural results of a life of dialogue, the useful plants referred to in 6:7. The phrasing of verse 10, however, could lead the reader to feel that God was just in that God rewards such good works with salvation. This feeling would be a disastrous relapse into the sort of "dead works" mentality the author has opposed throughout his exhortation. The wording aims instead at showing that God is not responsible for the sort of slothful lapse into death of which the author has warned. God faithfully responds to sustain dialogical energy, directed Godward, and the expression **for his name** indicates that such deeds of **work and love** are performed in response to the grace of the divine covenant partner. The author has already effectively barred the misuse of such ethical response to provide the basis for religious security: he has defined Christian repentance as turning away from such works of righteousness toward the living God (6:1). The recipients of such **ministering**, however, are the **saints**, which might lead one again to the conclusion that a rather narrow view of Christian solidarity is evident here. But at least it is clear that the author does not have in mind a small group of leaders or superlative Christians. As the argument in chapter 10 makes plain, the whole Christian community has received sanctification as a result of the Christ event. So **continuing to minister** to the **saints** would imply the remarkable impulse for sharing and sustaining one another that marked the early church.

The author's **desire** for the congregation is summarized in verses 11 and 12, wherein the argument of this entire section from 5:11ff. is succinctly drawn together, and the motif of the **promises** is announced. What the author desires is not merely the attributes or qualities, but rather the actions of pilgrims: they are to **demonstrate the same striving,** that is by the actions of **work** and **love** mentioned in verse 10, in order to gain the **full assurance of hope.** It is very odd that **striving** could be thought to produce **full assurance,** for one can only strive for that which is not yet complete and assured. Some exegetes and *The New English Bible* eliminate this oddity with the strained translation "to show the same eager concern, until your hope is finally realized." It is probable, however, that the author has in mind the same sort of experiential confirmation of faith or hope alluded to in 11:1, namely, that in the very impulse and action of **work** and **love**, one receives confirmation in the present moment of the validity of the promises. Just as in 1 Thessalonians 1:2–7, where the "work of faith and labor of love and steadfastness of hope" are viewed as primary signs of the presence of the kingdom, so here the author of Hebrews feels that **full assurance** is possible for those who understand their work not as an avenue to status, but as a sign of the spirit's presence. If they **strive** to maintain this dialogical activity, the dialogue will be its own reward and **assurance.** It is interesting to note, however, that the author offers **full assurance of hope** rather than "certainty." It was surely the latter that the Lycus Valley religionists promised. If one takes seriously the structure of dialogue with the transcendent God, as does Hebrews, it is obvious that "certainty" is presumptuous and idolatrous. All one can have is an **assurance** deriving from day-to-day experience that what is hoped for will come to pass. Finally, it is no accident that verse 11 ends with the eschatological proviso, **until the end,** which stands guard against the presumption of enthusiastic "certainty." Whereas the Lycus Valley heresy sought to secure a safe path for the elect as they passed through the threatening cosmic spheres at the end of life, the author is content to leave **the end** in God's hands, so that hope in God is the sole basis of **assurance** then as now. In **striving** to hold fast to vital dialogue, the congregation would avoid that **sluggish**ness described in such dreadful fashion in 5:11ff. Since the two are exact opposites, as Marcus Dods points out, to do the one is to avoid the other; thus the author does not have to devise a complicated, Pharisaic list of dos and don'ts. There is a profound, dialogical simplicity in Christian existence described here, particularly when one compares it with the pseudosophistication of the Lycus Valley religion.

To maintain this simple, dialogical pilgrimage is to be **imitators of them who through faith and patient endurance**

inherit the promises. The idea of imitation here is derived from Hellenistic philosophy, as Erich Grässer has shown, but defined in a unique way by the dialogical context. The author does not begin with an abstract definition of the virtues of the ethical ancestors as in the Hellenistic tradition, and there is certainly no equation here between being **imitators** and having **faith,** as Grässer maintains. The term **faith** is used here, as elsewhere in Hebrews, to depict the holding to relationship that marks those who have responded to God's word. And **patient endurance** relates to the trials the author considers typical for a pilgrim existence in this deteriorating world. Since it is not until the following verses, and more specifically chapter 11, that the author describes in detail the forebears in the faith, it is apparent that in contrast to the Hellenistic imitation ethic, the content here is provided before the characteristics of the models are sketched. And with the reference to **inheriting the promises,** the unique word-orientation of Hebrews is brought to the fore. The present tense of **inherit** implies, as did 4:10, that response to the word brings one into the rest not just at the end, but during the course of the pilgrimage. As the following verses make plain, it is only through trust in the dialogue partner's promises that one can approach the divine presence and avoid the apostasy which lurks as a dreadful precipice beside true pilgrim existence.

With verses 13 to 15 the author opens up a discussion that leads through to the end of chapter 7, concerning the promise and oath given to Abraham. Helmut Köster has shown that the tradition about the oath given to Abraham was drawn from Hellenistic Judaism, and that there is precedent for relating this material, as Hebrews does, to the description of maturity and the issue of second repentance. He also notes that the theme of Abraham's promise is concluded by verse 15, before the matter of the divine oath is taken up in detail in 16ff., so that the latter oath can be explicitly defined in the new Christian sense in terms of the priesthood on the order of Melchizedek (7:17-22). It is therefore clear that Abraham is not used here merely as an example of faith or for a promise-fulfillment scheme, but rather to show a correspondence between the Abraham oath and the Melchizedek oath to Christ at the point of God's word. In both cases God acts through a promise that is not only fulfilled in the present, but also opens up relationship for the future. This section thus carries forward the assumptions about God's word laid down in chapter 1, and more particularly in chapters 3 and 4, wherein Christian pilgrimage was defined as response to the word of God.

Within this context, then, the first point in verse 13 is that the promise to Abraham was authenticated by God through the oath. **God . . . swore, by himself,** which indicates that the validity of the word heard in the midst of the pilgrimage rests solely in the integrity of God. God is true to the divine self, and the only thing attaining to God's truthfulness is God's own word. For **he had no one greater by whom to swear.** In verse 14 the author cites the promise given to Abraham in Genesis 22:16ff., but with a characteristic alteration of the Septuagint text: instead of "I will multiply your seed" our text has **I will multiply you.** This may be motivated by the fact that Hebrews does not wish to build a case for the Christian community as the true seed of Abraham, as in Galatians 3:16, tending instead to downgrade "bodily descent" (7:16) as characteristic for the old cult that has been displaced by the Christ event. This alteration is one more indication that the author is not working with a promise-fulfillment scheme, as argued by Friedrich Bleek and others, whereby the Christian community becomes heir to the ancient promises. Verse 15 describes Abraham's response to the promise in terms drawn from verse 12, **and so having patiently endured, he obtained what was promised.** In other words, it was Abraham's holding fast to dialogue in the midst of adversity that the author emphasizes rather than, for example, his obedience as suggested in the Genesis account (Genesis 22:18). He held to the promised word of God, even though there was no earthly substantiation of its validity, and even when the only earthly possibility of fulfilling the promise of an heir was in jeopardy, with Isaac on the altar. It is consistent with this dialogical perspective that the author would have no qualms about stating flatly **he obtained what was promised,** although in 11:13 and 39 the patriarchs are said to have "not received what was promised." It is necessary at this point to incorporate Käsemann's helpful insight that the distinction between fulfilled and unfulfilled promises in Hebrews derives from the fact that fulfillment is always in the form of the proclaimed word, which can be lost if one departs from it. Although the pilgrim "obtains" the promise over and over again along the way, he or she never "possesses" it in the sense that its future, dialogical aspect is eliminated. For if dialogue is not renewed in the future, it is lost.

Verses 16 to 20 lead from the theme of the oath to the unique structure of Christian pilgrimage, responding to the oath about Jesus the high priest and entering into relationship with the Holy of Holies. The first verse reaches back in an explanatory fashion to verse 13, with the motif of swearing **by what is greater than themselves** leading to a renewed affirmation about the self-authenticating character of God's word: **when God willed to show . . . the unchangeability of his purpose, he guaranteed by means of an oath.** In the midst of the constant flux and uncertainty of pilgrim existence, it is this **promise** or **oath** alone that is unchanging and dependable. Yet it is a dynamic type of unchangeability, quite different from the esoteric magic of the Lycus Valley cult. It is an **unchangeability of his purpose,** a firmly established historical will that guides history toward its rightful end of righteousness. This is why the body of believers in verse 18 can be termed **pilgrims,** or literally, "we who have fled for refuge." This is why the goal of their pilgrimage can be termed **the hope set before us.** It is a life that strains always toward the future, moving from encounter to encounter, sustained by hope rather than by certainty. The **exhortation to seize the hope** is contained in the divine word itself, the **two unchangeable things,** which probably mean the oath of sonship and the oath of priesthood:

Thou art my Son, today I have begotten thee [Heb. 5:5, RSV].
Thou art a priest for ever, after the order of Melchizedek [Heb. 5:6, RSV].

In other words, it is the significance of Christ's work that leads the pilgrim community forward through history. The following chapters will set forth in detail the meaning of Jesus' sonship and priesthood, but the thesis of Hebrews is that none of this doctrine can be understood if the community is not holding fast to the dialogical pilgrimage it has been given. The crucial fact about Jesus, therefore, is that he is the **leader for us,** leading through the secular world and all its alienation to the very **inner side of the veil,** to the Holy of Holies, where he brings the pilgrim community with him into the presence of God. His priestly atonement must be understood on this basis. And the shape of Christian existence falls into heretical distortion if this is lost from view.

With this tremendous pilgrim vision, the exhortation that began with 5:11 is brought to an end, and the discussion of Jesus, the **high priest for the aeon after the order of Melchizedek,** can be taken up. For the shape and basis of Christian maturity has been laid out, the "dialogical maturity" that is required for comprehending a dialogical atonement and priesthood. The section ends on the key aspect of any system of maturity, namely, the source of confidence that gives one courage to face adversity. In this instance, it is defined as a **hope . . . which we have as an anchor of the soul, safe and firm, and entering into the inner side of the veil.** The character of this hope can only be explained on a dialogical basis: it is inaugurated by the **powerful exhortation** of God's word, and it leads one to **enter** into dynamic relationship with the hidden, transcendent God. Since it moves from present response to the word to renewed future response to the word, it provides the only **anchor** for a pilgrim community. It is an **anchor of the soul,** not in the sense of guaranteeing the immortality of the soul, because the term **soul** is probably used here with the connotation typical for the Pauline letters, namely, the observable life of a human. For the hope of entering into significant relationship has a stabilizing effect on the whole person; it is a basis for mental health in a world that seems to defy sanity; and it holds **safe and firm** when everything else deteriorates. The enormous significance of such hope was highlighted in the work of Viktor Frankl in the German concentration camp situation. He writes: "The prisoner who had lost faith in the future—his future—was doomed. With his loss of belief in the future, he also lost his spiritual hold; he let himself decline and became subject to mental and physical decay." He recounts examples of friends who succumbed very quickly after giving up such hope, and offers this generalization: "What man actually needs is not a tensionless state but rather the striving and struggling for some goal worthy of him. What he needs is not the discharge of tension at any cost, but the call of a potential meaning waiting to be fulfilled by him." It is this sort of hope, rather than the spurious "certainties" offered by the Lycus Valley cult, that grounds the maturity needed to grasp the great mystery of Jesus' high priestly work.

Chapter Six

The Melchizedekian Priesthood (7:1-10) of Christ (7:11-19) Provides Superior Atonement (7:20-28)

7:1 FOR this Melchizedek, king of Salem, priest of the most high God, who met Abraham returning from the slaughter of the kings and blessed him, ²to whom also Abraham apportioned a tenth part of everything (being first, by interpretation, "king of righteousness," and then also king of Salem, that is, "king of peace"; ³fatherless, motherless, lacking genealogy, having neither beginning of days nor end of life, but made to resemble the Son of God), remains priest continually. ⁴Consider how great he was, to whom Abraham the patriarch gave a tenth of the best spoils. ⁵Now those of the sons of Levi that receive the priesthood have a commandment to take tithes from the people according to the law, that is, from their brethren, though these have come out of the loins of Abraham. ⁶But he who has not their genealogy took tithes from Abraham and blessed him who had the promises. ⁷And it is beyond dispute that the lesser is blessed by the greater. ⁸And while here it is humans who are dying that receive the tithes, there it is by one of whom it is testified that he lives. ⁹One might even say that Levi himself, who receives tithes, paid tithes through Abraham, ¹⁰for he was still in the loins of his ancestor when Melchizedek met him.

We come now to what the author considers the central,

mysterious message of his "word of exhortation." It was alluded to in 2:17-18 and 4:14-16, where Jesus was described as a "great high priest," and its groundwork was laid in 5:1-10, where the citation from Psalm 110 concerning the priesthood "after the order of Melchizedek" was made. With the development of this mysterious doctrine having been interrupted by the warnings about maturity in 5:11—6:20, the audience's curiosity and attention are sharpened. The author's thesis about the significance of the Christ event is about to be revealed.

The mystery unfolds with a discussion of the Old Testament figure of **Melchizedek,** mentioned in Genesis 14:17-20. This figure, as we now know, stimulated elaborate speculation in various Hellenistic and Jewish circles. My audience hypothesis suggests that a version of this Melchizedek speculation was current in the Lycus Valley. He was likely viewed as an angelic figure who offered atonement by revealing the secrets of the spiritual cult of bread and wine. Those who followed his cultic instructions would be protected by him against the malevolent angelic forces, thus allowing the elect to ascend to their heavenly homeland. If this hypothesis is correct, several aspects of the author's discussion of Melchizedek gain vital, polemical significance.

First, it would then be apparent why the Melchizedek doctrine was postponed until a warning about apostasy and a theory of dialogical pilgrimage could be developed. After mentioning the high priesthood of Christ in 2:17; 4:15; and 5:10, the author inserted the remarkable section about apostasy in 5:11—6:20 on grounds that "the word has much to say to you which is hard to explain, since you have grown sluggish in hearing" (5:11). I would submit that the difficulty in explaining the Melchizedek doctrine was caused by the existence of a very alluring, heretical Melchizedek teaching in the Lycus Valley. Since the author had to build his case on the same exegetical foundations in the Old Testament as used by the Lycus Valley heretics, it was necessary to preface his discussion with an elaborate rebuttal of the manipulative, nondialogical, religious assumptions of the heretical position.

Second, a notable omission in Hebrews' discussion of the Melchizedek tradition takes on significance. F.F. Bruce notes "that one of the things that is said about Melchizedek in the Genesis narrative is passed over by our author without mention—his bringing forth bread and wine for Abraham's refreshment. Few typologists of early Christian or more recent days could have resisted so obvious an opportunity of drawing a eucharistic inference from these words." Bruce does not suggest a reason for this remarkable omission, but it is apparent, if my hypothesis is correct: the author eliminated the cultic aspect of the Melchizedek tradition because it was antithetical to his own version of Christian existence as a secular pilgrimage whose worship is the moment-by-moment encounter with the word of God.

A *third* anomaly of this text is similarly explained. Hans Windisch, Gottfried Wuttke, and others have noted that the rhythmic structure of the Melchizedek discussion, especially in verses 2 and 3, as well as the rather esoteric character of the divinity attributed to Melchizedek, seem to reveal the use of a previously established Melchizedek poem of some sort. Gottfried Schille has worked out the most elaborate hypothesis at this point, suggesting that with the excising of the prose lines, a three-strophe hymn stands out in verses 1 to 3. He pointed out the mythological aspects of this hymn and showed how the author historicized it by means of the prose insertions and the interpretation in the rest of the chapter. Although Schille's suggestion that this was a hymn to Christ as the Melchizedekian priest is less than satisfactory, because Christ is not mentioned in the reconstructed version of the hymn, the hypothesis fits in quite well with my reconstruction of the Lycus Valley angel speculation. With the discovery of the Melchizedek fragment in Qumran, the possibility of such an early speculative tradition is enhanced, and it can now be suggested that the author is actually citing the Lycus Valley creed at this point. He is willing to accept the idea of an immortal Melchizedek but uses this to substantiate his theory of a unique noncultic priesthood of Christ. For him, Melchizedek has no intrinsic significance as a revelatory or redemptive figure; his sole significance is as a prototype for Christ. In a highly effective condescension to the thought form and terminology of his Lycus Valley conversation partners, the author advances his own case on grounds that they would accept, yet distinguishes his position effectively from the heretical aspects of the Lycus Valley theology. With this historical reconstruction of the background in mind, the detailed exegesis of chapter 7 may proceed.

As a whole, chapter 7 is a typical Jewish midrash that, according to Friedrich Schröger, interprets the Melchizedek tradition by combining Psalm 110:4 and Genesis 14:17-20. The interpretation proceeds in typological fashion, with the similarities between Jesus and Melchizedek being used to show that they constitute a new and superior order of priesthood. In these first ten verses, however, the basis for the typological comparison is set forth. The author's perspective is most easily discernible when one begins with the alteration of the Melchizedek hymn in the first three verses. As reconstructed by Schille, the citation is as follows:

7:1a This Melchizedek,
7:1b   King of Salem,
7:1c   Priest of the Most High God,
7:2b First by interpretation King of Righteousness,
7:2c   And then also King of Salem,
7:2d   That is King of Peace,
7:3a Fatherless, motherless, lacking genealogy,
7:3b   Having neither beginning of days nor end of life,
7:3d   Remains priest continually.

While this hymn pictures Melchizedek as a thoroughly mythological figure, preexistent, immortal, combining kingship and priesthood, the author of Hebrews historicizes him by the insertion of material from Genesis. In verses 1d to 2a it is noted that he **met Abraham returning from the slaughter of the kings and blessed him.** The fact that Abraham **apportioned a tenth part of everything** to Melchizedek is also adduced. This historical material lacks any speculative content, yet provides the substantiation for the argument later in the chapter in favor of a Melchizedek-Jesus priesthood that abrogates the legal priesthood of the Old Testament. The most remarkable insertion in the Melchizedek hymn is 3c, **but made to resemble the Son of God.** Schille showed this line was not originally part of the Melchizedek hymn, because it tends to limit the extent of Melchizedek's preexistence affirmed elsewhere in the hymn, and it breaks the logical and stylistic continuity between 3b and d. Furthermore, there is a polemic aspect of the term **made to resemble,** as noted by Epiphanius, which is enhanced by the fact that this term was used in the Jewish tradition to portray the mere resemblance of idols to the living God. The priority thus remains with Christ, who, according to the opening chapters of Hebrews, is superior to any angelic figure. The significance of this insertion for the Lycus Valley adoration of Melchizedek is obvious. It limits Melchizedek to a historical archetype pointing forward and backward toward Christ. But the usefulness of this detail is clear: Jesus himself could claim no priestly descent and only by his congruence with the nongenealogical, immortal Melchizedek could his priestly office be argued. Since the hymn claims that Melchizedek **remains priest continually,** the ground is laid for claiming eternal priesthood for Christ in 7:24-26.

In verses 4 to 10 a midrashic argument is developed to show the superiority of Melchizedek over Abraham and the subsequent priestly law of Judaism. The comparison is drawn in the next section, whereby this superiority is claimed for Christ, the priest after the order of Melchizedek. Given the length of this section and the four closely related arguments for superiority, it is clear that this point is vital for the author. The superiority of the Melchizedek-Christ priesthood over the

Levitic-legalistic priesthood is in William Manson's terms "the central pivotal idea on which the great thematic argument of the writer turns." **How great** Melchizedek was is indicated by the fact that **Abraham gave a tenth of the best spoils** to him. While the **sons of Levi** are entitled to tithe only **their brethren,** Melchizedek took it from someone from a completely different tribe. Next, the fact that **he blessed him who had the promises** indicates his superiority, because **it is beyond dispute that the lesser is blessed by the greater.** Furthermore, while the descendants of Levi are **humans who are dying,** Melchizedek's superiority is indicated by the fact that he **lives** forever. And finally **Levi himself . . . paid tithes through Abraham,** since he was yet unborn **in the loins of his ancestor when Melchizedek met him.** At every step in this argument, the unique perspective of the author manifests itself, especially when compared with the Melchizedek speculation of his time. This is the only example we have of a Melchizedek midrash designed to shatter the finality of the Levitic law and, ultimately, the cult itself. It establishes a basis whereby the cultic practices of the Lycus Valley can be radically undercut and replaced by a new, secular form of Christian piety.

7:11 Now if there was perfection through the Levitical priesthood (for under it the people received the law), what further need would there be for another priest to arise according to the order of Melchizedek, and not be reckoned after the order of Aaron? [12]Now the priesthood having changed, there is necessarily a change in the law as well, [13]for he about whom these things are said belonged to another tribe, from which no one has attended the altar. [14]For it is manifest that our Lord sprang from Judah, and Moses never mentioned priesthood in connection with that tribe. [15]And it is even more abundantly evident when another priest arises according to the likeness of Melchizedek, [16]who has become (priest), not according to the law of fleshly commandment but according to the power of indestructible life.

[17]For it is witnessed that
"You are a priest for the aeon,
after the order of Melchizedek."
[18]For on the one hand, a former commandment is annulled because of its weakness and uselessness [19](for the law made nothing perfect); on the other hand, a better hope is inaugurated, through which we draw near to God.

In these verses the typological comparison is drawn between Melchizedek and Christ. Since Christ is the other priest to arise according to the order of Melchizedek, the author infers that both the Levitic priesthood and the Mosaic law have been abrogated. In verse 11 perfection and the law are brought into relationship, for the law that came with the Levitical priesthood presumably offered perfection for its adherents. So the fact that a new priest has replaced the Levitical priesthood is used to argue that perfection had in fact not been achievable before Christ. The result of this argument is presented in verse 19, in a succinct formula that expresses the "pivotal idea" in this section: for the law made nothing perfect. The terms need to be defined to show the implications for the Lycus Valley controversy. Law was the essence of the old high priestly activity, according to this passage. One became a high priest on the basis of law and performed high priestly duties according to the law. But for Hebrews, as for the Pauline tradition reflected in 6:1; 10:38, and elsewhere, the law has no power to make perfect. This term must be defined in biblical fashion: the perfect person is the one who stands in proper relationship to God as a covenant partner. Since humans in a state of sin are alienated from God, they are "imperfect" and cannot enter into such relationship. The perfect person is thus one in whom sin no longer rules. The thing one must avoid in thinking about this matter is any form of the abstract, moralistic approach to perfection. To be perfect is not to conform perfectly to some ideal or law. Such conformity can be completely unrelated to God as a covenant partner. In fact, experience and the implications of this passage in Hebrews indicate that such is the rule rather than the exception. The law—thought of as a standard for human behavior—cannot lead to relational **perfect**ion, because it encourages human self-dependency, pride, and self-righteousness. This was precisely its effect in the Lycus Valley, for in following the cultic regulations in order to enhance the security of passage to the divine realm, they fell into a manipulative, alienating relationship with God.

This is the sense in which the terms **weakness and uselessness** are applied to the **former commandment** in verse 18. The law is **weak** in the sense that it is unable to provide the **perfection** it presumes to offer, and it is consequently **useless.** As derogatory terms depicting the cultic regulations the Lycus Valley Gnostics derived from the Old Testament law, they would be very effective. The term **weakness** was related in the gnostic mind to the lost and evil realm of the flesh, while its opposite, "'strength" or "power," was associated with the divine realm of "spirit." Similarly, the expression **useless** would have a polemic impact on those who held compliance with the cultic regulations to be "essential" for the spirit to regain its true heavenly homeland. The Gnostic would be shocked to hear that his or her vaunted, esoteric regulations were afflicted either with **weakness** or **uselessness.** But the shock waves would be equally felt today in the modern church, for which branch of the church has not suggested that compliance with ritual and moral **law** was a powerful, effective guide to the good life? Fearful that freedom from the law inevitably produces license, releasing the individual from the benevolent control of the church, the **law** has been reinstated, at first merely as a useful guide to morals, but ultimately as the straitjacket for Christian existence. And the prophetic line from verse 19 is forgotten or reinterpreted: **for the law made nothing perfect.**

To support this daring attack on the effectiveness of the **law,** the author infers from his typological comparison between Christ and Melchizedek that the very presence of **another priest . . . according to the order of Melchizedek** abrogates both the law and the priesthood of Aaron. Verse 12 states this clearly: **Now the priesthood having changed, there is necessarily a change in the law as well.** This idea is developed in subsequent verses on the grounds that since **our Lord sprang from Judah,** from which no priests were to come, according to the Mosaic law, it follows that a new principle of priestly descent has emerged to shatter the old. This is summarized in verse 16, wherein Christ, the new Melchizedekian priest, has received his office **not according to the law of fleshly commandment but according to the power of indestructible life.** Although this term **fleshly** would have a very negative connotation to the Lycus Valley Gnostics, it is uncertain whether Hebrews is following technical Pauline usage at this point. The fact that Paul and Hebrews are the only New Testament sources to use this term would seem to indicate some interrelationship. In any event, it is clear that the **law of fleshly commandment** and the law with **the power of indestructible life** represent two mutually exclusive spheres, the one offering **perfection** and the other countering it. So with the appearance of Christ, the priest according to the order of Melchizedek, the **former commandment is annulled.** The law is shown to be irrelevant for the new age; its validity is completely abrogated by God. Thus the very rules and regulations that the Lycus Valley religionists assumed reflected the will of God and the path to human fulfillment are shown here to have been eliminated by the Christ event. A yearning of first-century legalistic religion, involving an eternal Levitical priesthood that would serve God forever according to the perfect letter of the law, is here swept aside with sovereign power. The very appearance of Christ brings the era of the Law to an end.

How, then, does the author substantiate the position of this new Melchizedekian priest, whose appearance abrogates the Old Testament **law?** Here he reaches back to the assumption with which the Epistle to the Hebrews began, to the idea of God's creative and redeeming word. It is God's word addressed to Jesus that, in Hebrews' perspective, authenticates his priestly office: **For it is witnessed that "You are a priest for the aeon,**

after the order of Melchizedek." This promise, which was adduced in chapter 5, is seen by the author to be addressed to Jesus, even though it is cited from Psalm 110. Although it is very possible that this promise was included in an early Christian hymn, as Schille has argued, its authenticating power for the author of Hebrews lay strictly in the fact that it was God's word. It is not derivative of liturgical custom, human wisdom, or logical argument. It is, in a real sense, the first cause, the logical starting point of Hebrews' theology. It may be appropriate at this point to recall that the great accomplishment of the so-called "neo-orthodox theology" of Barth, Brunner, Bultmann, and others was to rediscover the centrality of this starting point, and to uphold it against the claims of natural or cultural theology. It was a creative source of power and independence on the part of these theologians, giving them the courage to disentangle theology from the web of European nationalism and totalitarianism, and also from the alluring grip of philosophic progressivism and idealism that dominated Western thought until the tragic developments of the twentieth century. In contrast to the stultifying effect of religious dogmatism, this sense of the dynamic action of the word of God can set the mind free to respond in a fresh, resilient fashion to the challenge of one's time.

With this appointment of the Melchizedekian priest, Jesus, by the word of God addressed to him, the author reaches his climax on the theme of dialogical hope. While God's word served to **annul** the **former commandment,** it **inaugurated** at the same time **a better hope.** The character of this **hope** is precisely defined in dialogical terms: it is a **hope . . . through which we draw near to God.** In other words, the **perfection** of new relationship that Christ provided is necessarily an openended, uncompleted perfection. Like any relationship, it is never achievable in a static sense but is always subject to the future, when it must be renewed or lost. **Hope** for Hebrews is precisely this sense of holding to a relationship through to the future. It is the basis on which the pilgrim turns toward the word that addresses her or him along the way through the wilderness, in the expectation that the dialogue will be opened again, with its life-giving power. Christ, the **priest after the order of Melchizedek,** is the inaugurator of this new relationship, for as 2:14-18 and 5:1-10 suggested, he dispelled alienation by sharing it. The result of this at-one-ing activity is that humans can now **draw near to God.** The worshipful approach that hitherto had been barred by the law is now made possible. The contrast here with the Lycus Valley religion is thus both precise and telling: the approach to God that they had hoped to guarantee through compliance with the cultic law is here proclaimed to be enabled solely on the basis of Christ's law-shattering appointment.

7:20 **And inasmuch as it was not without an oath—for they have been made priests without an oath,** [21]**whereas he (was made priest) with an oath through the one saying to him,**

"The Lord has sworn and will not change his mind,

'You are a priest for an aeon,'"

[22]**—just so much better is the covenant of which Jesus is the guarantor.** [23]**Also while they became priests in large numbers, because they were prevented from serving by death,** [24]**he has a permanent priesthood, since he continued "for an aeon."** [25]**Hence for all time he is able to save those who approach God through him, since he always lives to make intercession for them.** [26]**For such a high priest was also fitting for us, holy, innocent, undefiled, separated from the sinners, and exalted above the heavens,** [27]**who has no need, as the high priests, to offer sacrifices daily, first for his own sins and then for those of the people. For this he did once for all, when he offered up himself.** [28]**For the law appoints humans in their weakness as high priests, but the word of the oath, coming later than the law, (appoints) a Son for an aeon who has been made perfect.**

Having shown that Jesus' priesthood replaced that of the Levitical law, the author moves forward in this section to show its superiority at the point of ensuring atonement. Three separate arguments are developed to this end from the typological exegesis of the Melchizedek materials. The first is that while the Levitical priesthood lacked **an oath,** Jesus received an oath directly from God. Again, a citation from Psalm 110 is adduced to prove this: **"The Lord has sworn and will not change his mind, you are a priest for an aeon."** This material, which breaks into the middle of the sentence beginning with verse 20 and ending with verse 22, was alluded to in 6:13-18, where the ground of Christian hope was set forth in the dependable word of God. Because believers can be assured in their new relationship with Christ, grounded as it is in God's word, the new **covenant** in which they stand is **better** than the Old Testament one. This is the opening wedge of the radical reinterpretation of the idea of "covenant" in chapters 8 and 9 in the direction of a new relationship between persons and God. **Jesus is the guarantor** of this new **covenant** in the sense that he opened up this new relationship by sharing human existence and then bringing his comrades with him into the very presence of God (2:13; 7:19). In a form that differs quite sharply from the Lycus Valley security system, Christian existence thus has its **guarantor.** It is personal, dialogical, and thus not manipulatable, being the promise of new relationship rather than a way to gain security for the solitary soul. Its authority partakes of the ambiguity, the openness, and the relational quality of word, for it is based on the **oath** given to Jesus.

The second argument for the superiority of the Melchizedekian priesthood of Christ relates to the key element of the hymn cited in 7:3. While Melchizedek and Christ have **a permanent priesthood** that continues **for an aeon,** the Levitical priests fell prey to mortality. The significance of this claim is accessible when one notes the strange emphasis in verse 25: **Hence for all time he is able to save those who approach God through him, since he always lives to make intercession for them.** The fear in the Lycus Valley was apparently similar to that found in gnostic writings like Pistis Sophia, namely, that if Jesus or Melchizedek should be inactive, the spirits of the enlightened would be helpless before the power of the evil aeons. Thus Christ's Melchizedekian priesthood offered precisely what the Lycus Valley ceremonies sought to ensure: constant access to God. The movement of the Christian pilgrim into the presence of God has a measure of assurance in face of the threatening future. It is not a manipulatable certainty, but one based on the person of Christ **who lives to make intercession for them.**

The third argument for the superiority of Jesus the high priest is neatly woven into a climactic, almost rhapsodic section that ends Hebrews 7. The point of verses 26 to 28 is that this new Melchizedekian priest **was also fitting for us,** that is, he provided what was required for salvation. Since the form of this salvation was restated again in verse 25 in terms of gaining direct access to relationship with God, the attributes listed in this section are thought to facilitate Jesus' role in producing access, or at-one-ment. The listing of the attributes in 26b made such a hymnic impression on commentators like Otto Michel and Hans Windisch that a citation from an early Christian hymn, or possibly even the Melchizedek hymn reflected in 7:1-3, has been suspected. But as Schille has shown, this section lacks the formal and stylistic attributes of a true hymn and therefore must be attributed to the rhetorical skill of the author of Hebrews. Michel's observation that the five attributes of Jesus' priesthood in 26b correspond in structure to the five attributes of the word of God in 4:12 tends to substantiate this conclusion. The first four relate to priestly qualifications: **holy, innocent, undefiled** relate to the Old Testament and rabbinic law concerning priestly purity, both in the inner and outer aspects of the self. The expression **separated from the sinners** is also drawn from rabbinic regulations concerning the isolating of the high priest a week before the Day of Atonement. For Hebrews, of course, this relates to the present position of Jesus in the heavenly sanctuary and is not meant to eliminate that seemingly contradictory phase of his atoning work alluded to in 2:14ff. and 4:14ff., namely, his complete identification with human life. Both aspects fit into the priestly task, as far as Hebrews is concerned, for while Jesus "in the days of his flesh" dispelled alienation by participating in "flesh and blood," thus making possible the approach of the pilgrim community to God, he is seen here as guaranteeing precisely this access by his priestly "separation."

The climactic attribute in verse 26, as far as the Lycus Valley was concerned, is the claim that Jesus is **exalted above the heavens.** The **heavens** would denote cosmic forces to the Lycus Valley theorists, and to be **exalted above** them would mean to be completely beyond their malevolent grasp. Such a priest as this would be able to ensure access through the evil aeons of the universe. Even the term used here for **exalted** formed the basis, as Günther Bornkamm noted, for the Hypsistarian sect that worshiped the "heights" as the source of cosmic power in a manner quite similar to the Colossian, or Lycus Valley heresy. So the claim that Jesus was **fitting for us** would be substantiated in the minds of the Lycus Valley residents because he fit so perfectly into their need for redemption from the cosmic forces. Here is a Christology tailored for a particular time and situation, yet faithful to the traditions of the earliest Christian community. It is an indication of how far faith can go to make its message "relevant" to the mind of a particular group.

With extraordinary subtlety the following verse opens an attack on the cultic pretensions of the Lycus Valley, while pursuing the argument concerning the superiority of Christ. Against the repetitive aspect of the old cult, being required **to offer sacrifices daily,** stands the sacrifice which Christ **did once for all.** As Martin Dibelius has shown, this expression epitomizes the polemic drive of Hebrews against any cultic activity, in the normal sense of the word, being carried on after the Christ event. This verse provides a preview of the anticultic argument that dominates chapters 8 to 10 of Hebrews, and already at this inception it is clear that what remains of cult is simply the dialogical approach itself. Since the Christian pilgrims are defined in verse 25 as **those who approach God through him,** it follows that they have no further need for repetitive rites. The Lycus Valley religionists are thereby thrust out of their comforting enclave and onto the path of secular pilgrimage. Their new form of worship is to encounter the word of God moment by moment along the way and thus to enter into the heavenly sanctuary **through him.**

The final line in this climactic third argument for the superiority of Christ contains a double contrast between **law** and **oath,** and between **weakness** and **perfection.** Once again it is implied that since the **word of the oath** came to the new priest **later than the law,** it completely supercedes and eliminates it. At this point the pivotal argument for this entire section is restated, and the implication is plain: the legalistic ritual of the Lycus Valley has been abolished by the Christ event and thus cannot accomplish what it promises to its devotees. By confirming the validity of Christ's atoning activity with his **oath,** God places faithfulness on the path of pilgrimage and abrogates the path of pious, cultic works. Since God has placed the divine word behind Jesus, the path Jesus offers can be depended upon. Humankind is thereby encouraged to give up the desperate existence of self-dependency and self-righteousness, and to accept the new existence of relationship with God. But woven in with this contrast between **law** and **oath,** with their two mutually exclusive forms of existence, is a rather problematic contrast between being **weak** and being **perfect.** Here the fact that the Levitical priests were **humans in their weakness** is used in a derogatory fashion, quite in contrast with Christ's positive identification of himself with "weakness" earlier in Hebrews. In 4:15 it was stated that Jesus sympathizes "with our weakness" and in 5:2 that he fulfilled the role of the priest who "himself is beset with weakness." It appears that we have a situation here similar to the separation from the sinners in 7:26b. As far as Hebrews is concerned, both the identification with **weakness** during Jesus' earthly ministry and his transcendence above **weakness** in his exaltation were necessary for his priestly effectiveness. While in the earlier chapters of Hebrews, Jesus brought atonement by reconciling humans to their finitude by sharing **weakness,** here he assures atoning access by performing the heavenly liturgy (**he always lives to**

make intercession for them), which can only be carried out by **a son for an aeon who has been made perfect.** While the two aspects of this priestly work may seem sharply counterposed to the modern mind, the author obviously considers them as two sides of the same coin.

One route into Hebrews' remarkable conception is to follow the logic of the perfect passive verb, **has been made perfect.** This is clearly not the moralistic perfection Marcus Dods depicted, avoiding "the sinful yielding to infirmity exhibited by the Levitical priests," but rather, as Dibelius has shown, the primary sense of consecration for the sake of access. In accepting human weakness in its fullest sense, Jesus was accepted by God; he was given the **perfection** of access to the forbidden presence. This was stated in other terminology in 5:7, RSV, where Jesus' "loud cries and tears to him who was able to save him from death" were "heard." At the moment of sharing finitude most fully, he was granted the access implied here in 7:28. So the passive form of the verb is exactly expressive of the nonmoralistic concept of **perfection** the author wishes to convey.

Thus the great Melchizedek chapter closes on a motif that is intimately related to the level of "perfection" or "maturity" which the author felt was required to understand the doctrine. If the believers are to share in this perfection of access, entering into the sanctuary following the path of their pilgrim forerunner, they will do so in a way that is consistent with Jesus' Melchizedekian priesthood. By accepting their weak finitude and giving up all dreams of manipulating life through a legalistic cult, they can receive the perfection that is given but never earned, the perfection of open relationship. These themes, which are fully developed in the next three chapters, are therefore already contained in the teaching about Jesus the high priest after the order of Melchizedek.

Chapter Seven

Christ's Ministry (8:1-6) Inaugurates the New Covenant (8:7-13): Religiosity Versus Relationship

8:1 NOW the chief point in what we have said is this: we have such a high priest, who took his ruling seat at the right hand of the Majesty in the heights, ²a minister of the (holy of) holies and of the true tent which the Lord set up, not a human being. ³For every high priest is appointed to offer both gifts and sacrifices; hence the necessity for him to have something to offer. ⁴Now if he were still on earth, he would not even be a priest, since there already exist those who offer gifts according to the law. ⁵Such ones serve a copy and shadow of the heavenly (sanctuary)—as Moses was instructed as he was about to complete the tent: for he said, "See that you make everything according to the pattern shown you on the mountain." ⁶But as it is, (Christ) has obtained a ministry that is as much more excellent (than the old) as the covenant he mediates is better, since it has been enacted on better promises.

Having established the superiority of the Melchizedekian priesthood in the preceding chapter, the author develops in the next three chapters his picture of its superior **ministry**. The argument is based on the idea of atonement in the form of renewed relationship as developed earlier in the epistle. It therefore begins in 8:1-13 with the inauguration of a **more excellent . . . covenant** that replaces empty religiosity with valid relationship. Then, in 10:1-18, the author works out the implications of such new relationship in terms of obedience. One can easily lose one's way in this argument, with its welter of obscure cultic categories, unless this fundamental line of argument is kept in mind.

In verses 1 to 6 the themes of chapters 8 to 10 are related to the previous argument, including the Melchizedek discussion. The **chief point** in Hebrews thus far, having reached its definition in the Melchizedek chapter, is that **we have such a high priest.** This is the faith statement that grounds the critique of the Lycus Valley cult and provides the basis for the Christian pilgrimage into the sanctuary. But it is the **ministry** of this **high priest** that is of major interest now, and verses 1b and 2 describe this with considerable polemic finesse. First, Jesus the high priest **took his ruling seat at the right hand of the Majesty in the heights.** This line is cited from 1:3, which stood at the beginning of the argument against the adoration of **the heights,** the aeons, or any other angelic powers. The reader is therefore to relate this antignostic premise to the presently unfolding teaching about Christ's **ministry.** The **high priest** is at the same time the ruling Son, whose place is above all supposed cosmic powers. Given the Lycus Valley context, this affirms Christ's power to guarantee access despite their fears about the malevolent **heights** through which they must pass. But while verse 1b glances backward over the argument, verse 2 looks forward to the discussion concerning the **true tent** in chapter 9. The polemic that will be developed there against all earthly shadows of the heavenly cult is announced with the words **which the Lord set up, not humans.** The ministry in this **true** sanctuary, as opposed to the false sanctuaries of either the Jewish or the Lycus Valley varieties, is founded by the will of God and derives its effectiveness for its believers from that fact. The plural **holies** indicates clearly that the author has in mind the Holy of Holies, that symbol of direct and terrifying access to the living God, which is now open to the pilgrim followers of this great **high priest.**

In a somewhat clumsy fashion, the following verses

review some of the priestly assumptions that are to be developed in detail in chapters 9 and 10. That **every high priest is appointed to offer both gifts and sacrifices** is virtually cited from 5:1, and although it is based on the ritual law that the author otherwise wishes to supercede, this point is apparently made to show that Christ does have **something to offer** in a cultic sense as the heavenly **high priest.** As the following chapters make plain, he offers himself as a sacrifice in order to lead his people with him into the presence of God. The location of this sacrificial ministry is defined in verse 4 as being in heaven, and it could be that the peculiar logic in saying **there already exist those who offer gifts according to the law,** thus leaving no room for Jesus' priestly work **on earth,** points to a polemic intention. The earthly ministry is based on the law that chapter 7 showed had been set aside by the Christ event, so by implication any cultic activity this side of heaven is encumbered with procedures which are "weak and useless" (7:18). But whether there is a polemic jab here against the Jerusalem or the Lycus Valley cults, or both, the main point is to prove that the location of the true cult is in heaven. This is extremely important for the subsequent argument of Hebrews not only because it can easily be brought into contrast with any earthly cult, but also because it symbolizes the direct access to God that the congregation so earnestly sought. Yet in contrast to traditional conceptions of heaven, Hebrews insists over and over again that such access is opened by God's word addressed to the pilgrim community along its path through the secular world (4:1-16; 6:17-20; 10:19-22; 12:22-24).

In verses 5 and 6 the implicit polemic against earthly cults comes clearly to the fore: the earthly priests merely **serve a copy and shadow of the heavenly** tent. This terminology is reminiscent of Philo's philosophy of shadow and reality that is used to commend to the readers of *De Vita Mosis* the validity of the Old Testament law. Both Philo and Hebrews cite Exodus 25:40 in a similar fashion: **for he said, "See that you make everything according to the pattern shown you on the mountain."** But as Sidney Sowers notes, "the very text which

Philo uses to Judaism's defence was turned in Hebrews to its disadvantage. Hebrews sees the text as a clear indication that Judaism is based upon an earthly cult all of whose institutions are mere copies of heavenly archetypes." By treating the earthly cult as "a shadowy outline, a second-hand, inferior reproduction" of the **true tent,** as James Moffatt formulates it, Hebrews sets the stage for the critique in the following chapters. It strikes at the heart of the Lycus Valley religion, which presumed to have divinely authenticated rites mollifying the cosmic forces and ensuring access to the gnostic homeland. But rather than developing this critique immediately, the author turns to a theme that deserves priority, given the dialogical framework on which he is operating.

By climaxing this thematic preview with the reference to **covenant** in verse 6, the author picks up the motif mentioned in 7:22 and prepares the way for the remarkable, long citation from Jeremiah, in verses 8–12. As this citation makes plain, the **covenant** Hebrews has in mind is not the inauguration of a new system of religious obligations, but rather as F.F. Bruce has argued, a new, personal relationship. This is the basis on which the entire concept of Christ's heavenly liturgy is to be understood, for as the argument in verse 6 suggests, the superiority of his **ministry** is based on the superiority of **the covenant he mediates.** That the **media**tion of a **covenant** is an aspect of priestly ministry is a completely unprecedented claim on the part of our author, for the term mediator was normally linked with juristic procedure, or in Judaism, with the role of Moses and the angels in passing the law from God to humans. By opening his formal discussion of Jesus' **ministry** with this theme of mediating **covenant,** the author breaks new ground in the reinterpretation of cult and worship. He draws it out of the stale arena of esoteric ceremony and manipulative religiosity and places it squarely on the pilgrim path of encounter with God's word moment for moment. Thus it is fitting that verse 6 should end with the claim that the superiority of the new **covenant** is based on the fact that **it has been enacted on better** promises. It is the word—the spoken promise—of God that provides the basis for this new relationship.

8:7 For if that first (covenant) had been blameless, then no place would have been sought for a second. [8]For he finds fault with them when he says:
"Behold, the days will come, says the Lord, and I shall complete with the house of Israel and with the house of Judah a new covenant, [9]not according to the covenant I made with their fathers on the day of my taking their hand to lead them out of the land of Egypt, because they did not remain in my covenant, and I paid no heed to them, says (the) Lord. [10]For this is the covenant which I shall make with the house of Israel after those days, says the Lord: giving my laws into their minds, I shall inscribe them upon their hearts, and I shall be their God and they shall be my people. [11]And they will not each teach his fellow citizen and each his brother, saying, 'Know the Lord.' For they will all know me, from the least of them to the greatest, [12]because I shall be merciful to their unjustices and I will remember their sins no more."
[13]In saying new (covenant) he made the first obsolete. And what is becoming obsolete and senile is ready to vanish away.

The long citation from Jeremiah 31 that dominates this section has seemed rather enigmatic to exegetes, who sometimes skip over it with rather superficial comments. But the genial fashion by which the author has previously fit such citations into the very heart of his argument should lead us to suspect that Jeremiah was cited for more than general background. The significance of the citation is indicated not only by the fact that it precedes the detailed description of Christ's ministry announced in the previous six verses, but also by the fact that as compared with the use of this material in Philo, Qumran, and the rest of the New Testament, this is the most complete and lengthy citation that appears in ancient literature. One is driven to the assumption, therefore, that this five-verse Jeremiah citation plays a crucial role in the development of Hebrews' argument concerning Jesus' priestly ministry. As exegetical criteria in the effort to discover the character of this role, it is appropriate to take account of (a) the author's alteration of the wording from the Old Testament, (b) the points of comparison that are lifted up for discussion by the author in the immediate context, and (c) a definition of ideas and terms in the citation on the basis of the argument elsewhere in Hebrews. It would be inappropriate to interpret the Jeremiah citation in light of its own historical context seven centuries before Hebrews' time. As Markus Barth has argued, the author of Hebrews treats such texts not as documents of a previous historical period, but rather as statements addressed by the spirit to the congregation.

The citation is introduced by reference to the inferior character of the old **covenant** as compared with the one Christ mediates. The very presence of a **second** covenant is taken as evidence that the **first** had not been **blameless.** This negative note is strengthened by the line **he finds fault with them when he says. . . .** By introducing the citation in this way, an "undertone of reproach," in Friedrich Schröger's words, is inserted into the passage, leading the reader to pick up this less-emphasized motif within the citation itself. The citation is therefore designed to play a role in the critique of the non-Melchizedekian ministry, whose law, according to 7:18, was "annulled because of its weakness and uselessness." To be more precise, it is the devotees of that old **covenant** who are being blamed: the controversy is **with them.** Thus the point of emphasis in the first part of the citation is that the new covenant was required **because they did not remain in my covenant.** This calls to mind the rebellious desert generation described in chapters 3 and 4, who turned away from the word that addressed them and fell dead in the wilderness. But even in closer proximity to this section of Hebrews is the warning about apostasy in 6:1-8, in which those who have "tasted the goodness of the word of God" come to be slothful in hearing and fail to remain in vital relationship. As related to the Lycus Valley context, they fail to **remain in my covenant** because their interest has shifted to cultic manipulation of the forces of the cosmos. In a real sense, apostasy in chapter 6, as well as in this Jeremiah citation, is a matter of being immersed in an old cult that lacks the dimension of personal relationship.

This line of interpretation may be confirmed by the several alterations in the wording of the Jeremiah text. In verse 8 the **new covenant** is **completed**, rather than simply "inaugurated" as in the original, and in the following verse, the **covenant . . . with their fathers** was **made**, which represents a toning down of the somewhat stronger "inaugurated," which again appears here in the Septuagint. This appears to be an effort on the part of the author to contrast the level of personal commitment and permanency between the old and the new covenants, an issue discussed in detail in Bernhard Weiss' commentary. This correlates well with the statement **I paid no heed to them, says the Lord**, which follows the accusation in verse 9. The people's breach of covenantal relationship is here counteracted by the terrible withdrawal of covenantal possibility, in a manner strongly reminiscent of chapters 3, 4, and 6. In light of the argument of Hebrews as developed so far, the alternative is between legalistic manipulation of cult and vital personal relationship, the one being rejected by God and the other being established by the priestly ministry of Christ.

In striking contrast to the old **covenant**, with its impasse in terms of sustaining open relationship between human beings and God, stands the **new covenant** as described in verses 10ff. It reaches **into their mind** and is **inscribed . . . upon their hearts**, producing a new and vital relationship between the people and God: **I shall be their God and they shall be my people**. Again, the profoundly personal aspect of this new relationship is enhanced by the author's alteration of the Septuagint text, from "write" to **inscribe**. This was not intended to lift up the "permanent nature of the laws of the new covenant," as Schröger assumes, but rather to emphasize the internal, personal impression of God's will and presence upon the heart. This level of personal relationship is not to be reserved for the elite, as was typically the case for gnostic enlightenment, **for they will all know me, from the least of them to the greatest.** Even the teaching role, which the Lycus Valley elite apparently held in high regard (cf. 5:12), would be eliminated: **and they will not each teach his fellow citizens.** The essential, personal knowledge of God that can only be gained by personal experience will be given to each person. They will thus be transformed from legalistic manipulators into dialogical partners.

The citation closes with an emphasis on the priestly aspect of this new covenant, namely, the atonement for sins. The author has augmented verse 12 with the addition of **their sins,** a line that is unparalleled in either the Septuagint or the Hebrew text of this passage. While the term **unjustices** has a noncultic aura, this insertion brings the passage fully into the orbit of the great high priest's task of taking away **sins** (9:14-26). By leading his pilgrim people into this new relationship with God, the Melchizedekian priest dispels the alienation of sin. If no one can enter into personal dialogue unless such alienation has been overcome, it follows that to inaugurate dialogue is to wipe the consciousness of alienation away.

In summary, therefore, this citation suggests that the old legalistic covenant produced alienation between God and humans, while the new covenant of Christ the high priest inaugurates open, personal relationship that eliminates all barriers. In retrospect, the "first principles" of 6:1 lie at the heart of this argument. If one does not base life on the "foundation . . . of repentance from dead works and faith in God," one is irrevocably a devotee of the old covenant with its legalism, its alienation, and its death. Depending upon cultic works that are in reality dead, one falls into self-justification and self-dependency. And there is no hope until, under the impact of the word about the great high priest, one **repents** and turns in **faith** to God. At that moment the **new covenant** promised by Jeremiah becomes part of a person. The issue here is sometimes confused by taking the references to the **mind** and

heart to imply that "subjective religious experience" is the only solution. Under this assumption the **new covenant** announced by Jeremiah would be a matter of accepting God's will as a personal, subjective challenge. Another variation of this general approach holds that the **new covenant** involves a fresh motivation for doing what is right. Such interpretations cannot account for the cultic categories of this discussion in Hebrews. The author explicitly links this prophecy of a new covenant with the establishment of a new cultic **ministry,** i.e., the sacrificial work of Christ the high priest. Thus the content of the new covenant—that which makes the **mind** and **heart** at-one with God—is the sacrifice of Christ. But this event is the very opposite of the old cult that people performed in response to the law. For the Christ event, especially the events of his death and resurrection, leaves no space for independent work of self-justifying. In fact, as the Gospels reveal, it was righteous, law-respecting persons who put him on the cross. His word of forgiveness redeemed them without a single justifying act of their own. That which redeems humans in the Christ event is not its subjective impact, but rather its judgment and forgiveness of human self-justification. When this happens, people receive new **minds** and new **hearts** in relation to God and find that the performance of God's will becomes a joyous response (10:1-18). Such people are at peace with God, against whom they had formerly competed. They know the heavenly Father, upon whose mercy their life depends, and thus their **mind** is attuned to the truth. They find themselves open to the truth as it streams in on them from the Christ event, and discover the maturity of those who have accepted the "first principles" and made them the foundation of their lives. Even more amazingly, they find their heart new in the sense of willing the good and doing it. Rather than being set on the attainment of personal prestige, the new **heart** joyously wills to do the good and does it. Disobedience and **sin** are no longer the products of the heart, since it is no longer self-driven. It rejoices in its newfound master and discovers that **sin** is no more. Wesley's journal illustrates this new existence that

Hebrews proclaims. The day after the Aldersgate experience, these words were written: "But this I know, I have now peace with God. And I sin not today, and Jesus my master has forbid me to take thought for the morrow."

It might be appropriate to reflect on this reality a moment by asking how the church today seeks to lead its people into the **new covenant**. Obviously, churches today are not exactly filled with persons made new in **mind** and **heart**. In fact, given the power of the Christian proclamation, it is astounding that there are so few with this self-sustaining power of the **new covenant** within them, persons whose **minds** are hungry for the word of God and whose **hearts** never cease willing and marvelously performing the good. Why is this? It may relate to the way people are being exhorted today, and the comparison with Hebrews' "word of exhortation" (13:22) might be instructive. I would submit that the exhortation today is usually to perform some good deed or the other. This week it is to support the Boy Scouts and next week the hungry in Asia, while last week it was the tornado fund and last month it was the demonstration to halt the draft. Month after month the program of the modern church aims at organizing and procuring the good, and who is to complain that these causes do not all have their important places? But in the context of Hebrews, they seem to correspond to the legal requirements of the old cult, the mere "shadows" and "copies" of the good. And in promoting these shadows, the contemporary church may be unwittingly leading people deeper and deeper into the alienation the law always causes. Such exhortations lead persons into justifying themselves by their compliance, saving themselves by doing what religion seems to require of them. But their doom is the same as that of the desert generation and the apostates in the Lycus Valley. One wonders in light of this whether the pattern of exhortation in Hebrews might not be more promising, for it intertwines the good news about the **new covenant** inaugurated by Christ's high priestly ministry with the exhortation to hold fast and to move forward responsibly along the pilgrim path. When such a message takes root, and people come to respond to the restoring and atoning grace of God, they receive new hearts and minds, and thereafter need no law or program to evoke their action. It flows in a torrent of love and good will that far surpasses the pitiful results of the law.

In light of the either/or quality of true dialogue, the coming of the **new covenant** has the effect of exposing and shattering the old. So it is on this motif that chapter 8 closes: **In saying new (covenant) he made the first obsolete. And what is becoming obsolete and senile is ready to vanish away.** The tragedy of the Lycus Valley type of religion is that refusal to see the **obsolete** character of the cult it promotes. Rather than leading people into the enlivening dialogue of the **new covenant,** it directs faith toward what is **ready to vanish away.** Touting the innovations of cultic reforms and organizational charts, they find themselves caught up by what is already **senile,** to use Markus Barth's provocative translation. Lacking the renewal of genuine faith, should it be surprising that such churches and cults find themselves facing the prospect of diminishing vitality, indeed even of **vanishing away?**

Christ's Ministry Accomplished Purification: Rite Versus Restoration (9:1–28)

9:1   CONSEQUENTLY, the first (covenant) also had regulations for worship and the cosmic sanctuary. ²The foremost tent was equipped with the lampstand and the table and the bread of the Presence; it is called the Holy Place. ³And behind the second curtain (was) a tent, which was called the Holy of Holies, ⁴having a golden incense altar and the ark of the covenant covered all over with gold, which contained the golden urn holding the manna, and Aaron's rod that budded, and the tables of the covenant; ⁵above this were the cherubim of glory, overshadowing the mercy seat—about which we cannot now speak in detail. ⁶And being thus equipped, the priests enter continually into the first tent, carrying out the worship services; ⁷but into the second (tent) only the high priest goes once a year, not without blood which he offers for himself and for the errors of the people. ⁸By this the Holy Spirit declares that the way into the (Holy of) Holies was not yet disclosed as long as the first tent has status—⁹which is parabolic for the present critical moment, in that gifts and sacrifices are offered which are unable to perfect the conscience of the worshiper, ¹⁰(based) only upon foods and drinks and various baptisms, fleshly regulations imposed until the time of reformation.

This chapter shows how the sacrificial worship performed by Christ the high priest effected purification. This theme, like that in the previous chapter, is developed by contrasting his service with its ineffective counterpart in the old cult. In the first five verses a rather peculiar and thoroughly polemic description of the **equip**ping of the old cult is provided. In light of the Lycus Valley obsession with the cosmic forces, the use of the expression **cosmic sanctuary** in a rather derogatory context in verse 1 is quite striking. The term connotes worldliness, but the Hellenistic Jewish tradition of the sanctuary as symbolic of the whole cosmic realm lurks in the background of this usage. By refraining from developing the mythological possibilities of this **cosmic** symbol, and by arguing in verse 8 that the very presence of the inner tent indicates that access to the divine presence is barred, the author places a substantial bulwark against the Lycus Valley cult. Even the sequence of the list of cultic paraphernalia in verse 2 seems to bear the mark of this polemic concern; as Otto Michel has noted, the listing of the **lampstand** as the first of the sanctuary objects stems from the Hellenistic Jewish tradition in which, for example, Philo gives precedence to the seven-armed candlestick as symbolic of the planets and other cosmic forces. Furthermore, the peculiar reference to the **second curtain** in verse 3, implying that there were actually two separate tents—one for the **Holy Place** and the other for the **Holy of Holies**—is not derived from the Old Testament tradition of one tent with a divided section for the Holy of Holies. It stems from the Hellenistic Jewish tradition that thought of two tents as symbolizing heaven and earth as cosmic realms. As Michel says, "the distinction between the two tents had a definite cosmic sense for the Hellenistic source our author uses." In fact, there are many other points in the sanctuary tradition, noted by Hugh Montefiore, where the author could have followed his Hellenistic tradition to develop the sort of cosmic speculation his congregation in the Lycus Valley would have appreciated. The four-sided **incense altar** could have been used to speculate on the four elements of matter; the proportions of the **ark** could have provided material for symbolizing the mysterious power and purposes of God; the **manna** in the **golden urn** could have symbolized the mystery of perception; and the **cherubim** could have provided a basis for speculating on the cosmic hemispheres. But, Montefiore concludes, the "author abjures here this allegorical method of interpretation." Such things are not to be spoken of **in detail.** Avoiding all the positive speculative comparisons that could have been made, he turns instead in verses 6 to 10 to develop a devastatingly negative argument against the validity of this ancient cult.

While the first five verses dealt with the equipment of the sanctuary, here the **worship services** of the **priests** are in view. The details include the repetitive character of this ritual, the priests **entering continually,** and the **high priest** entering the **second (tent)** . . . **once a year.** The negative possibilities of this repetitive service are developed later in chapter 9. Also there is a rather fearful aspect of the wording in verse 7, for although the **high priest** can enter once a year, it is **not without blood which he offers for himself and for the errors of the people.** The implication is that he dare not enter without such atoning means to dispel the wrath of God, which was thought to center in the forbidden holy place. This negative motif comes to dramatic expression in verse 8: **By this the Holy Spirit declares that the way into the (Holy of) Holies was not yet disclosed as long as the first tent has status.** In other words, the very existence of the enclosed tent is taken as an indication that humans had no real access to God. The expression **not yet disclosed** in relation to a **way into the (Holy of) Holies** stands quite close to Philonian and gnostic usage concerning the revelation of the path of the soul to its spiritual homeland, as Ernst Käsemann points out. If the path is not revealed, it cannot be found through human effort, and consequently, one is lost. This denies the central premise of the Lycus Valley heresy, namely, that through cultic manipulation conforming to Old Testament regulations, access to the spiritual realm would be ensured. As long as they depended upon something analogous to the **regulations** of the **first covenant,** this essential secret of the path to God would be hidden. And given the context of the Lycus Valley controversy, to say that **the first** tent has status means to have a significant role in a cultic method of salvation.

The polemic application to the Lycus Valley cult is even more visible in verses 9 and 10. Despite the complexity of translation, the focus on the controversies there is unmistakable. The author sees the closed tent and the barred access as **parabolic for the present**, that is, the moment of writing the letter, and the choice of the term *kairos,* meaning **critical moment,** suggests "the idea of a present crisis," as Brooke Foss Westcott puts it. If my historical reconstruction of the situation in the congregation is accurate, the shape of this "crisis" is obvious. The author sees the **Holy Spirit'**s revelation concerning the barred access in the old cult as pertaining to the Lycus Valley effort to ensure access to the divine homeland through performance of esoteric rituals that would appease the hostile cosmic forces. This interpretation is confirmed most powerfully by the inclusion of the seemingly irrelevant details in verse 10. What do **regulations** concerned with **foods and drinks and various baptisms** have to do with the author's previous description of the **gifts and sacrifices** of the old cult? Hans Windisch has noted this odd irrelevance, and the effort to relate these coherently with the sacrificial system as such has completely failed. When one takes account of the appearance of this curious plural **baptisms** in 6:2 and the polemic against **foods** in 13:9, as well as the congruence between these cultic items and those mentioned in Colossians as part of the Lycus Valley heresy, it becomes apparent that the author is alluding to ceremonies current in the congregation addressed by his epistle.

In light of this direct, polemic, allusion to the Lycus Valley cult, the antithesis between **perfect the conscience** and **fleshly regulations** is extremely apt. While the Gnostic typically identified the **conscience** with the inner, spiritual person, which could be **perfect**ed by knowledge of its spiritual destiny, he classified the **flesh** as the physical source of corruption. Consequently, the Lycus Valley Gnostics probably sincerely believed that their esoteric knowledge and cultic compliance would **perfect** this inner self, freeing it from the bondage to **flesh** and corruption. The author turns this precisely on its head, denying that such a cult could **perfect the conscience of the worshiper** and charging that it was simply based on **fleshly regulations** whose validity only lasted until the new age appeared.

What a devastating critique the author issues against the well-meaning religion of his day! In seeking to improve humans and give them some rules to increase their chances of entering the heavenly homeland, it was actually barring their access to God. In leading them to perform the ritual duties with the hope of achieving salvation, it closed the door of relationship with God. It achieved just the opposite from what it intended. This is what is so shocking about Hebrews' argument: despite the good intentions of religious leaders and the earnest desire of religious devotees, the harvest is nothing but thorns. Who would have thought that such sensible regulations as those about **foods and drinks and various baptisms** in the Lycus Valley would lead to such appalling results? After all, isn't cleanliness next to godliness? Is it not appropriate to abstain from **drinks** to provide a good example for the weak? Are not such **regulations** quite sensible, particularly when one eliminates their gnostic rationale and reduces them to sensible modern forms? Despite what idealists may say, does the flesh not need some **regulations** imposed upon it? But here the author of Hebrews has the audacity to state that such religious acts are not only unable to **perfect the conscience of the worshiper,** but actually reveal that the way to God's presence is **not yet disclosed.**

Would the same charge be leveled against the religious duties we impose upon ourselves today? Would the author of Hebrews class our moral regulations and program directives along with the **regulations** for the old sanctuary? Would he compare our beautifully balanced organizational schemes for local churches, state conferences, general assemblies, and general conferences with the magnificent but useless equipage of the old **tent?** Is there any chance that he would compare the

continual activity of the priests going in and out, back and forth, restlessly performing their **worship services** with our ceaseless busyness on behalf of the program of clubs and churches? Would he charge that our activities and concerns bar the very gates of God's house in our faces?

Perhaps one way of answering such questions is to discover whether these modern forms of cultic activity actually succeed in bringing persons to God. Are those who are busiest with the work of the church today succeeding in their personal approaches to the **Holy of Holies?** Are they reposed and full of numinous joy while at prayer? Do they have a growing awareness of God's will for them as persons? Or are they hasty at prayer, distracted at worship, at flight in their leisure, and so intent in their endeavors as to eliminate that openness and watchfulness to God's new activity that their master enjoined upon them? In short, does the modern religious activist have an inexplicable sense of the absence of God? It would be beyond the scope of a commentary like this to attempt to answer such questions, but the words of Hebrews stand as a provocative challenge to those who do: **By this the Holy Spirit declares that the way into the (Holy of) Holies was not yet disclosed.**

Verse 10 ends with the thought that the activities and the effectiveness of the old cult last only **until the time of reformation.** There has been considerable discussion as to whether this is earlier or later than **the present critical moment,** and whether it is contrasted with it. In light of Hebrews' argument in chapter 7 that the new Melchizedekian priest has abrogated both the ancient priesthood and the ancient law, it would appear that the **time of reformation** is the Christ event itself. The appearance of this new high priest annuls the "former commandment" and inaugurates a "better hope" (7:18f.). Thus the period from the Christ event until the author's time would be included in the **time of reformation,** and that which makes the **present . . . moment** so **critical,** in his view, is that the Lycus Valley Christians are tempted to carry on as if that **reformation** had never taken place. In his view, the **time of reformation** is the new aeon, when the busy religious activities required by the law are replaced by pilgrimage that enters moment by moment into the presence of God. It is the era when the Old Covenant that led to self-righteousness and alienation is replaced by a new and more personal relationship. It is necessarily a **reformation** brought about not by the reforming zeal of leaders, but by God's immeasurable grace. The task of the church in the Lycus Valley, therefore, is to carry through with this **reformation.** Those who live in the **time of reformation** are called upon to accept the judgment upon the old institutions and regulations, to accept the new institutions of grace and faith that Christ established in his high priestly ministry. If the author of Hebrews is correct, the old cult cannot be renewed or made more relevant; it must instead be abrogated. The tabernacle cannot be revitalized by trying harder, by polishing up the golden ark, or by scurrying more diligently from tent to tent. All this would simply reinforce the false claims of the old cult and eliminate more effectively the access to the living God. Instead, the congregation is called upon to concur in the divine abolition of the religious methods of self-justification, and thus to participate in the continuous **reformation** of the age of grace.

9:11 **But Christ having appeared as high priest of the good things that are come, through the greater and more perfect tent not made with hands, that is, not of this creation, ¹²and not through blood of goats and calves, but through his own blood, he entered once for all into the sanctuary, securing an eternal redemption. ¹³For if the sprinkling of the defiled with the blood of goats and bulls and the ashes of a calf sanctifies for the purification of the flesh, ¹⁴how much more shall the blood of Christ, who through the eternal Spirit offered himself unblemished to God, purify your conscience from dead works for service to the living God?**

Having shown the powerlessness of the old cult, the author moves on in these four verses to depict the effective sacrifice that Jesus the high priest performed. The atonement day imagery is used to explain and interpret the death on the cross, whereby the Good Friday event and the ascension are drawn together, as Michel observes. Since the idea of salvation through the blood of Christ may strike the modern ear as meaningless jargon, it is important to penetrate through the imagery to the author's thought about the significance of this death. In particular, it is crucial to bear in mind the assumptions the author himself has laid down in the earlier chapters of Hebrews, particularly the idea of atonement through participation (2:14-18; 4:14—5:10). Hebrews sees the at-one-ment effected through Christ's sharing of human finitude, dispelling its threat and alienation, and reconciling persons to themselves and their creator. As 2:14 made plain, Christ's sharing of human death was an essential aspect of this reconciling activity, but its effectiveness was not in terms of assuaging divine wrath at human sin, but rather in terms of dispelling the alienation of finitude, thus opening up the way to relationship with God. On these premises the unique and nonmythological description of Christ's sacrifice may now be discussed in detail.

In the first long sentence comprising verses 11 and 12, the Christ event is viewed from the perspective of the death, as would be expected if sacrificial categories are to be utilized. Consequently, the very **appear**ance of **Christ . . . as high priest** is linked with his entrance **once for all into the sanctuary** at the moment of his death. The **tent** he entered, however, was viewed as the heavenly sanctuary, the **more perfect tent not made with hands.** In other words, at the very moment of his death, he entered into the presence of God—of which the heavenly sanctuary is the symbol. The **eternal redemption** he secured gains its definition in the earlier argument of Hebrews: as 2:13 made plain, he brought his "children" with him into the presence of God. Since it was the sharing of humanity that cost Jesus his life, his death can be viewed as the event which secures this dialogical **redemption.** The emphasis on the **eternal** character of this at-one-ment fits the requirements of the Lycus Valley yearning for secure access to God that is beyond the scope of the malevolent cosmic powers. The same term is used here as is elsewhere translated "for an aeon." A simple, dialogical reality, therefore, lies behind this atonement-day terminology. The **good things that are come,** with an explicit emphasis on the present tense, describe the new relationship between the pilgrim community and the word that addresses it on the path through the secular world along with the other related eschatological gifts depicted in 6:4-5.

The price paid for this **redemption** is fully honored by the atonement-day imagery. It was a price paid in **blood.** At this point Hebrews' interpretation correlates well with the historical event as reconstructed from the Gospel accounts. Christ voluntarily remained in Gethsemane, where he knew he would be captured by the temple police, led by Judas. By so doing he made himself a sacrificial victim. He died at the hands of those he came to redeem; he was despised and deserted by the people whom he loved. And he uttered the word of redemptive forgiveness, at the moment of the shedding of his own **blood,** to the very ones who executed him. Looking back on this cross event, the early church felt that Jesus had in some mysterious sense taken the place they should have occupied as sinners worthy of death. They felt they had been responsible for his death, and that their guilt was cleansed by his word of forgiveness. They recognized that their self-righteousness had led them into rejection and murder of God's envoy of grace, and they experienced his redemptive acceptance of even this enmity. In short, men and women felt that Christ's death on the cross was redemptive for them personally, and it is this that Hebrews attempts to express with the atonement-day imagery of **redemption . . . through his own blood.**

In the second long sentence in this section, the effect of the high priest's sacrificial death is described. The typical contrast between the old cult and the new is included in this important statement, along with the antithesis noted above, in verses 9 and 10, between the **flesh** and the **conscience.** Yet the formulation of this antithesis carries the interpretation of Christ's death farther, linking it explicitly with the "first principles" and with the inauguration of dialogue.

While the ancient cult had merely provided **purification of the flesh,** Christ's sacrifice served to **purify your conscience from dead works for service to the living God.** On the one side is the conformity of the **flesh** with the laws and regulations of the old cult, but as the argument in the preceding chapters has shown, this cannot serve to eliminate the alienation of self-righteousness and self-dependency that it established. On the other side is an act of worship performed by Christ that deals with the **conscience.** The curious thing is that our author does not focus on the overcoming of "bad conscience." Instead, the **conscience** is to be cleansed **from dead works.** Westcott and Käsemann see in this expression a reference to the efforts of natural human beings to reconcile themselves with God by doing **works,** and given the Lycus Valley context, one would have to say cultic **works.** This would correlate well with the significance of this expression in 6:1 and also with the perverse results of the ancient cult as described in 9:9. At every point in Hebrews' argument, the **works** of religiosity, whether they be moral or cultic, are pictured as misguided efforts to redeem oneself. They are an expression of pride and sinful self-reliance that deepen rather than overcome peoples' alienation from God. These **works** are called **dead** because they lack the power to lead people to the life-giving dialogue. They isolate individuals as self-righteous units, leading to a life that is hard and inflexible, self-enclosed and self-satisfied—the marks of spiritual and personal "deadness."

Yet the puzzling thing about the author's expression **purify your conscience from dead works** is that the works of the self-righteous do not prick their **consciences.** What religious person feels his or her **conscience** aroused in the performance of the works of cult and moral duty? One may feel guilty about one's evil deeds, or about the good deeds left undone, but it is highly unusual to feel guilty about the deeds performed in the very name of religious law. What, then, does the author have in mind with this idea of **dead works** making the **conscience** impure? My suggestion is that these words point to the propensity of religious **works** to corrupt and delude the conscience. They give people a false sense of security and make them comfortable in their alienation and rebellion. For who has a more rigid and yet more erroneous sense of eternal rectitude than the Pharisaic person? One thinks of the Pharisee in the temple in Jesus' parable as being absolutely certain of his righteousness in tithing and fasting twice a week; his conscience told him that he was infinitely superior to the publican who stood with his head bowed, uttering a prayer for mercy. But Jesus pronounced that the proud conscience of the Pharisee was in error: "I tell you, this [publican] went down to his house justified rather than the other [Luke 18:14]." This parable coincides with Hebrews 9:14 in lifting up the tendency of punctilious performance to encourage the kind of conscience that is unaware of its own prideful alienation from God. In this connection, it is a curious thing that modern church people, who are probably the most active, concerned, and busy Christians the world has seen, are accused by a whole generation of preachers and prophets of being complacent. Although in one sense it is a strange allegation to make against those who are busy seven nights a week with meetings and organizations to accomplish various good works, it may also coincide with Hebrews' perception that pious busyness can mislead the conscience. The sacrificial death of the great high priest purified your conscience from dead works in the sense that the self-righteous are enabled to perceive therein both judgment and forgiveness. Once the impact of that death becomes clear, the conscience is sensitized to its burden, freed from the deadening weight of self-satisfaction, and thus made healthy again.

The result of such transformation, or redemption, is a new motivation for good works. Such a person begins to serve the living God. Rather than being active in the Lycus Valley sense in order to guarantee access to heaven, or earning the esteem of superiors, she or he begins to respond to God's will. This corresponds to the alteration in the direction of the self in the "first principles" of 6:1—"repentance from dead works and faith in God." Rather than doing things because the cult requires them, such a person responds spontaneously to a divine desire to meet the needs of others, which is what it means to serve the **living God.**

9:15 Because of this he is mediator of a new covenant, in that a death having occurred for redemption from the transgressions under the first covenant, they that have been called may receive the promise of the inheritance for an aeon. [16]For where there is a covenant, the death of the one who made it must be established. [17]For a covenant takes effect at death, since it has no force as long as the one who made it lives. [18]Hence even the first covenant was not inaugurated without blood; [19]for after Moses had announced every command according to the law to all the people, he took the blood of calves and goats, with water and scarlet wool and hyssop, and sprinkled the book itself and all the people, [20]saying, "This is the blood of the covenant that God prescribed for you." [21]And in the same way he sprinkled blood on the tent and all the liturgical vessels. [22]And almost everything is purified with blood according to the law, and without the shedding of blood there is no remission of sins.

In this section the sacrificial death of the high priest is correlated with the **new covenant** idea developed in chapter 8, while explaining the necessity for **death** and **blood** to free humans from alienation. Verse 15 opens with the claim that Christ's **death** made him the **mediator of a new covenant.** Here the sacrificial concepts drawn from the atonement-day tradition are joined with the Jeremiah 31 tradition of a new, personal relationship between people and God. The reader is thereby led to recall that the **new covenant** concept was laid out as the presupposition of the sacrifice idea, with the consequence that certain, superstitious theories of the atonement would seem to be eliminated.

From legal and biblical tradition the author develops two arguments to explain the necessity of the **shedding of blood** in a system of salvation. The first is that a **covenant** in the sense of a will provides its benefits only when the testator has died. The second is that in the Old Testament tradition, the Mosaic covenant was sealed by the **sprinkling of blood** over the people and the cultic objects. This tradition is elaborated in verse 22a with the claim that **almost everything is purified with blood according to the law.** Then, in a sweeping statement that serves to summarize the argument of this entire section, the author draws it together this way: **without the shedding of blood there is no remission of sins.** Now this is not a hard and fast biblical rule, and the author himself probably knew there were exceptions in the old covenant. But it is a fundamental principle as far as he is concerned, and if one generalizes, as he does, from the Christ event to develop his entire system of thought, it is easy to see from whence it is derived. The question that has moved theologians concerning this statement is what doctrine of the atonement Hebrews is advocating. It is obvious that the theory of a victory over the devil, won by the death of Christ, is not in view here. And there is no hint of the more modern moral example theories in this section. The traditional theory frequently associated with this text is that God requires blood to satisfy a divine abstract demand for justice which had been offended by human sin. But even this has no decisive support here, because the wrath of God is not mentioned, and Hebrews seems to be against the sort of legalism presupposed by such a theory. In place of these traditional theories of the atonement, the argument of Hebrews thus far points in the direction of atonement by participation. To relate this passage to the earlier sections of Hebrews, including the chapter on the **new covenant,** it is Christ's participation in human life that dispels its alienation and opens the possibility for renewing relationships with God. But if one operates on this theory of the atonement, what is the sense of emphasizing the necessity of **blood?**

The suggestion that rises out of this study is that the author uses this symbol to express the high cost of human redemption, a cost that was required not because of divine reluctance, but because of human intransigence. The author had to confront the same fact as modern theology and social theory does, namely, that the price of **purification** was paid in **blood.** It took the shedding of Jesus' **blood** to reveal the final enmity and depravity of religious self-righteousness. And if the Lycus Valley cult is any indication, this price was necessitated not to appease God, but rather because of the perennial perversity of humans. The author has in view what Robert Penn Warren calls "the ancient cost of our redemption." The price is paid both on the religious and the social levels, as the tragedy of the Civil War was interpreted by Warren and others, and as anyone can read from the assassinations of noble leaders like Lincoln, King, the Kennedys, and others. The author of Hebrews states the principle in very general terms, that **without the shedding of blood there is no remission of sins,** because alienation and hatred cannot be overcome by anything short of sacrificial love. Love that is willing to shed its own **blood** to achieve reconciliation is required to heal the grievous wounds inflicted upon one another in this or any other society, which is what 13:13 has in mind with the reference to "bearing abuse" for Christ.

In summary, it is human pride and self-righteousness that necessitated **blood** as the means of redemption, and those who comprehend this will be realistic about the price of overcoming sin in a broken world. They will know that **without the shedding of blood there is no remission of sins.**

9:23 Now while it was necessary for the copies of the heavenly things to be purified by these (sacrifices), the heavenly things themselves required better sacrifices. ²⁴For Christ entered, not into a sanctuary made with hands, an antitype of the true one, but into heaven itself, to appear now in the presence of God for our sakes. ²⁵Nor was it to offer himself repeatedly, as the high priest enters the sanctuary every year with blood not his own; ²⁶for in that case he would have suffered repeatedly since the foundation of the world. But now, once, at the close of the aeons, he has appeared to abolish sin through his sacrifice. ²⁷And just as it is appointed for humans

to die once, and after that (comes) judgment, [28]so also the Christ, having been sacrificed once to bear the sins of many, shall appear a second time, apart from sin, to them that eagerly are awaiting him for salvation.

In this climactic section, the antithesis between the repetitive rite of the old covenant and the single sacrifice of the Melchizedekian priest, producing restoration for humans, is set forth. Two aspects of this argument are particularly noteworthy: the references to the complete **abolition** of **sin** and to the **purification** of the **heavenly things** in 23b. The latter point is particularly puzzling to exegetes, for although it is clear why the **copies of the heavenly things** would need to be **purified** according to the Old Testament law, as alluded to in 9:15-22, it is very odd that the **heavenly things** themselves would require such redemptive activity. The effort to explain this problem away by suggesting, as F.F. Bruce does, that the cleansing of the human conscience would have the effect of eliminating the defilement of the heavenly sphere avoids the clear implication of this verse, for the author does not consider the conscience to be one of the **heavenly things.** Michel has pointed in the right direction by mentioning the references in the apocalyptic tradition to the purification of heaven by casting out Satan, but notes that this passage appears to presuppose a great deal about the **heavenly things** that has been left unsaid. It would seem, however, in light of the previous argument in Hebrews against the adoration of heavenly forces, that the author has provided sufficient background for the understanding of this remarkable assertion. One must keep in mind the apocalyptic and Hellenistic traditions concerning the disobedient angels cast from heaven because of pride and hardness of heart, leading humans astray, and seeking self-adoration. As James A. Sanders has shown, the early Christian hymns such as Philippians 2:1-11 celebrated the triumph of Christ over these "dissenting deities," just as the Melchizedek fragment found in Qumran looks forward to triumph over such evil "angels." There are definite parallels to terming such a triumph over the malevolent angels a "cleansing from defilement" (cf. Ethiopian Enoch 10:20-22); Hans Dieter Betz has traced the tradition—in closely related Hellenistic, gnostic, and apocalyptic materials—of salvation in terms of "purifying" the cosmic elements from defilement which marks at the same time the inauguration of the age of righteousness. Taking this broad tradition into account, it is clear that Hebrews does indeed feel that the **better sacrifice** of Christ the Melchizedekian high priest served to cleanse not only earth, but also the cosmic spheres of sinful disobedience. His entrance into **heaven itself** before **the presence of God** at the moment of his sacrificial death was at once a purification of, and a triumph over, these cosmic forces. The union of these priestly and kingly motifs will be elaborated in more detail in the next chapter, and is so central a concern for the author of Hebrews that it was stated in the opening lines of his "word of exhortation": "Having made purification for sins, he took his ruling seat at the right hand of the majesty in the heights, having become as much superior to angels as the name he has inherited is more excellent than theirs [1:3-4]."

It must be noted, however, that this affirmation of Christ's sacrificial cleansing of the **heavenly things** is developed in antithesis to a form of cultic cleansing along the lines of the old covenant. In verse 23 the cleansing of the cosmic forces required a ritual that was **better** than the one described in the Old Testament. In verse 24 the location of Christ's cult is not **a sanctuary made with hands, an antitype of the true one,** an extremely polemic formulation, as Sidney Sowers observed. And in verses 25ff. The **once** for all character of Christ's sacrifice is contrasted polemically with that of a **high priest,** who **enters the sanctuary every year.** Given the Lycus Valley context, this polemic strikes very hard against the cult being practiced there. The implication is that the cosmic forces cannot be touched by such an **antitype,** and that all the earthly **sanctuary** seeks to accomplish has already been done by the sacrifice of Christ. This polemic focus explains why the discussion in verses 23 to 28—which has seemed to many exegetes as cosmological nonsense—was left until the climactic end of this argument. For the effectiveness of cult upon the cosmic forces was the central issue for the Lycus Valley. In light of this situation, the sweeping claim that Christ's sacrifice served to **abolish sin** makes sense. By triumphing over the demonic forces and at the same time leading believers into the **presence of God,** Christ overcame the alienation that had afflicted humankind. This overcoming of **sin,** however, has nothing to do with the cultic obligations performed to gain sanctification. The initial abolition of alienation is not the work of humankind, repeated day after day by cultic and ethical activities, but Christ's work **for our sakes,** done once for all.

Consistent with this radical doctrine of sanctification is an eschatological perspective that comes clearly to the fore in the closing lines of this section. The Christ event is defined as having taken place **at the close of the aeons,** and it establishes a form of existence that stands **eagerly . . . awaiting him for salvation.** The coming of Christ **a second time** is clearly in view here, modifying the doctrine of sanctification in a decisive fashion. Although it is a gift rather than an achievement, it cannot be received or possessed in a static manner, and it does not eliminate the conditions of finitude. To enter freely into the presence of God in dialogue with God's word is to remain in subjugation to time, to waiting, and even to the **judgment** referred to in verse 27. Sanctification for Hebrews is to take part in an eschatological form of pilgrimage, enjoying the reconciliation that has already taken place, but **eagerly . . . awaiting** the final **salvation** at the end of time.

Chapter Nine

Christ's Ministry Produces Sanctification: Piety Versus Perfection (10:1–18)

10:1 **F**OR since the law has a shadow of the good things to come and not the very image of the things, it can never, by the same sacrifices continually offered year after year, perfect those who draw near. ²Otherwise, would they not have ceased to be offered, as the worshipers, having once been cleansed, would have no more consciousness of sin? ³But in these (sacrifices) there is a reminder of sin year after year. ⁴For it is impossible for the blood of bulls and goats to take away sins. ⁵Consequently, when he comes into the world, he says,

"Sacrifices and offerings you did not desire, but a body you prepared for me. ⁶In burnt offerings and sin offerings you took no pleasure. ⁷Then I said, 'Behold I have come,' as is written in a volume of a book about me, 'to do your will, O God.' "

⁸When he said above, "sacrifices and offerings" and "burnt offerings and sin offerings you did not desire, neither had pleasure," which are offered according to the law, ⁹then he said, "Behold I have come to do your will." He eliminates the first in order to establish the second. ¹⁰And by this "will" we are the sanctified through the "offering" of the "body" of Jesus Christ once for all.

In this chapter the polemic contrast between Christ's ministry and that of the law is brought to conclusion. Although the argument parallels the preceding chapter to a large extent, several fresh points are scored, principally revolving around the combination of Psalm 40:7-9 in this section and the reiterated citation from Jeremiah 31 in the next section. The entire pericope 10:1-18 seems to contrast the useless piety of the old cult with the obedience and sanctification of the new.

With the pejorative use of **shadow** as descriptive of the Old Testament **law**, verse 1 argues that the old cult with its **sacrifices . . . offered year after year** is unable to **perfect those who draw near.** The expression **those who draw near,** of course, depicts the devotees of a cult who seek to approach the divine presence. For such devotees to gain **perfection** would imply, in the definitions provided by the previous argument in Hebrews, that they gained the desired access to the heavenly throne. But the exact opposite is affirmed by the author, implying that the devotees of the Lycus Valley cult or any other such cult cannot achieve such a goal by depending upon corrupt **shadows of the good things to come.**

This assertion is substantiated in verses 2 and 3 with a penetrating exposé of the impact of repetitive sacrifices. The argument in short is that if the old cult had provided **perfection,** the devotees would have had no further need for practicing the cult. The assumption of this argument is provided in verse 2, that the attainment of perfect access to God eliminates the **consciousness of sin.** To be **cleansed** is to be restored to proper relationship so that the feeling of alienation disappears. As a result, the continuation of sacrifices in a cultic system proves that such relationship has never really been restored, for **in these (sacrifices) there is a reminder of sin year after year.**

This argument not only uncovers the illusion of the Lycus Valley cult, but also strikes to the heart of a modern religious issue. The typical premise of modern preaching is that one must first arouse a **consciousness of sin** before the good news can be effectively proclaimed. The Protestant sermon ever since the time of the Great Awakening begins with damnation in order to end with grace. More recent practitioners begin with the "problem" described in terms of the guilt and sloth of the congregation or society; only then do they move to the "solution," which usually amounts to the urge that they try harder. Hearers are thereby robbed of any residual sense of wholeness in grace, and are placed back in the position of the Lycus Valley cult in which the ever-renewed **sacrifices** for religion simply **remind** them **of sin year after year.** To be sure, temporary successes are achieved with this technique. Just make people feel guilty for having eaten a substantial breakfast, or having comfortable homes, or being absorbed in their work or their families, and they will make certain sacrifices to rid themselves temporarily of their uncomfortable feelings. But one thing is clear, in light of this passage: such **sacrifices continually offered year after year** cannot **perfect those who draw near.** These techniques may succeed in keeping charitable institutions going for a while, though on a grudging and penurious level, but they cannot produce life-giving dialogue with God. They leave the worshipers empty and isolated, feeling that something crucial is somehow missing in their experience of religion.

Verse 4 is a general summary of the point made in the previous verses, but it serves at the same time as a transition to the following citation from Psalm 40. When one takes the flow of the argument from verses 5 to 10 into account, the reason why the **blood of bulls and goats** cannot **take away sins** is that God does not desire it. This point is derived from the Septuagint translation of the psalm, which at several points is somewhat distant from the Hebrew original. In particular, the rendering of "ears you have dug out for me," with **a body you prepared for me** offers the author a point of contact with the high priestly ministry he is attempting to describe. The contrast he derives from the citation, however, is clear and fits his purpose very well. What Christ the high priest says **when he comes into the world** is that **"Sacrifices and offerings you did not desire. . . . In burnt offerings and sin offerings you took no pleasure."** Instead, he affirms of God that **"a body you prepared for me. . . . 'Behold I have come . . . to do your will.' "** It is cultic rite versus obedience, the useless sacrifices that God hates contrasted with the bodily service and self-sacrifice that God desires. And as verse 9 puts it, **he eliminates the first in order to establish the second.** This **eliminates** the Lycus Valley cult and any other cult based on the same principles. It strikes out every form of religious manipulation and self-saving. It shatters the human effort to earn atonement and make the self more acceptable to God. As Martin Dibelius puts it, it implies the abolition of every cult, either religious or secular.

The use of **body** in verses 5 and 10 has occasioned considerable debate, with Ernst Käsemann suggesting that the author utilizes at this point the gnostic conception of the "body of Adam," which Christ put on in order that the curse of its inevitable death might be overcome. The usage appears to stand closer, however, to that in Romans 12:1, where "body" is the locus of obedience in the new aeon inaugurated by the death and resurrection of the "body of Christ" (Romans 7:4). This positive use of **body** in Hebrews seems atypical for gnosticism, which viewed the "body of Adam" as the source of human corruption. It seems to be a point where the Pauline tradition of the author shines through rather clearly. On this basis the concept of obedient self-sacrifice fits in very closely with the idea of atonement that was developed in chapters 2, 4, and 5. The redemptive activity was a matter of faithful participation in the human plight, a sharing of the weakness and anxiety of the **body** in the fullest sense. This dispelled the alienation that kept humans from God and opened the possibility for the enlivening dialogue before the throne of grace.

The result of this high priestly performance of God's **will** is described in this section in terms of **sanctification.** In fact, the author goes so far as to call the Christians **the sanctified** ones. **And by this will we are the sanctified through the offering of the body of Jesus Christ once for all.** To be **sanctified,** of course, means to be made able to stand before the holy God in dialogue. It implies a complete transformation of the person, and the argument in this chapter, as well as the foil of the Lycus

Valley piety, provides some basis for describing the shape of this. It is a matter of being freed from the self-involution of the old cult, with its encouragement of self-righteousness and its constant consciousness of guilt and alienation. And it is at the same time a restoration, through grace alone, of open relationship with God. This implies an elimination of further **consciousness of sin.** This is precisely the shape, by the way, of Wesley's remarkable Aldersgate experience. It was a giving up of the futile effort toward self-justification through pious works and a sudden realization of the boundless love of God, which accepted Wesley exactly as he was and made him new. A short citation from Wesley's journal may help to illustrate the shape of Hebrews' conception of the **sanctified** ones:

> In the evening, I went very unwillingly to a society in Aldersgate Street, where one was reading Luther's Preface to the Epistle to the Romans. About a quarter before nine, while he was describing the change which God works in the heart through faith in Christ, I felt my heart strangely warmed. I felt I did trust in Christ, Christ alone for salvation; and an assurance was given me that he had taken away my sins, even mine, and saved me from the law of sin and death.

It was from this experience that Wesley's doctrine of "scriptural holiness" developed, and given the argument of Hebrews, there was considerable justification in calling it "scriptural." At its inception, this doctrine was based strictly on grace. Holiness was viewed as an aspect of justification and therefore as a gift rather than a human achievement. Wesley's residual moralism and a lack of conceptual clarity in his day, particularly in understanding either biblical relationalism or early Christian eschatology, led to the corruption of this doctrine. The effort to provide ethical guidelines for holiness, or to measure its presence, tended to drive it back into the arena of the old cult. And the attempt to give expression to the ongoing character of Christian existence by the phrase "going on to perfection," tended to be understood in a moral progressivist fashion and ultimately to undermine the gift quality of **sanctification**. Perhaps the elaboration of this doctrine in the following section of Hebrews may provide some basis for stating Wesley's insight in a more adequate fashion.

10:11 **And while every priest stands daily at his service, offering repeatedly the same sacrifices which can never take away sins,** [12]**he, having offered a single sacrifice for sins, took his ruling seat for all time at the right hand of God,** [13]**then to wait until his enemies were made a stool for his feet.** [14]**For by one offering he perfected for all time the sanctified.** [15]**And the Holy Spirit also bears witness for us; for after saying,**
[16]**"This is the covenant that I will make with them**
   after those days, says the Lord, giving my laws on their
   hearts, I shall inscribe them upon their minds."
[17]**(then he adds,)**
   "And their sins and their misdeeds I shall remember no
   more."
[18]**Now where these are remitted, there is no more offering for sin.**

This section draws to a conclusion the argument concerning the ministry of Christ the high priest that began in 8:1. It substantiates the sanctification and purification that this ministry provided by joining the sacrificial motifs with those of kingly rule over **his enemies**. Beginning with the now familiar references to the **daily . . . repeated sacrifices** of the old cult that were unable to **take away sins,** verses 12 and 13 link the themes of priest and king in a striking fashion. Christ, **having offered a single sacrifice for sins, took his ruling seat for all time at the right hand of God, then to wait until his enemies were made a stool for his feet.** This use of the triumph motif from Psalm 110 relates very closely to the reference in 9:23 to cleansing the angelic forces and subjecting them to the control of the Melchizedekian priest. On the basis of the Jewish and Hellenistic parallels, as well as the Lycus Valley context, there is little doubt that the **enemies** would be the disobedient cosmic forces that were thought to cause the bloodshed and depravity of earthly life and were expected to hinder the passage of the elect to the heavenly presence. Thus to **offer** the **single sacrifice** that dispels human alienation and leads men and women to God is at the same time to triumph over these **enemies**. The significance of this assertion in the Lycus Valley would be to make the salvation offered by Christ dependable in the sense of ensuring access to God despite any hindrances from malevolent cosmic forces. The phrase **for all time**, used earlier (7:25) as an assurance that Christ would not cease his intercessory work and allow the faithful to slip back into the power of evil, fits well into this framework. As is characteristic for Hebrews, the assurance lies entirely in the Christ event itself as proclaimed by the word; no objective evidence is offered that the cosmic forces have been defeated, and no subjective points are made about the confirmation of this triumph in their Christian experience.

At this point the argument of Hebrews throws some light on the problem of holiness theology since Wesley's day. The concern about the "second blessing" of the spirit and about being "under conviction" by the spirit relates to this matter of assurance that one is really **perfected** and **sanctified,** using the terms of verse 14. But intensive reflection on such experiential aspects of the faith can easily lead to a new form of legalism, to pride and self-concern, and it can scarcely do justice to the wide diversity of human personality and experience. Hebrews avoids such problems by concentrating the source of assurance strictly on Christ, insisting that the work of **perfecting** is not for humans, but for the great high priest. Since the great high priest guarantees our access by the sacrifice of himself, there is no further need for introspective proof, which is so distractive for the life of faithful dialogue.

An important consequence of Hebrews' approach to **sanctification** and theodicy is that it allows for a realistic acceptance of adversity. The experience of a pilgrim community in the hostile, secular world is necessarily one of anxiety and tribulation, with tragic events and the uncertainties of the human consciousness conspiring against any sort of euphoria. The time after the Christ event is, after all, a period when even Christ must **wait until his enemies were made a stool for his feet.** The implications of this for Christian ethics are set forth in the great final section of Hebrews, which begins with 10:19. But the premise of that section is clarified here, namely, that the ground of Christian confidence is solely in Christ's high priestly work.

A compressed but fertile summary of the result of Christ's ministry is offered in verse 14: **For by one offering he perfected for all time the sanctified.** The emphasis on the single act of self-sacrifice, along with the permanent quality of its achievement, fits into the polemic against the repetitive cult in the Lycus Valley, insisting that since access has been ensured **for all time,** further cultic activity is irrelevant. But in a sweeping fashion, this summary claims that the goal of the religious quest has been achieved not by human striving, but by the self-sacrifice of Christ. The past tense **perfected** implies a completion performed entirely by Christ himself, and this stands in striking tension with the present participle with a progressive implication—**the sanctified.** The two terms have virtually identical definitions in the usage of Hebrews, but in this sentence they are used to express the dynamic tension between the absolute givenness of renewed relationship and the requirement to hold fast to that relationship through the vicissitudes of existence in a world where one must **wait** for the final triumph of righteousness. In this context, therefore, **perfection** is the act of restoring open dialogue between people and God, done once for all by the great high priest. The ones being **sanctified** are those who, having been given the enlivening dialogue by God's word, hold fast to the relationship they have been given. With either term, however, the activity remains with Christ so that Hebrews stands as a bulwark against the moralizing and quantifying of holiness that has so debilitated the pietistic tradition. When either perfection or sanctification are made into a human achievement and abstracted from their relational context, the result is a reversion back into the legalism of the old cult that Christ replaced.

The question raised by this great affirmation in verse 14 is how the **perfection** and **sanctification** are communicated. If the method of Hebrews is any indication, it is by the hearing of the "word of exhortation." By proclaiming the glorious worship of Christ the high priest, the author evokes the congregation's response of worship—a matter that comes to the fore in the very next section of Hebrews. But given the assumptions about the spirit's activity within the word as set forth in chapters 1 and 2, it is clear that the author does not feel that the exhorter elicits this response. It is the spirit of the living God that encounters the congregation as it hears the marvelous proclamation. Thus the next verse in chapter 10 insists that **the Holy Spirit also bears witness for us** in the promise of the new covenant cited once again from Jeremiah. Through the word of the scripture, the congregation is to hear the **Spirit's witness** within their **hearts** and **minds.**

This corresponds to a typical Protestant concern for the internal witness of the Spirit which "convicts" one that one is accepted by God. But it is word-oriented rather than experience-oriented; it directs the pilgrims toward the word that encounters them along the way rather than inward, toward the elusive voice of their own consciousness. **Perfection** and **sanctification** are therefore not states of mind or human achievements; they are not peculiar to the spiritual athlete or the genius. They are interpreted here in terms of new **covenant,** or relationship. This involves both a vivid sense of God's will that God **inscribes** on the innermost self and an assurance that even the **remembrance** of **sins** and **misdeeds** has been wiped away. Nothing whatsoever stands in the way of open relationship, and the people entering into it do so as restored creatures, with healthy senses of values and clear consciences. There is nothing subservient about creatures thus **perfected** and **sanctified.** They enter with dignity into a status of "participation" or "partnership" (3:1, 6, 14), with an autonomy that is absolutely essential for life in the secular world. Having the law within them, they have no need to stop to ask for instructions at every turn of the path; their **minds** are freed to wrestle effectively with the issues at hand. And they are neither imprisoned by nor worried about the past **sins** and **misdeeds** that they have done. They are set free for effective service along the pilgrim path that lies before them.

This section of chapter 10 concludes—and with it the entire middle section of Hebrews, which starts with 4:14—with a final jab against superfluous cultic activity. It is a summary that is consistent with the secular autonomy suggested in the preceding verses and the pilgrim ethic that follows. **Now where these are remitted, there is no more offering for sin.** If the sins of the past have been overcome and forgotten, replaced by a new relationship inaugurated by the great high priest, then the human effort to secure human happiness by certain **offerings** is simply eliminated. The grandiose effort of the Lycus Valley religion, with its mysterious laws and ceremonies, and its promise of manipulating the cosmic forces for the sake of human achievement, is exposed and dropped. And each modern equivalent of the Lycus Valley cult is similarly thrust into nothingness. The cult of "happiness," secured by following the promises of Madison Avenue to purchase a promising new product in the drugstore; the cult of "progress," secured by voting for the right party or buying the right new refrigerator; the magazines' dream of a "perfect marriage," securable by adhering to the cult of glamour; the cult of the "number one nation," secured by higher military spending and unanimity of opinion; the cult of paradise, with the lures of a perfect climate, an ideal home, and no troublesome neighbors—all these and their countless private equivalents are set aside. Those who are freed for secular pilgrimage by the Christ event have no further need of such silly and deadening rituals. They learn to live without "lasting cities" and to accept the conditions of life in a hostile and deteriorating world. They are freed from the delusions of their culture and from the dead weight of accumulated obligations its cults placed on their consciences. They can travel light, like the protagonist in *Pilgrim's Progress* after burying his "burden" at the foot of the cross. So they are ready now to hear the magnificent exhortation to take up the pilgrim existence of daily worship in the secular world.

Chapter Ten

The Positive (10:19-25) and Negative (10:26-31) Exhortation to Take Up Worshipful Pilgrimage

10:19 **H**AVING therefore, brethren, the boldness (to take) the way into the sanctuary by the blood of Jesus, [20]by the fresh and living way which he inaugurated for us through the curtain, that is, his flesh; [21]and (having) a great priest over the house of God, [22]let us approach with a true heart, in full assurance of faith, with hearts sprinkled clean from bad conscience and bodies washed by pure water. [23]Let us hold fast the confession of our hope without wavering, for he who promised is faithful; [24]and let us notice each other, to stimulate love and good works, [25]not deserting our assembling together, as is the habit of some, but exhorting (one another), and all the more so as you see the Day drawing near.

With the positive and negative exhortation in this section, the author brings his great central argument of Hebrews, which began with 4:14, to a conclusion. It provides the closing bracket to the doctrinal exposition about the great high priest, showing its practical significance for the Christian community. The exhortation opens with a call to participate in the high priestly ministry of entering and **approaching** the living God. The **boldness** to enter the **sanctuary** has been given by the preceding proclamation, showing that the cosmic forces no longer bar access, and that the alienation caused by sin has been overcome. The cowering spirit of the Lycus Valley cult has been eliminated by Christ's work, symbolized here with the expression **by the blood of Jesus,** thus providing a rightful courage to approach the formerly forbidden sanctuary. It is a **boldness** given in the throes of the adversity and insecurity that mark pilgrimage in the flesh. So it is within this context that the much debated identification of **his flesh** with the dividing **curtain** should be understood. Eduard Schweizer provides a succinct summary of the alternative explanations of this passage, agreeing with Ernst Käsemann that the **curtain** is the barrier of materiality which Christ took upon himself in the incarnation, freeing humans from its alienation by escaping from it in the ascension. This approach accounts more adequately than any other yet suggested for the gnostic background of identifying the **curtain** with the **flesh,** but it shifts the locus of Christ's high priestly ministry from its vital and redemptive sharing of human life in the **flesh** to its resultant exaltation to the seat above the principalities and powers. Hebrews has argued, and reiterates by reference to the **blood of Jesus** in verse 19, that what really redeemed humankind was Jesus' sharing of its plight, not his escaping from it. When this argument is properly understood on the basis of 2:14-18 and 4:14—5:10, the antignostic thrust of the passage under discussion can be seen. The Gnostics felt, as Käsemann has shown, that the only way to overcome the barrier of the **flesh** was to transcend it, allowing the spirit to return to its homeland. Hebrews has argued in contrast that Christ overcame the barrier of the **curtain** by accepting the **flesh,** even dying in the flesh as high priest, thus reconciling humankind to its life in the flesh and **inaugurating . . . the fresh and living way** in the midst of secular existence to encounter with God. Although the use of **flesh** in this context is incomprehensible outside of the context of a gnostic discussion, it contains an antignostic polemic that would have been sharply felt in the Lycus Valley.

There is a fine wordplay in this passage, with the **way into** (=*eisodos*) in verse 19 being qualified as a **fresh and living way** (=*odos*), in verse 20. Here the **way**faring character of Christian existence is qualified with cultic imagery: the pilgrim

way is a **way into** the Holy of Holies moment for moment. The life that the pilgrim community leads "outside the camp" is therefore a constantly repeated act of worship in which the daily path is thought to be the **way into** the heavenly sanctuary that one enters over and over again. Pilgrimage is worship, and the encounter is not postponed until the entering into the "heavenly city" at death. It takes place whenever the pilgrim community hears the word and responds. Thus the **way** is always **fresh.** The encounter of yesterday can never suffice: "Today . . . today . . . today, when you hear his voice" (3:7—4:7). The path is never really the same and the encounter can never be taken for granted. It partakes of that **fresh**ness of all vital relationship. Thus it can also be called the **living way.** It is radically different from the life of "dead works," which for the author of Hebrews characterizes the life under the old covenant. For the obligation to the covenant partner can never be encapsulated by laws or dogmatic formulations, and one is never encouraged to lapse back into that deadening self-enclosure of works righteousness. The path partakes of that magnificent openness to both the present and the future which has always marked the true pilgrim, celebrating a **fresh and living** relationship along the **way,** yet being constantly open to the restoration of that relationship in a different form in the next "today." This is why **having . . . the boldness (to take) the way** can be placed in such parallelism with **(having) a great priest over the house of God,** the two accusative expressions being controlled by the same verb, **having,** as James Moffatt shows, in verse 19. For to take this pilgrim **way** is to stand in relationship with Christ the **priest.**

In line with this vision of dialogical worship, both the work of Christ and the transformation of the believer are described with cultic categories. The term translated with **he inaugurated** in verse 20 is drawn from Old Testament cultic language meaning "to consecrate and inaugurate and thus render valid and ratify," using Nils Dahl's definition. To thus consecrate a **way . . . through the curtain** is to lead people directly to the presence of God, which is the same as confirming the new covenant—mentioned in the preceding verses. To **approach with a true heart** is to take part in the new cultic activity of relationship with God, but to do so with the inner self made new by the Christ event. The gift of the new covenant that transforms the **heart** (8:10, 10:16) is here united with the technical terminology of **approach** to the sanctuary. Similarly, the expression **in full assurance of faith,** associated elsewhere in Hebrews with the experiential confirmation that comes after one responds to God's word (4:2; 6:11-12; 11:1-39), is integrated into the cultic context of **approach** to the sanctuary. These two expressions, which are ordinarily noncultic in their connotations, are placed in parallelism with two additional expressions drawn from the previous discussion of the old and the new priestly ministries. The **hearts sprinkled clean from bad conscience** are those cleansed by the priestly activity of Christ from their previous corruption through reliance on "dead works" (cf. 9:14). The expression **bodies washed by pure water** is also cultic in background, referring, as Dahl suggests, to Christian baptism. Such a positive reference to cultic activity, even in connection with the new Christian era, is quite unusual for Hebrews. One thinks not only of the categorical rejection of cultic activity implied by the argument of chapters 7 to 10, but also of the seeming rejection of sacramental practices in 13:9ff. One is inclined to suggest that this positive expression is inserted mainly for the purpose of carrying out the antignostic polemic of 10:5, 10, and 20, implying that the material **body** is not a barrier to **approach**ing God, and that the simple act of Christian baptism is sufficient to **wash** it clean enough for participation in the new secular liturgy of dialogue. At any event the author pictures the whole person, not only the inner portion highly valued by the Gnostics, but also the **heart** as the center of intentionality and the **body** as the agent of activity and relationship, as entering into the worship along the pilgrim **way.**

In the second long sentence comprising this exhortation, a call to disciplined participation in Christ's ministry is made. It is a discipline with explicitly communal aspects. The **holding**

fast the confession of our hope probably refers to the public baptismal affirmation to the faith, but the implication is that the entire community is consciously to commit and re-commit itself. In light of the relational character of this particular cult, there is necessarily a future dimension depicted here with the word **hope,** resulting in an intrinsic requirement to enter and re-enter the relationship. This may be done with confidence, **for he who promised is faithful.** Consequently, this dialogical discipline is quite different from usual concepts of self-discipline. Dialogical discipline is turned outward without anxiety toward the partner, and it implies communal responsibility, for as 3:13 suggested, its vitality depends on each one uttering the word of exhortation to the other every day along the pilgrim path.

The communal aspects of this dialogical discipline come particularly to the fore in verses 24 and 25. Unlike the Gnostic who is isolated from the unenlightened by her or his heightened self-consciousness, the members of Hebrews' congregation are to **notice each other, to stimulate love and good works.** This wording seems to imply not only the mutual exhortation to do such charitable **works,** but also to take note of one another's needs and moods so that in **love** one might weep with those who weep and laugh with those who laugh. This fits rather closely with the next expression, **not deserting our assembling together, as is the habit of some.** As Martin Dibelius has noted, this expression for the early Christian worship service is strikingly noncultic—even secular in its connotation. Since its sole purpose seems to be to exhort one another to hold fast to the faith, Dibelius seems quite justified in issuing the judgment that "the author speaks of Christian worship like an old Calvinist or Methodist."

A vital question is what led **some** to take up the **habit** of **deserting** the congregational meetings in the Lycus Valley. It was probably a matter of preferring another kind of meeting that was organized to perform the elaborate cult aimed at manipulating the hostile cosmic powers. It was surely more than a simple preference for a more liturgical style of worship than that of early Pauline churches. The issue was not whether "low church" or "high church" forms should be followed, but whether the worship celebrated the **fresh and living way** that Christ had already **inaugurated for us through the curtain.** The alternative was a meeting designed to release its participants from the burden of history as contrasted with one that sustained a daily pilgrimage through adversity. The author was convinced that the latter was more necessary than ever, because the entire cosmos was moving toward a historical climax that no one would be able to escape: **exhorting (one another)** . . . **all the more so as you see the Day drawing near.** The shaking of every foundation was imminent, and even the most sophisticated cult would not be able to withstand its tremors. The better alternative was to continue that worshipful **approach** to the divine covenant partner, responding to the **blood of Jesus** that was shed to bring genuine reconciliation and to make possible the creative pilgrimage of worship in the secular world.

10:26 **For if we sin deliberately after receiving the knowledge of the truth, there no longer remains a sacrifice for sins, ²⁷but a fearful prospect of judgment and a zealous fire about to consume the adversaries. ²⁸Someone violating the law of Moses dies without mercy at the testimony of two or three witnesses. ²⁹How much greater punishment, so you think, will he deserve who tramples underfoot the Son of God and considers profane the blood of the covenant, by which he was sanctified, and outrageously treats the Spirit of grace? ³⁰For we know him who said, "Vengeance is mine, I will repay." And again, "The Lord will judge his people." ³¹It is fearful to fall into the hands of the living God.**

The negative exhortation that begins with these verses is the perfect counterpart to the more positive preceding section. With relentless logic, the author pictures what it means to refuse the exhortation to take up worshipful pilgrimage. To **sin deliberately** is to say "no" to the dialogue that has been offered.

This concept of deliberate sin was derived from the Old Testament, according to Otto Michel, and was current in Hellenistic Judaism, where it implied not only the willing, but also the permanent rejection of the message of salvation. This message, set forth in the first ten chapters of Hebrews, offers the knowledge of the truth, a formulation that the Lycus Valley Gnostics would have appreciated, although it later became the typical expression for the orthodox Christian message (1 Timothy 2:4; Titus 1:1). But this **knowledge** about the ministry of the great high priest inaugurates a form of existence that is different from that envisioned by the Gnostics in the Lycus Valley. Its inexorable alternatives derive from the nature of dialogue itself.

The alternatives, as described in this section, are either to accept the life of dialogue or to become one of **the adversaries.** There seems to be no neutral ground. As the wording implies, the one who turns away becomes an enemy. This motif is elaborately developed in verse 29 with a threefold description of the action of the **adversaries.** First, such a person **tramples underfoot the Son of God.** The verb connotes the highest degree of personal disdain, a "contempt of the most flagrant kind," in James Moffatt's words. To do this to the exalted **Son of God,** named to this position by the divine word of acclamation (cf. 1:5; 5:5), under whose feet even the principalities and powers have been placed (cf. 1:13; 10:13), would be utterly reprehensible.

Similarly, to **consider profane the blood of the covenant, by which he was sanctified** is to turn against the atoning sacrifice that has made one new, thus confirming its sacred power. It is to deny, contrary to one's own personal experience of transformation, that the life and death of Jesus, symbolized here by the **blood,** inaugurated the new **covenant.** It is to say that his death had no more significance than that of any other person, for to **consider profane** is to view as common.

The third expression of contempt is drawn from the classical Greek tradition, with its concern about *hubris,* "pride." To **outrageously treat** *(en-hubrizō)* **the Spirit of grace**

179

is to act with the "insolent self-assertion" that marks the tragic Greek hero. As Brooke Foss Westcott puts it, this expression "combines arrogance with wanton injury." But again, the incongruous quality of the action is depicted by combining this self-assertive action with its virtual opposite, the **Spirit of grace,** which imparts itself selflessly and without qualification. In all three expressions, the opposition is pictured as a highly personal, though utterly incongruous, state of enmity. Clearly, there is no friendly parting when it comes to dialogue; to turn away is to affront the partner, **deliberately** and **outrageously.**

If one undertakes to become an **adversary** such as this, the consequences are inexorable, as far as the author of Hebrews is concerned. First, he asserts, **there no longer remains a sacrifice for sins.** In other words, there is nothing the grace of God can do for someone who remains in this state of active enmity to grace. It belongs to the very nature of dialogical salvation that it is impossible to restore one to dialogue if one refuses it. The **sacrifice for sins** that Christ the high priest made to reconcile persons in their finitude to the living God can have no effect when they refuse to acknowledge their finitude and set off on a path of prideful enmity that presumes to be more than human. Instead, the path ends where the great Greek tragedies as well as the profound insights of secular and biblical literature envision it: in **a fearful prospect of judgment and a zealous fire about to consume the adversaries.** The author substantiates this point in verse 30 with the citations from the Old Testament, emphasizing that God is involved in such retribution, even though it may on the surface appear to be simply the tragic nexus of cause and effect. In the Lycus Valley situation this repeated emphasis was vitally necessary. For in that gnostic milieu the eschatological dimension of judgment, both within history and at its end would have been absent. The Gnostics considered that they had already passed through the judgment of bondage to materiality at the moment of enlightenment, and since they thereby recovered their divine inner nature, any further judgment was eliminated. Time itself was annulled in the ecstatic discovery of the divine spark, so that the future no longer continued in a linear or circular fashion, but rather was overcome in the ascent to the timeless, heavenly sphere. Consequently, there was no room for future judgment, either within history or at its end. For one thus enlightened, the possibility of pride was enormously enhanced. There was a natural tendency to consider oneself superior to others and to demonstrate this by condescension, haughtiness, and outrageous violations of normally accepted standards. It is highly probable, therefore, that the enlightened Lycus Valley religionists lacked a **fearful prospect of judgment,** and that their sophisticated rejection of dialogical responsibility was a natural consequence.

It is interesting to note in this connection, however, that verse 26 includes the writer and the loyal members of the congregation in the sweeping first person plural: **if we sin.** This allows no room for mutual accusations between congregational factions, nor for hostile allegations against those who happen to oppose the viewpoint of the author. Everyone stands before this inexorable bar of **judgment,** not only in the eschaton, but also in the course of historical experience itself.

The exhortation ends, just as the similar passage in 4:11-13 did, with a reminder about the **living** quality of the divine partner in this new covenant: **It is fearful to fall into the hands of the living God.** The partner in dialogue cannot be reduced to an "it." God cannot be manipulated, as the Lycus Valley religionists had hoped to manipulate the cosmic forces; and one cannot presume on divine mercy and make God a plaything of human whim. For God is **living,** the dynamic force sustaining the universe and carrying out timely purposes of righteousness with relentless but impartial power. If one refuses to take up the dialogical partnership that God offers through the ministry of the great high priest, then one inevitably **falls into** God's **hands.** It is either/or: either mercy that is taken up responsibly in the relationship of the new covenant, or **judgment** that shatters human illusions. In light of these inexorable alternatives, there is a proper form of

Christian **fearful**ness. According to Walter Bauer, this term *phoberos*, found in the New Testament only in Hebrews, denotes that which causes "fear," is "fearful, terrible, frightful." As its use in 12:21 implies, this **fearful** quality particularly adheres to the old cult and should be overcome for the members of the new. But it should not be eliminated from the consideration of personal and historical possibilities. Although such fear has been replaced for believers by the "boldness (to take) the way into the sanctuary" (10:19), it still remains as the character of an alternative, incapable as the old cult itself to redeem, but providing impetus for the nurture of dialogical realism.

Just as the Lycus Valley theology lacked a proper appreciation of this **fearful** quality of divine justice, so it can be said that one of the most pressing needs of contemporary American thought is to balance the emphasis on the unconditional love of God with a corresponding insistence upon the righteous **judgment** of God. Despite the complexity of such doctrinal reflection, the results for the individual are clearly discernible. When one knows only the **fear** of God, one recoils in anxiety and loses one's autonomy. One is apt to lapse into an obsessive works-righteousness to prove that one is not liable to the judgment of God, and correspondingly to express the savagery one fears in the form of cruelty to others. But when one knows only the love of God, one tends toward euphoria and fails to come to grips with the tragic dimensions of life. One is apt to lack seriousness in dialogue or in moral purpose; one lacks the sense of humor that comes from an ironic grasp of finite limitations. When, like the author of Hebrews, someone knows the love of God yet can glimpse through the justice implied by that love to the end point of **fearful . . . judgment,** that person can be both liberated and humane.

When one thinks about the implications of this tremendous vision of the **living God,** the examples of the great heroes of faith in the following chapter of Hebrews come to mind. One is struck not only by their faith, but also by their courage, grounded in the conviction that God is **living.** There is a sense in which fear of the living God can dispel the fear of anything else and provide the basis for impressive secular courage In face of the greater fear of falling out of covenantal relationship, the pilgrim of Hebrews is ready to accept whatever humans have to threaten: "raging fire . . . the sword . . . [being] tortured . . . mocking and scourging . . . chains and imprisonment. They were stoned, they were sawn in two, they were killed with the sword; they went about in skins of sheep and goats, destitute, afflicted, ill-treated [Heb. 11:34-37, RSV]." Like the soldiers in Cromwell's army, they feared not humans because they feared God most of all. Properly understood, this sense of the fear of God as Hebrews portrays it produces champions of justice rather than cowering religionists. Courage in face of mortal dangers is in fact one of the conspicuous attributes of the great pilgrims of English and of American history, most of whom fought their battles without military weapons. Such persons remain cool and effective in the most adverse circumstances, looking after the lives of the innocent and acting responsibly to bring order out of chaos. It is to these great pilgrim heroes of the past that the next section of Hebrews turns.

Chapter Eleven

Pilgrim Faith in the Secular World (10:32—11:40)

10:32 **N**OW recall the former days when, having been enlightened, you endured frequent struggle with sufferings, [33]sometimes being made a spectacle by insults and afflictions, and sometimes becoming partners with those so treated. [34]For you sympathized with those in bonds, and you accepted with joy the plundering of your possessions, knowing that you have a better and lasting possession. [35]Therefore do not toss away your boldness, which has a great reward. [36]For you have need of endurance so that having done the will of God you may cash in what is promised.

[37]"For in a little, a very little now,
the coming one will arrive and not delay.
[38]But my righteous one shall live by faith,
and if he shrinks back, my soul takes no pleasure in him."
[39]But we are not of those who shrink back to destruction, but (those who) by faith preserve (their) life.

At the beginning of this third major section of Hebrews, it would be well to review briefly the path that has been followed and to show how it relates to the path that lies ahead. The ministry of Christ the great high priest calls for a response on the part of the recipients of the gospel. This response is essentially one of worship, but a worship that takes the form of pilgrimage through the secular world, encountering the word of God moment for moment along the way. The Christian is called to approach the formerly forbidden presence of God not so much within the hallowed ground of the church as within the secular world. This has some far-reaching implications. To worship in the hushed and sheltered sanctuary surrounded by fellow believers may not involve great risk, and thus it does not demand courageous faith. But to worship in the secular world, with its threats, its uncertainties, and its inevitable suffering, requires a constant and assured faith. So our author climaxes his great "word of exhortation" in these last major chapters with a discussion of the life of faith in the secular world. He argues that faithful worship receives the divine promises that it celebrates. It therefore provides a fulfillment of human existence in the course of the worldly pilgrimage.

In the opening verses of this section the author recalls the difficult early days of faith in the Lycus Valley. Despite the efforts of Martin Dibelius to show these remarks are unrelated to the life of any specific church, the use of the second person plural indicates an appeal to their own experience. The early history of this congregation revealed a paradox about Christian existence that was vitally important for the author's purpose: the moment they were **enlightened** they began to **struggle with sufferings.** When one takes account of the background of this term **enlightened** in Hellenistic mystery religions and gnosticism, it appears likely that it would carry a connotation of apotheosis in the Lycus Valley. It implies the kind of redemptive self-discovery that frees one from bondage to the treadmill of the flesh. That such connotations were alive in the Lycus Valley is indicated by the fact that the people considered tribulation antithetical to full Christian maturity, seeking to counter it by manipulating the cosmic powers causing evil. The author's point, therefore, is that their own experience documents the fact that **enlighten**ment provokes **sufferings.** The two belong together, because the place of Christian existence is not in the heavenly realms, but on this deteriorating and hostile earth that Jesus the high priest shared. Consequently, Christians can recall what it meant to be made a public **spectacle,** and to be made **partners** with the outcasts of society. Their experience is paralleled by that of other pilgrims in the early church and down through the generations. The neighbors whom one loves will hate and persecute in return, and the authorities for whom the pilgrim community prays will respond with harassment.

There is a healthy realism that comes from taking this remarkable juxtaposition between **enlightenment** and **suffering** into account. It is quite naturally a matter that the Christians in the Lycus Valley would have liked to avoid. And it is a mark of the frivolous quality of much of contemporary religion that this reality is denied. How often do well-meaning counselors of the soul affirm that if people just accept their message, all troubles will cease? How fervently do our positive thinkers promise that faith will lead to success and security. A veritable library of "how to achieve success and popularity" tracts lead people astray with this fallacious and shallow assumption. Be kind and loving to others, and they will respect you, love you, etc. Yet our experiences as individuals and as a nation belie this belief in automatic reciprocity. That persons and nations bite the hand that feeds them is apparently a perennial feature of human experience. A world operating under the pretensions of the old cult, either in its religious or its secular guise, will react with hostility to anyone who is truly free and **enlightened.** As long as people refuse the unpleasant reality of which Hebrews speaks, believing that faith will produce success and happiness, there is no possibility for genuine faith to emerge.

In verse 34 the congregation is reminded of an aspect of its early experience that was even more remarkable. They had responded to the **sufferings, insults,** and **afflictions** in a manner that defied all human expectations. They had used the opportunity of being in prison to express human **sympathy** for **those in bonds,** finding a common ground with elements in society with which they had perhaps not formerly been closely associated. Rather than complaining about **the plundering of** their **possessions,** they had **accepted** it **with joy.** This was so remarkable that it required the explanation suggested in 34c: **knowing that you have a better and lasting possession.** This is understood by Hugh Montefiore and F.F. Bruce in the sense of being sure of a heavenly reward, but the present tense of the verb implies that something more than a future paradise is in view. In light of the previous argument in the letter and of the context of the present discussion, it is more probable that the author thinks here of their new and abiding dialogue with God, based on "having" the great high priest and the boldness to enter the sanctuary with him (10:19-21). To put it briefly, it was their faith in God that gave them the remarkable joy in the loss of their possessions. For their security in life was no longer based on their jobs, their social position, and their belongings. With faith in God, they gained the power to respond with resilience to the arbitrary abuse of a hostile world. It was not a matter of lethargically accepting their fate because their thoughts were on the next life. They had not been mystical drifters who convinced themselves that no pain in the flesh could touch their immortal souls—although the Lycus Valley theology was nudging them in that direction. Mystagogues of that sort would hardly have demonstrated the presence of mind to minister to the well-being of nonsympathizing cellmates, as the congregation had done. Nor would they likely have been capable of the full-bodied, earthly joy of which our author speaks. No, it was the this-worldly realism of the early experience that the author wished to lift up, because in his view, it indicated that faith gives people the capacity to be responsive and at the same time to be sustained with joy, even in face of the worst that fellow humans were capable of inflicting upon them.

What then is the **great reward** for **boldness** in verse 35? Again, it is possible to think of this in terms of the gifts that will come in the afterlife to those who are faithful through persecution. But this interpretation can scarcely be based on the preceding argument of Hebrews. I would suggest in contrast that the present tense of the verb **has a great reward** implies that the eschatological rest comes to the pilgrim community along the way. As in the earlier chapters of the letter, it is "today . . . today . . . today" that the author has in mind. One might even go so far as to say that the sort of

boldness implied in this verse, having gained a dynamic definition in terms of confident approach to God in 3:6; 4:16; and 10:19, provides its own reward. It reveals the presence of a vital sense of autonomy and self-respect that is essential to survival under pressure. For if one remains **bold** enough to approach the throne of grace, one will surely be able to face life with a similar spirit.

In contrast, verse 36 appears to speak clearly about the eschatological fulfillment that draws the pilgrim toward the future and keeps open the dynamic character of a dialogical **promise.** The vernacular translation **you may cash in what is promised** is an attempt to capture the sense of the verb *komizō*, which is frequently used in the context of receiving wages or recovering possessions. Despite its lack of elegance, this translation conveys the author's sense of holding fast to the new relationship in order to receive it again in the future. The **need of endurance** must therefore be understood in a dialogical sense, for the **will of God** as shown in the preceding argument of Hebrews is that humans retain the living sense of the new covenant inaugurated by the high priestly ministry. The eschatological horizon of this exhortation has frequently been in view earlier in the letter (1:2; 2:3; 7:7f.; 10:25-31).

To summarize, the Christian community finds fulfillment in adversity, for every moment offers a renewed opportunity to approach God. Just as the great high priest approached the Father's throne at the moment of his death, so his people are brought by him in moments of mortal vulnerability to the very presence of God. This encounter is the present **reward** and the future **promise** by which human life is fulfilled.

In verses 37 and 38 the matter of holding fast during the eschatological crisis is developed by use of Old Testament citations combined from Isaiah 26:20 and Habakkuk 2:3-4. The analysis of the author's combination and alteration of the Septuagint text by Friedrich Schröger, Otto Michel, and others indicates that verse 37a is designed to depict an extremely short time until the eschatological fulfillment, while 37b is altered so that **the coming one** refers explicitly to the returning Christ.

Furthermore, 38a and 38b have been reversed by the author, so that there is no possibility of identifying the he who **shrinks back** with **the coming one** in 37b. In its resultant form the citation has a heightened eschatological tension with a clear reference to the parousia. It implies that the **need of endurance** in the verse before the citation is qualified by the proximity and certainty of the eschatological fulfillment. But more than that, it proves that the existence of the community in the meantime is to be shaped by **faith.** In this sense verse 38a provides the theme for the entire chapter: **but my righteous one shall live by faith.** The alternative is to **shrink back to destruction,** as verse 39 explains. The path that the pilgrim community should follow is the one marked by a **faith** that serves to preserve **life.**

The interpretation of this great thematic announcement based on the Isaiah and Habakkuk citations has been deeply entangled, ever since the time of Luther, with the question of its relation to the normative Pauline doctrine of faith. The study of the problem by Erich Grässer is based on the conviction that **faith** is used here simply as an ethical attitude of standing fast. His position does not take adequate account of Hebrews' use of **faith** as the "first principle" understood in a relational sense of "faith in God"; nor does it take with sufficient seriousness the polemic in 7:10 against the law and the old cult. The author of Hebrews stands close to the Pauline doctrine in affirming that **faith** is a gift of God communicated by the gospel, as indicated by passages like 2:1-4 and 4:1-10. To conclude, as Grässer does, that the differences from Paul prove there is nothing specifically Christian about **faith** in this passage seems inappropriate in light of the Christological alteration of the Habakkuk citation, the heightening of the parousia expectation, and the previous argument against cultic law and works righteousness in Hebrews. The point of the Isaiah-Habakkuk citation in its present context is that the imminent return of the great high priest and the current eschatological crisis produce a situation in which those made **righteous** by the Christ event must **live by faith.** They must hold fast to the relationship they have been given.

There is no denying that **faith** in this passage is used in the sense of "faithfulness," as noted by Grässer and others, moving at this point toward the traditional Old Testament usage. It is fair to point out, however, that such usage is closely paralleled by Pauline passages such as 1 Corinthians 16:13, Romans 3:3 and 4:18f., and 2 Thessalonians 1:4. One would be ill advised either to attempt to disguise the differences or to overlook the Pauline orientation of the concept as a whole. The expression "pilgrim faith" is suggested in this chapter to describe Hebrews' extension of an essentially Pauline doctrine. It presupposes the earlier argument in the epistle showing that this **faith** was inaugurated by the gospel concerning the ministry of the great high priest, that it involves taking up the proffered new relationship with God, and therefore that it is a matter also of turning away from the self-involution of "dead works." In other words, despite the arguments of Grässer and others, I am convinced that the author of Hebrews is completely serious about both the centrality and the relational quality of **faith** as depicted in 6:1: "faith in God." What he develops in the present chapter is not a definition of **faith** by which that earlier usage must be interpreted, as Grässer assumes, but an application of an already established doctrine of **faith** for the requirements of pilgrimage in the Lycus Valley.

On this basis it is possible to discern the aspect of **faith** that the author wishes to develop and apply in verses 37 to 39. It is that those who have been given the **faith** relationship are called upon to **live** it out in the secular world, running the gauntlet between eschatological judgment and the hostility of their fellow humans. It is a pilgrim **faith**, lacking in normal securities and comforts, but encountering the life-giving word that brings them into the "rest" momentarily along the way. While verses 32 to 35 describe in a realistic fashion the gauntlet of hostility, verse 39b lifts up the sustaining power of **faith** in face of such dangers. That the pilgrims **by faith preserve (their) life** has frequently been misunderstood and mistranslated in the sense of "saving their souls" in the next life, as Brooke Foss Westcott asserts. The Greek word *psychē* in this context denotes not "soul" but rather **life**, as indicated by parallels in Luke 21:19 ("By your endurance you will gain your lives") and in Pauline passages (1 Thessalonians 2:8; Romans 11:3; 16:4; 2 Corinthians 1:23). The eschatological context of this statement would seem to point to the matter of surviving as God's elect despite the woes and tribulations of the last days. In this context, to **preserve . . . life** might include passing successfully through the future judgment of God. But again the author seems to have a more present reality in view. Both the reference in verse 36 to the **need of endurance** and this reference in verse 39 to the preservation of **life** appear to indicate an interest in the actual physical survival of the community during the period of running the gauntlet. He is implying that **faith** provides the ability to endure and to keep life intact.

Those who retain **faith** despite adverse pilgrimage experiences maintain a life-preserving sense of meaning and purpose. As they hold fast to the relationship of worship, they receive "rest" in the midst of tribulation. They find opportunities to worship through service and praise in every situation, no matter how grim. There is, consequently, a possibility of joy despite troubles and of humane relationship despite alienation. The faithful enjoy, though as pilgrims, the supreme gift of a meaningful life, and thus they endure.

11:1 Now faith is an assurance of things hoped for, an evidence of things not seen. ²For in it the elders had witness borne to them.

³"By faith we perceive that the aeons were created by the word of God, to the end that the visible (was known) to be made out of that which cannot be seen.

⁴"By faith Abel offered God a more ample sacrifice than Cain, through which he was witnessed as being righteous, God bearing witness by accepting his gifts, and through this he still speaks (though) dead.

⁵"By faith Enoch was taken up so that he never died, and he was not found because God had taken him up. For before he was taken up, it was witnessed that he had

pleased God. [6]But without faith it is impossible to please (God), for it is necessary for the one who draws near to God to have faith that he exists and that the reward comes to those who seek him out.

[7]"By faith Noah, being warned about the things which were still unseen, moved by reverence, he constructed an ark for the saving of his house; by this he condemned the world and became an heir of the righteousness that comes by faith.

[8]"By faith Abraham obeyed when he was called to go out to a place that he was to receive as an inheritance; and he went out not knowing where he was to go.

[9]"By faith he sojourned to the promised land as in a foreign (land), dwelling in tents, with Isaac and Jacob, co-heirs with him of the same promise."

[10]For he looked forward to the city having foundations, whose builder and craftsman is God.

[11]"By faith Sarah herself received power to conceive when she was past the age for it, because she considered faithful him who promised. [12]On this account from one man (virtually) dead were born descendants like the stars of heaven in number and as countless as the sand on the seashore."

[13]These all died in faith, not having cashed in on the promises, but having seen and greeted them from afar, and confessed that they were strangers and pilgrims on the earth. [14]For those who speak thus reveal that they are seeking out a homeland. [15]If they had thought of the land they left behind, they would have had time to return. [16]But now they desire a better (country), that is, a heavenly. Therefore God is not ashamed to be called their God, for he prepared for them a city.

Chapter 11, which I propose to divide into several major sections because of the length of material, has long been suspected as being a citation from an example catalog. The most penetrating and thorough analysis of this question by Gottfried Schille shows that an early Christian baptismal catechism was used by the author in part of this chapter, with the insertion of his own qualifying comments in verses 1-2, 10, 13-16, and 39-40. Following observations by Otto Michel, Schille notes that verses 13 and 39 insist that the forefathers did not inherit the promises, while in verse 5 Enoch is referred to as having actually been **taken up** into heaven, and in verse 33 the Old Testament saints are said to have "received promises." These contradictions reflect different viewpoints within the chapter, with the verses containing typical qualifications in the author's terminology standing against other material that appears to be traditional. In one instance, the author's qualifications (verses 13 to 16) interrupt the Abraham material from verses 12 and 17 that would fit together beautifully without the insertion. Schille discerns a stylistic uniformity in this traditional material, with double-membered sentences organized in five strophes of six verses each. He suggests that this material originated in a Jewish setting as a confession of the faith of the fathers, similar to materials found in Jubilees, the Damascus Document, and the Manual of Discipline from Qumran, but was then adapted for early Christian use as instruction for baptismal candidates. Since the author does not appear to alter the citation, preferring to place his qualifying insertions at the beginning, middle, and end, Schille suggests that it must have been accepted by the congregation as an authoritative confession of faith. In other words, the author probably utilizes in this chapter a portion of the baptismal catechism used in the Lycus Valley. The indented material in my translation, provided with quotation marks, delineates the scope of this catechism used by the author.

If this hypothesis is correct, verses 1 and 2 must be understood as a qualifying and interpretative definition by which the following catechetical citation is to be understood. Although the style is that of Hellenistic philosophical definition, as Michel observes, it is important to keep in mind the use of the term **faith** in the earlier theological argument of Hebrews, especially in 6:1. In other words this interpretative definition rests on fuller foundations earlier in the letter and aims at qualifying the material that follows, To use 11:1 as the fundamental definition of **faith** in Hebrews, qualifying it by the cited materials that follow, as Grässer does, is methodologically improper and leads to a misunderstanding of the author's argument.

Since it is generally agreed that verse 1b is in explanatory apposition to 1a, it would seem appropriate to begin the analysis with **evidence of things not seen.** Since the term *elegchos* is never used in the sense of subjective conviction, it depicts the objective proving of the reality of the **things not seen.** The idea is that the miraculous presence of **faith** in pilgrims buffeted by opposition serves to validate in an objective fashion the **things not seen.** Their adverse experience may seem to contradict the sovereignty of God, but the inexplicable existence of **faith,** based not on their virtue but rather on the action of the spirit, affirms it. The expression **things not seen** relates directly to the following citation, particularly verses 3b, 7a, and 27b. Whereas the citation seems to imply that these mysterious realities are actually **perceived** or **seen,** verse 1 states that **faith** itself is the sole evidence of their reality. It functions as a Pauline type of caution against the enthusiastic or gnostic claim of possessing the spiritual reality in the perception or "knowledge" of it. It is possible that the unusually flat term **things,** which Michel shows is not so much descriptive as evasive, would be understood as including the divine mysteries that the Lycus Valley presumed to possess.

With this foundation it is possible to reason backward to discern the intention of 1a: **Now faith is an assurance of (things) hoped for.** There are four major alternatives in translating *hupostasis:* as a "substance" or "presentation" of the eschatological reality that one presently possesses in the spirit; as the "conviction" of the validity of eschatological reality; as a "guarantee" that objectively affirms the eschatological reality; or as a "firm stance" in relation to this reality. The last alternative cannot be precisely translated with the genitive plural **(things) hoped for;** since the best Grässer can do in rendering this is to paraphrase it as "a firm stance in that for which man hopes," this option should be eliminated. The first alternative directly counters the effort in verse 1b to caution against any flat identification of present experience with eschatological reality, so it also should be rejected. This leaves the two middle alternatives, of which the translation as "conviction" or **assurance** is slightly preferable, because it comes closer to matching the aforementioned caution. Whereas "guarantee" seems to imply an absolute degree of certainty unfitting for pilgrim conditions as set forth thus far in Hebrews, the translation with **assurance** correlates quite well with the qualifying second clause, **an evidence of things not seen.**

The point of this qualifying definition is that the very presence of **faith** provides the **evidence** and **assurance** of eschatological reality. It is not some certified content of this **faith** or the dogmatic conviction with which it is held, but rather the very existence of **faith** in adverse circumstances that provides an experiential proof of the presence of the new age. Such **faith** is evoked by the gospel that was accompanied by miraculous outpourings of the spirit (2:4), and it therefore comes to be synonymous with the new relationship that marks the "age to come" (6:1-5). **Faith** in this sense is far from being a human virtue or one of the "dead works" of religious performance. Its very presence is a sign of divine intervention in human life—unexpected and transforming. It therefore offers a sort of minimal but effective confirmation to a pilgrim community. As 10:32-39 indicates, the congregation had experienced this inexplicable reality within their own lives when they cheerfully submitted to plunder and found the power to sympathize with their fellow prisoners. Such faith had miraculously sustained them through their persecution, for they have already been described by Hebrews as "(those who) by faith preserved (their) life." Faith so transforms people that it provides a sort of confirmation, though short of "certainty," of the faithfulness of God. This is what gives the pilgrim community such remarkable power, not to escape tribulation, but to endure.

In verse 2 this theme is carried out in sharp and unequivocal fashion. Substantiating the previous verse (For . . .), it lifts a single dialogical motif from the catechism about to be cited. **For in it** (i.e., faith) **the elders had witness borne to them.** Since the author returns to this term **witness** at the end of his citation, in verse 39, it serves as an interpretative bracket for the catechism. On the one hand it lifts up the witness motif in verses 4 and 5 as having crucial importance for the understanding of the catechism; because of the intrinsic connection of this motif with God's word of promise (7:8, 17) and the Spirit's word from the scripture (10:15), it lifts up these same motifs in the lives of the heroes of faith. On the other hand, as Schille notes, verse 2 tends to limit the level of fulfillment reached by the **elders.** They did not achieve perfection through their **faith,** nor did they really "cash in" on the promises (11:13, 39); instead they received a **witness** in **faith** that pointed to the power of God's future. And thus they enjoyed the dialogical fulfillment that comes from hearing God's word and responding to it. This emphasis appears to pick up the antignostic thrust noted in connection with verse 1, countering any idea of apotheosis through "seeing" the divine reality.

With this limiting, interpretative framework established, the author begins citing the Lycus Valley catechism, each section opening with *pistei*, **by faith.** The rough transition from verse 2 to verse 3 indicates the beginning of cited material. The subtle differences between this catechism and the author's position, as well as the striking similarities to the Lycus Valley theology visible elsewhere, need to be lifted up. Verse 3 implies that the person of **faith** is able to **perceive** the mystery of the creation of the **aeons.** While this verb is not used elsewhere in Hebrews, it is widely used in Hellenistic Judaism and gnosticism to depict the capacity of the spiritual core of a person to recognize divine reality by means of fundamental affinity. The purpose of this creation was **to the end that** the enlightened might know that **the visible** came from **that which cannot be seen.** The use of Hellenistic philosophic terms like

the visible, found nowhere else in the New Testament, points to the independent sophistication of the Lycus Valley catechists. Taken by itself, verse 3 leans in the direction of gnosticism, but with the author's qualification in verses 1 and 2 that all one really receives in **faith** is the dialogical **witness** of God rather than complete insight into divine mystery, the citation plays a positive role in the author's argument. It even serves to remind the congregation that their own tradition affirmed the **aeons** were not ultimate, but rather were **created by the word of God,** so that worship must now consist of maintaining dialogue with that **word** rather than attempting to manipulate the cosmic **aeons.**

Verse 4 seems to conflict even more strongly with the previous argument of Hebrews, for **Abel** is pictured as achieving **righteous**ness by presenting **God a more ample sacrifice than Cain.** Since the author has argued at length in chapters 7 to 10 that sacrifices cannot perfect the worshiper, it is a sign of his respect for the Lycus Valley tradition that this portion of the catechism is included at all. The Abel passage would have provided excellent justification for the cultic service in the Lycus Valley. Yet the qualifying introductory verses serve particularly well in this instance, implying that the fulfillment Abel received was strictly a matter of receiving a **witness** from God that made him an acceptable dialogue partner. Furthermore, as the author's interpretative insertion in verse 13 emphasizes, Abel died in the midst of such dialogue. At this point, the tradition blends fortuitously with the realistic emphasis on the risks of pilgrimage. The person of **faith** does not transcend finitude, as the Lycus Valley Gnostics sought to do, but rather receives a fulfilling **witness** even in face of his own death at the hands of a murdering brother. It is this realistic message that the author hears Abel **still speak (though) dead.**

Directly opposed to such realism, at first glance, is the description of **Enoch** in verses 5 and 6. For he achieved precisely what the Lycus Valley mystics desired: **Enoch was taken up, so that he never died. . . . For before he was taken**

up, it was witnessed that he had pleased God. This tradition of Enoch's "trip" directly into the heavens provided the inspiration for the apocalyptic and mystical traditions, and would have provided a valid precedent for the Lycus Valley effort to overcome finitude, to achieve union with the divine, and to **please God** in order to accomplish this through the performance of the cultic rites. It is no accident that this idea of being **taken up** is most closely paralleled in Colossians 1:13, "He . . . has transferred us to the kingdom of his beloved Son." So the author circumscribes the Enoch story very tightly by the interpretative brackets that he provides. He implies in verse 2 that the fulfillment resided strictly in the matter of God's **witness** that one takes on faith, and this tends to discount the matter of a trip directly into the heavens. Even more shockingly, he insists in verse 13 **These all died in faith, not having cashed in on the promises.** In other words, the author of Hebrews denies that Enoch was really taken up into the heavens without dying. All that remains of the Enoch myth when one takes the interpretative brackets into account is the **witness** that **by faith** Enoch **had pleased God.** This is the point that the catechism had reiterated in verse 6, that **it is impossible to please (God)** without such **faith.** This fits in so perfectly with the author's argument that he can afford to accept without qualification the dry dogmatic formula, **it is necessary . . . to have faith that** God **exists,** and even to quote the legalistic statement about **the reward** being given only **to those who seek** God **out.** That these statements are uncharacteristic for Hebrews is clear when one recalls the relational definition of **faith** in 4:2 and 6:1, and its inauguration not in the religious quest of humans, but rather in the gospel about the great high priest (1:2; 2:1; 3:1, etc.).

Although the term **witness** does not occur in the Noah passage, in verse 7, it is implied by the expression **being warned about the things which were still unseen.** The verb translated with **warned** is a typical expression for divine announcement, and Noah is pictured as being **moved by reverence** and obeying the word of God. By so doing, he **became an heir of the**

199

righteousness that comes by faith, a technical expression for salvation in the Pauline tradition. This portion of the Lycus Valley catechism is therefore well suited to the author's argument, with the possible exception of one point: Noah escaped the kind of disaster that, in Hebrews' perspective, strikes particularly hard at those holding a pilgrim **faith.** Although this correlates well with 10:39 and the idea that those who keep their **faith** will also save their **lives,** it is bracketed with a healthy dose of realism by verse 13: **These all died in faith, not having cashed in on the promises.** If **faith** provides the power to endure the storm, and even to **condemn the world** in the process, it nevertheless does not lift the limits of finitude.

The greatest example of **faith,** as far as Hebrews is concerned, is set forth beginning with verse 8. **Abraham** received a divine witness when he received the word **to go out to a place that he was to receive as an inheritance. By faith** he responded to this **call** and took up a pilgrim existence that provides a magnificent precedent for the Lycus Valley congregation. Rather than seeking the security of a cultic enclave or attempting to build some "lasting city," he took up a pilgrim trek into the unknown. **He went out not knowing where he was to go.** To leave the certainties of the past and the familiar, to break away from the bonds of family and nation, and to move courageously into the unknown is the requirement for both maturity and creativity. Rollo May relates this requirement implicit in **faith** to mythical and psychoanalytic experience. After discussing Oedipus, Orestes, Prometheus, and other great figures associated with the quest for the unknown and for maturity, May reflects:

> It often occurs to me that the reason Freud was able to work with such courage and unswerving purpose throughout the last forty years of his life was that he won the battle of being able to grow and work alone in that first solitary ten years, when, after he had separated from Breuer, he pursued his explorations into psychoanalysis with neither colleague nor co-worker. It seems to me, further, that this is the battle the

creative ethical figures like Jesus win in the wilderness . . . the temptation . . . to throw himself down from the mountain to prove that God was protecting him. . . . When one has been able to say "No" to the need that he be "borne up," when, in other words, he is able not to demand he be taken care of, when he has the courage to stand alone, he can then speak as one with authority.

The courage required to **go out not knowing where** one **was to go** is provided by the sort of **faith** Hebrews has in mind; it is the inauguration of vital relationship that dispels the anxiety which chains people to the past or to a futile quest for security. It draws the pilgrim inexorably toward the future, when the dialogue will again be invigorated and when the outlines of the "city which is to come" begin to give creative shape to present projects. So the person of **faith** must necessarily be a pilgrim, breaking resolutely from the illusion of security and moving courageously toward the unknown.

The epitome of Abraham's pilgrim existence is depicted in verse 9, for even when he arrived at the ostensible goal of his pilgrimage, he remained essentially an outsider. **By faith he sojourned in the promised land as in a foreign (land), dwelling in tents.** This particular citation from the Lycus Valley catechism is one of the most provocative and profound statements in the entire literature of pilgrimage. It counters the theocratic illusion that gripped much of first-century Judaism just as it has at times captured the soul of America. The illusion is that one should be able to dwell with complete security and at-home-ness in a **promised land.** This illusion played a role in the grandiose effort of the first-century Zealots to rid the **promised land** of its external and internal enemies, ending up in an interparty warfare that surpassed in violence even the vengeance finally exacted by the Roman legions. One can trace the effects of such illusions in the efforts of Americans to rid themselves of the heretics, the witches, and the Indians who appeared to threaten the security of the divine commonwealth. As we experience the collapse of the hollow promises of politicians and military experts to provide such security, we are driven to learn the hard way that it is necessary to **sojourn in the promised land as in a foreign (land).** We cannot assume that the task of enacting its **promises** is ever completed or that we shall ever be completely at home within its boundaries. Abraham, the person of **faith,** is presented by the catechism as a suitable model at this point. He **sojourned,** ready to fight or change or move on, but was never rooted irrevocably to the culture of feudal Canaan. His **dwelling in tents** is a fitting symbol of this pilgrim attitude: ready to move on, to travel light, to move toward better pasture, to adjust to new circumstances. The ideal includes a sense of responsibility for others and for the future, as hinted by 9b: **dwelling in tents, with Isaac and Jacob, co-heirs with him of the same promise.**

What is it that makes **sojourning** necessary, even for the **co-heirs** of the **promised land?** Why is an uneasy exile required by **faith?** It must be more than the natural enmity between those who are truly free and others who wish them to conform, and it must be more than the reaction to the deteriorating character of the world, for the alienation implicit in both of these was overcome by the work of the great high priest, according to the argument of Hebrews up to this point. Verse 10 provides a succinct answer to this question, implying that the continual dissatisfaction of the pilgrim is due to the vision he or she carries of **the city having foundations, whose builder and craftsman is God.** In this insertion by the author, Abraham is pictured as being driven on his pilgrimage by the fact that **he looked forward** to this **city.** This sense of tension between the divine realm and the place in which one lives, no matter how high its pretensions, is an expression of what Herbert N. Schneidau calls "sacred discontent," the crucial contribution of Hebrew thought to Western culture. "It created a sacredness of spatial emergence rather than one of continuity, and it leads eventually to the great literary theme of the journey or quest, including picaresque versions which are full of implicit social criticism." The Abrahamic venture is sacred because it is evoked by that which is truly permanent in this life—**the city having foundations.** Although those who **sojourn** in this sense appear at times to be rootless and marginal, their vision is the potential source of cultural revitalization.

When the author returns to his citation of the catechism in verses 11 and 12, a certain garbling of the text occurs, with **Sarah** inexplicably becoming the subject of the expression **received power**, which is usually reserved for male participation in conception, and being described as **considering faithful him who promised**, which does not jibe very well with her sarcastic laughter in response to the news of her future conception (Genesis 18:12). Possibly the subject of this sentence was originally **Abraham**, with the reference to **Sarah** in the dative rather than the nominative; at any rate, it is he rather than she who is again the subject of verse 12. The implication of these verses, however, does not correlate too well with Hebrews' purpose, because the implication is that **Sarah's** belief in the **faithfulness** of God was rewarded by the birth of her son. Such miraculous **power**—a term used elsewhere in Hebrews as characteristic of God and not as the possession of humans (1:3; 2:4; 6:5; 7:16)—is not held out in 10:32 or elsewhere as the reward for pilgrim existence.

The possible misunderstanding of the **Sarah** and **Abraham** example is immediately allayed, however, by the insertion of the author's interpretative remarks in verses 13 to 17. Despite the **power** that they were given and the long-lasting historical results of their lineage, both **Sarah** and **Abraham** are included in the sweeping assertion of pilgrim finitude: **These all died in faith, not having cashed in on the promises.** This characteristic expression of the author, used in 10:36 and again in later portions of chapter 11, denies a final reception of the eschatological gifts in the sense of possession to which one is entitled. While the catechism itself implied that **faith** makes one somewhat more than finite, emphasizing the acceptable sacrifice of Abel, the ascension of Enoch, the escape of Noah, and the miraculous power of Sarah and Abraham, the author retains a very realistic grasp of their transient pilgrim quality. They, like the pilgrim community of the Lycus Valley, received not a divinizing gift, but rather a **faith** relationship in which the

promises of God continue to lead toward the historical future. They have only **seen and greeted** the eschatological fulfillment **from afar.** So with complete realism, the people of **faith** in the Old Testament **confessed that they were strangers and pilgrims** on the earth.

This is the model the author suggests for his congregation, one which has beckoned with powerful force from the *Canterbury Tales* and *Pilgrim's Progress* down to the novels of Steinbeck and Faulkner. It has inspired Christian folksongs from "Lonesome Valley" to "Swing Low, Sweet Chariot." And at times of crisis, when the life of **faith** leads into conflicts with authority and public opinion—even in the **promised land**—this image speaks with powerful realism. It counters the euphoric dream of a world being made "safe" for faith; it stands in judgment against the shallow hope that **faith** in the form of positive thinking will solve life's problems; and it belies the discouragement that often strikes a **faith** which assumes that God's children are simply held in the protective hollow of God's hand. To the contrary, those who respond to the gospel with **faith** often become **strangers** to their families and their colleagues. They are torn away from the incestuous bonds that tied them to country and familial solidarity. They become **pilgrims** within their own communities, drawn by their dialogical vision toward that which is new and better. Like Abraham, they learn to live even **in the promised land as in a foreign (land).**

Verses 14 and 16 reiterate the decisive force drawing the **faith**ful into pilgrimage: their yearning for **a homeland** and for **a better (country), that is a heavenly.** This is usually interpreted in terms of a yearning for the heavenly reward, which reduces earthly pilgrimage to "temporary object-lessons pointing to the saints' everlasting rest," in F.F. Bruce's words. This other-worldly version of Christianity, which has done so much to vitiate the pilgrim character of **faith**, fails to take adequate account of the sustaining power and social responsibility of **faith** in the present, and tends to lapse back into a program of working for the heavenly reward that resembles the ancient cult which Hebrews opposes. The **heavenly** land that the **pilgrims desire** is, after all, the spot to which they already have been brought by the great high priest when he drew them with him through the forbidden curtain into the presence of God. It is not just a future reward and reality, but rather a present experience in **faith**, for **faith** is the gift of being placed in relationship with the Holy of Holies. Working hard as a pilgrim so one can get to heaven is unnecessary for those who have responded in **faith** to the good news about the heavenly liturgy of Christ, for they are given thereby a dialogue that is at once "rest" (Hebrews 3—4) and heavenly "worship" (12:22-24). But since this is a dialogue, it can never be possessed and must always be entered into every day. The pilgrims stand in a relationship that draws them constantly forward: they are constantly **seeking** and **desiring** the renewal of dialogue and the approximation of the **better** (**country**) in their own lives and communities. Gripped by a vision that is rooted in dialogue, they move realistically and responsibly toward the future, refusing to settle for any promise of absolute security or any mere certainty of a future reward.

The dialogical character of the eschatological fulfillment is insisted upon in 16b: **Therefore God is not ashamed to be called their God, for he prepared for them a city.** This wording picks up the new covenant motif developed in chapter 8, in which a new relationship would be established in which "I will be their God, and they shall be my people [8:10, RSV]." The essence of the heavenly city, for Hebrews, is dialogue, not golden streets and golden slippers. To respond to that **city** is to take up the **pilgrim**age of dialogue that realistically accepts finitude but never ceases to strive for the gradual though never final approximation of its qualities in whatever locale one happens to live.

11:17 **"By faith, being tested, Abraham offered up Isaac, and he who had received the promises was offering up his only begotten son, 18to whom it was said that 'in Isaac shall your** seed be named,' ¹⁹having reckoned that even from (the) dead God (is) able to raise up. Hence he did get him back, parabolically.

²⁰"By faith also Isaac gave a blessing concerning the future to Jacob and Esau.

²¹"By faith Jacob, when dying, blessed each of the sons of Joseph, and bowed in worship over the head of his staff.

²²"By faith Joseph, at (his) end, thought about the exodus of the sons of Israel and gave instructions concerning his bones.

²³"By faith Moses, after birth, was hidden for three months by his parents, because they saw the child was beautiful, and did not fear the decree of the king.

²⁴"By faith Moses, when grown up, refused to be called the son of Pharaoh's daughter, ²⁵choosing rather ill-treatment with the people of God than to enjoy the fleeting pleasures of sin, ²⁶accounting the reproach of Christ greater riches than the treasures of Egypt, for he looked forward to the reward.

²⁷"By faith he left Egypt behind, not fearing the anger of the king; like one seeing the invisible one, he endured.

²⁸"By faith he kept the Passover and the sprinkling of blood, in order that the Destroyer might not touch their first-born.

²⁹"By faith they crossed the Red Sea like dry land, while the Egyptians, attempting the same, were drowned.

³⁰"By faith the walls of Jericho fell down, having been circled about for seven days.

³¹"By faith Rahab the harlot did not perish with the unfaithful, having received the spies in peace."

In this last major section of the Lycus Valley catechism cited by the author we shall attempt to discern the implications of the interpretative brackets in 11:1-2, 10, 13-16, and 39-40, discovering, if possible, the relationship of these examples to the Lycus Valley situation and to the argument of the author. In the offering of **Isaac** in verses 17 to 19, the "witness" motif appears in the references to the **promises**, the citing of the oracle—**in Isaac shall your seed be named**—and particularly in his **parabolic** release from death to life. This release is related in the catechism to the doctrine of the resurrection in which Abraham is pictured as setting his reckoning. In gaining back Isaac from death, as it were, Abraham received a "witness" of the faith he had in the resurrection. There is an emphasis on the present reward of faith that fits in well with 10:32–39, and the possible misunderstanding of this example in the sense of assuming that resurrection is more than **parabolic** in the present is adequately countered by the insistence in 11:13 and 39 that fulfillment does not eliminate finitude.

In verses 20 to 22 the effect of faith on the future is described, with Isaac and Jacob giving a **blessing** to their sons, and Joseph making provision for the **exodus** generations before it occurred. The typical biblical idea of the **blessing** is in view here, whereby the power of prosperity and happiness can be bestowed by great persons, producing a state of well-being and fullness in the minds and fortunes of the recipients. This is an extension of the idea in 10:39, that **faith** "preserves life" in the present eschatological crisis, for it reaches creatively into the future. It bespeaks that pilgrim yearning for the future of the city and the earth in which they are aliens, an effective concern that the dialogical promise of the "city which is to come" might enrich the future.

According to Otto Michel, verses 23 to 31 comprise a tightly knit unit concerned with Moses and the movement from Egypt to the promised land. The motif of civil disobedience is at the forefront of this section, with the pilgrim people **in faith** courageously opposing the political power of a would-be "lasting city." **By faith** Moses' parents **did not fear the decree of the king,** hiding their child in the bulrushes. This lack of **fear,** derived from a **faith** in the unseen God, led them to respond to the fundamental experience of parents—**they saw the child was beautiful**—rather than to the fearsome decree of a dictatorial government. A powerful re-ordering of priorities derives from such **faith,** because once the **fear** of a majestic and all-powerful government is dispelled, the pilgrim gains a clear sense of what must be done and an effective will to accomplish it. This theme is carried out in verses 24 and 25, with **Moses** identifying with his own people rather than with **Pharaoh's daughter, choosing rather ill-treatment with the people of God than to enjoy the fleeting pleasures of sin.** Identifying with the exploited and refusing to collaborate with the corrupt power-holders are logical results of pilgrim **faith.** They derive from the re-ordered scale of priorities intrinsic to pilgrimage, drawn as it is by the vision of the "city which is to come" that stands in judgment of the oppression in **Egypt.** The antithesis between **the reproach of Christ** and the **treasures of Egypt** places this question of priorities in a particularly poignant form: on the one hand are the magnificent material, artistic, and spiritual heritages of a great empire, compelling but inhuman, and on the other hand is the **reproach** the messiah would assume in sharing the plight of the oppressed. That **Moses** here would be pictured as participating proleptically in the Christ event is a rather typical motif in the Pauline church (cf. Colossians 1:24; 1 Corinthians 10:1-4), probably based on the idea of the preexistence of Christ (Hebrews 1:2-3).

Once this order of priorities impresses itself upon the person of **faith,** the path of civil disobedience stands as an open possibility. It was a path that **Moses** did not hesitate to take. **By faith he left Egypt behind, not fearing the anger of the king.** Again, it is the **fear**less quality of **faith** that is the premise of the action he takes. The pilgrim is so drawn by the image of the "city which is to come" that he lacks the disabling awe of the seemingly omnipotent government that marks most oppressed peoples. His sense of the **invisible** king of righteousness dispels the illusion that the **Pharaoh** is either just or, as he claimed, divine. On this basis the pilgrim can, when necessary, make plans to set his people free. Despite the disparity in strength and power, it was not the **Pharaoh** but Moses who **endured.** He was able to persevere against the worst the government could do, which is not to say that he escaped the generalization of verses 13 and 39: "These all died in faith, not having cashed in on the promises." To **endure** is not to become immortal or infallible, but rather to be borne from fear to effectiveness by a pilgrim calling.

Moses not only determined to **leave Egypt behind,** but returned to lead his people past the power of the Destroyer through the **Red Sea.** The pilgrim who takes Hebrews seriously will not delude himself or herself that the sea will always become **like dry land,** that the **Egyptians attempting the same** will always be **drowned,** or that the **walls of Jericho** will collapse after merely being **circled about for seven days.** Yet Moses provides a magnificent example in times of oppression. Even the prostitute **Rahab** participated in this process, sheltering the **spies** of the Israelite vanguard from the police of her own city: so this sort of pilgrim **faith** is not a matter of protesting merely for the sake of abstract principles, but of acting in behalf of the concrete advancement of the oppressed. It lacks the crystalline rigidity of the ideologue who opposes authority simply because it is authority, or who willingly sacrifices people in a hopeless cause to satisfy his or her zeal. It partakes of that pragmatic effectiveness of the pilgrim whose illusions are overcome, whose idolatrous attachments have been displaced, and whose goals are the possible augmenting of human freedom and the advancement of justice in the direction of the "city which is to come."

One recalls in this connection the remarkable interaction between pilgrimage and civil disobedience marking our history. One thinks of John Bunyan writing in prison, of Roger Williams departing because of his dissent from the practices of the commonwealth, of Henry David Thoreau refusing to pay taxes to an unjust state, of the often anonymous Quaker dissenters in the South and border states protesting against the institution of slavery, of Martin Luther King, Jr. in the Birmingham Jail, and of the Berrigan brothers in solitary confinement for their actions against an oppressive draft system. The list of pilgrim heroes and heroines could go on at length and encompass people of every nation, like Johannes Schneider and Dietrich Bonhoeffer in the Nazi prisons, Chief Albert Luthuli under the ban in South Africa, and Mahatma Gandhi suffering in prison for the independence of his people. These persons are as finite as any others and at times are beset with the most distressing human failures. But they are people of faith who were driven by circumstance not only to be pilgrims, but to follow this path to its extremity of disobedience to the kings of would-be "lasting cities." It is to such a company of heroic figures that the author turns in his magnificent conclusion of chapter 11.

11:32 **And what more shall I say? For time will fail to tell about Gideon, Barak, Samson, Jephthah, of David and Samuel and the prophets—**[33]**who through faith conquered kingdoms, worked for righeousness, received promises,** [34]**shut (the) mouths of lions, quenched (the) power of fire, escaped the mouths of (the) sword, from weakness made strong, in war made mighty, put foreign armies to flight.** [35a]**Women received their dead by resurrection.**
[35b]**But others were tortured, not accepting the release, that they might obtain a better resurrection.** [36]**But others suffered mocking and scourging, but in addition chains and prison.** [37]**They were stoned, they were burned, they were sawn in two, they died by slaughter of sword. They went about in sheepskins and goatskins, destitute, afflicted, ill-treated—**[38]**of whom the world is not worthy—wandering over deserts and mountains and caves and gullies of the earth.**
[39]**And these all having been witnessed to through the faith did not cash in on the promise,** [40]**God having forseen something better for us, that apart from us they should not be perfected.**

With a characteristic change of style, the author moves from the citation of the Lycus Valley catechism into his rhetorical conclusion. First, he provides a catalog of victors, but then in the final, emphatic position he moves on to the catalog of martyrs, concluding the section with the two-verse bracket in 39 and 40. The antithetical **but** in 35b indicates clearly the demarcation between these two catalogs, with the list of martyrs providing a certain corrective to the image of pilgrimage as an all-conquering procession.

The victor catalog in verses 32 to 35a, with its series of

military conquerors and heroes, is unparalleled in the New Testament, which in general tends to downplay the zeal for holy warfare. Yet it fits, with qualifications, into the author's emphasis that **faith** not only provides a witness to the validity of the promises, but also gives the pilgrim community power to endure. When circumstances demand it, such **faith** provides the cool effectiveness that is essential to **conquering kingdoms** and **working** for **righteousness**. Quite obviously, the concept of Christian existence as pilgrimage included the possibility of breaking with the pacifist tendencies of the early church. There is a vital link here with the holy war tradition in the Old Testament whose vitality reached down to the Zealot and the Essene movements of the first century. The vision of the righteous "city which is to come" can lead the adherent of this tradition into violent opposition to the evil of the present age. Even against heavy odds, this ideology can provide the motivation for action, as indicated by the disastrous Zealot-Roman War, from A.D. 66–70.

The participants in holy warfare do not act entirely on the basis of pragmatic considerations: typically, they take account of the **promises** they feel their movement has received, hoping for the miraculous intervention that can **shut (the) mouths of lions, quench (the) power of fire,** and protect them from **the mouths of (the) sword.** In this configuration, **faith** can provide a powerful motivation to stand against the forces of evil. The tales of the warriors in the Old Testament and in the intertestamental literature provide considerable substantiation of this. The deep feeling of moral conviction, the certainty of ultimate victory, and the willingness to abandon one's life for the sake of righteousness are inherent in such a **faith.** Consequently, it does have the power to transform a **weak** person into one who is **strong,** to make one **mighty in war,** and even at times to succeed in putting **foreign armies to flight.** The history of the Jewish people and of Christianity give some indication of the martial effectiveness of such a **faith.** But history also indicates the suicidal lack of political realism, the tendency to stereotype the enemy, the barbaric propensity to use any

211

means to accomplish the end, and the destructively alienating capacity of such **faith**. It is for this reason that one is impressed by the context in which the author has placed this catalog of victors. It follows the proviso in verse 13—"These all died in faith"—and it is countered by the subsequent inclusion of the martyr catalog that indicates clearly that one had better not expect miraculous interventions if one is to take up the sword of holy warfare. This realism is an essential part of the world view of those called into pilgrimage by the great high priest, for he did not overcome alienation, after all, by means of holy warfare against the enemies of righteousness. The result is that although the pilgrim community may occasionally be forced by circumstances to take up the warfare of faith, it must not delude itself about the probable consequences, and it must not assume that the human race can thereby be redeemed. It remains as a last resort in which a person of **faith** may be effective not because she or he expects divine intervention, but rather because she or he realistically counts the odds and still acts without **fear** (11:23, 27).

The catalog receiving the emphasis of the author by being placed in the last position in the chapter is the one containing the martyrs. The tradition of the Maccabean era is particularly in view here, with the seven brothers and their mother of 2 Maccabees 7 being **tortured** on the wheel, refusing to **accept release** at the price of denying their faith, for the sake of the eschatological **resurrection**. The experience of **mocking and scourging . . . chains and prison** typified the martyrdom of **faith** from the time of Jeremiah through the Maccabean period down to the early church. It was said that Zechariah and Jeremiah were finally **stoned;** some of the Maccabean martyrs were **burned;** Isaiah was supposed to have suffered the death of being **sawn in two;** and the traditional fate of the prophets from the time of Elijah to John the Baptist was the **slaughter of sword.** Even when they were not being murdered, these typical people of **faith** led a pilgrim existence in every sense of the word. They resorted to the makeshift clothing of the desert wanderer like Elijah, wearing **sheepskins and goatskins.** Like the apostle Paul, they knew what it meant to be **destitute** (cf. Philippians 4:12); and like most of the early Christian missionaries, they were **afflicted** and **ill-treated.** These great persons, **of whom the world is not worthy,** knew from bitter personal experience that pilgrimage is a risky and uncomfortable business: **wandering over deserts and mountains and caves and gullies of the earth.**

This then is the realistic climax of **faith.** It is not simply a matter of triumph or success; it is not quite an "endless line of splendor"; and those called to it must not expect that **faith** will provide much more than "an assurance of things hoped for" and "a proving of things not seen." But this is enough. For in doing this the **faith** relationship in which the pilgrim stands provides a noble courage and pragmatic adaptiveness in face of circumstances that drive lesser persons to self-defeating compromises and despair. This is why the catalog of martyrs, with all its dreadful detail, provides so exhilarating a climax to the chapter on **faith.** It grips the hearer because it takes the tragic dimension of human existence with complete seriousness, and yet reveals a resistance to evil and a sense of calling that are so dynamic and firm they accomplish more for the human race than all the military victories of history. It reveals to the bewildered Christians of the Lycus Valley, who were so shocked at the continued presence of persecution and trouble in the new age that they tried to devise a cultic means to manipulate the forces of evil, that the course of **faith** leads straight into this tragic dilemma. It is not a shelter from the storm. It leads instead directly into the eye of the storm. But it leads with power and without alienation.

Verses 39 and 40 are the final interpretative bracket by which the author indicates how the catalogs of victors and of martyrs, as well as the traditions about the forebears are to be understood. Each of them, no matter how miraculous the escape or exploit, participated in the pilgrim structure of moving from **witness** to **witness** but never achieving the fulfillment in any final sense: **these all having been witnessed to through the faith did not cash in on the promise.** Here the author insists once again that **faith** is not a formula for success, but rather an enlivening relationship. It is a matter of living with God's word, which utters its **witness** not only through the "word of exhortation," but also in the spirit-inaugurated experience of **faith** itself. The result is that until the eschaton no person of **faith** can claim to have **cashed in on the promise.** This expression, which was used in 10:36; 11:13, and 19, depicts a final possession that eliminates the yearning for the future. In the author's opinion such fulfillment will not take place until the eschaton. Neither the triumph of the holy warrior, nor the ecstasy of the martyr; neither the insight of the Gnostic, nor the vision of the mystic; neither the sweep of technological progress, nor the defeat of one's most recent enemies will eliminate the finitude that keeps **faith** a matter of pilgrimage. Thus the fulfillment of history in the eschaton, that **something better for us** which God envisioned, will include all pilgrims of every period and nation. The idea that **apart from us they should not be perfected** seems to point to the interconnected, cumulative weight of human history, in which the rich experience of the past seems to drive history on toward the future, and in which the fulfillment toward which the very cosmos strains is that omega point—in Pierre Teilhard de Chardin's term—of Christ who stands at the end of time. The pilgrims in the Lycus Valley are not alone, therefore, as they face their trials and uncertainties. They stand with the great pilgrims of the past and the future, sharing the enlivening **witness** and participating in the righteous momentum driving history toward its fulfillment in the "city which is to come."

Chapter Twelve

Pilgrim Discipline (12:1–17) and Worship (12:18–29) in the Secular World

12:1 THEREFORE, since we are surrounded by so great a cloud of witnesses, laying aside every weight and the easily ensnaring sin, let us run the race which lies before us with patient endurance, ²looking attentively to Jesus the leader and perfecter of faith, who for the joy set before him endured the cross, despising the shame, and has taken his ruling seat at the right hand of the throne of God. ³Consider him who patiently endured such hostility from sinners against himself, so that you not grow weary (and) faint-hearted. ⁴You have not yet resisted to the point of blood(shed), struggling against sin, ⁵and have you forgotten the exhortation which dialogues with you as sons?

"My son, do not think lightly of the Lord's discipline,
    nor lose courage when punished by him.
⁶For the Lord disciplines whom he loves,
    and chastises every son whom he receives."
⁷For the sake of discipline you must patiently endure. God is treating you as sons. For what son is there whom the father does not discipline? ⁸If you escape discipline, in which all have participated, you are bastards and not sons. ⁹Besides this, we have had fleshly fathers disciplining (us) and we respected (them). Shall we not subject ourselves much more readily to the Father of spirits and live? ¹⁰For they disciplined us for a short time according to their lights, but he does so for (our) profit that we might receive our share of his holiness. ¹¹Now all

discipline does not appear at the time to be joyful but rather sorrowful, but afterward it pays back the peaceful fruit of righteousness to those trained by it.

Some form of discipline is required to raise pilgrimage above the level of mere nomadism. The author envisions both individual and communal effort in coping with the threats of existence in a hostile world. It is rather similar to what Peter Marin describes as "the long march" away from the "demons of the age" toward a more viable future: "The most difficult task of all is to steer between exhaustion and illusion, between resignation and escape into dogma." Hebrews undertakes this task by placing pilgrimage within a meaningful framework of historical significance and movement. The community is **surrounded by so great a cloud of witnesses,** described in the preceding chapter. They are the victors and martyrs mentioned in the preceding chapter who fulfilled their callings despite all obstacles. The community is drawn forward by **Jesus the leader,** who strides ahead of them in the race. History both past and future is viewed here as entering into intensive relation with the pilgrim community: the past **witnesses** to the present. So intensive is the historical interaction that Alexander C. Purdey concludes "the throng of witnesses . . . are not mere spectators, but, in a sense, fellow participants (11:40)."

What Hebrews presents in this image is quite different from historical determinism, in which the past so dominates the present that human initiative is eroded. It is also in contrast with a characteristic American belief that the present moment is absolutely new and superior to any past. History both past and present is viewed instead as the arena of human initiative, where the decision to **run the race** in a particular manner makes all the difference. Present troubles and challenges are not completely unlike those of past generations, yet their answers cannot be our answers. Each pilgrim generation must take the path that lies at hand, and the courage to act comes in part from the sense of participating in a rich but tragic tradition, of hearing the **witness** of those who faced unique challenges and kept the faith.

Encouraged and sustained by the great pilgrims of the past, the Lycus Valley Christians are exhorted to **lay aside every weight and the easily ensnaring sin,** much as a runner must shed all excess poundage for the race. It is a magnificent image for traveling light, avoiding the encumbrances of possessions, prestige, and comfort. John Bunyan takes up this image with Christian's "burden" of self-righteousness that is finally cast down at the foot of the cross. This stands rather close to the probable meaning of verse 1b, for the **easily ensnaring sin** in the Lycus Valley was the pious cult that promised to render the devotee safe from the threats of the cosmic forces (cf. 3:13; 6:1-8; 10:1-31). The appeal of such **sin** was in the nostalgic yearning to be rid of pilgrimage itself, to arrive at some safe refuge by cultic means. But as antithetical as **sin** and **weight** are to pilgrim existence, the wording of the sentence implies that they are simply to be laid **aside.** The grim, introspective battle required by asceticism is not in view here, for that isolates the self by riveting attention on the dubious condition of the heart. Pilgrims must direct their attention outward, toward the path **which lies before** them, conscious of the cheering of the **cloud of witnesses** and of **Jesus the leader** before them on the track. This enables the pilgrims simply to drop the "burden" and go on, to shed one **weight** after another because the grace of Jesus Christ has made it superfluous.

The translation **looking attentively** emphasizes the Christocentric orientation of pilgrimage, which achieves its fulfillment by relating to the **leader** along the way. The call for concentration was particularly required because of the temptation in the Lycus Valley to be distracted by the problem of the cosmic powers. Jesus is the **perfecter of faith,** because he experienced the same dilemmas of cosmic insecurity that the community now faces. The life of **faith,** the author insists, is life under the **cross.** It would involve **shame and hostility** for the Lycus Valley Christians just as it did for Jesus himself. But it also involves the creative tension between current circumstances and the **joy set before him,** that is, the celebration in the heavenly Jerusalem portrayed in 12:22–24. Such tension between current ill-treatment and "the city which is to come" is constitutive for the life of **faith,** as chapter 11 showed. In this instance the **joy** is not a future reward for good behavior, but rather the ecstatic moment of genuine dialogue that gives pilgrims the power to **patiently endure.** The entire perspective is dynamic rather than moralistic; faith is the movement along the path Jesus struck through the secular world; and as Hugh Montefiore noted, the perfect tense **has taken his ruling seat** stresses "that while Jesus' death was a single past event, his heavenly session is a present reality." The **leader** still retains the dynamic role stated in the opening verses of the epistle, ruling the world "by his powerful word" (1:3). The relation with him is what raises the role of Jesus as a pilgrim **leader** above that of mere example, and raises pilgrim discipline above that of moralistic achievement.

The content of the **exhortation which dialogues with you as sons** is derived from Proverbs. The citation had an acute relevance, because the Lycus Valley Christians viewed their threatening circumstances as proof that the cosmic powers were able to separate them from God. But if **the lord disciplines whom he loves, and chastises every son whom he receives,** their suffering would not produce the element of alienation. In every negative experience **God is treating you as sons.** The relational aspect of suffering is argued in detail with the analogy between **fleshly fathers** and **the Father of spirits.** To refuse **discipline** is to break relationship, to become **bastards and not sons.** Even the reward of discipline is relational in verse 10, **that we might receive our share of his holiness.** Both **holiness** and the **righteousness** in verse 11 are relational terms, connected with standing in openness and frankness before God. To accept this relation as **sons** means to view adversity with the secure vision of children who are certain of the love of their unseen **father.**

12:12 Therefore lift up the drooping hands and the palsied knees, [13]and make straight paths for your feet, that what is lame may not be dislocated but rather healed. [14]Seek after peace with all persons and for the sanctification without which no one shall see the Lord, [15]taking care that no one fail to keep up with the grace of God, that "no root of bitterness spring up and cause trouble" and thereby the many become defiled; [16]that no one be immoral or profane like Esau who for a single meal sold his birthright. [17]For you know that afterward, when he desired to inherit the blessing, he was rejected; for he found no chance to repent, though he sought it with tears.

With strenuous motifs about pilgrimage from Isaiah and Proverbs the author exhorts his congregation to communal responsibility. Passivity in face of daily threats is the great danger countered here. For the Lycus Valley Christians were attempting to deal with **drooping hands,** hindrances on the **paths,** and **lame** joints by removing external impediments to safe journeying to the spiritual homeland. By eliminating the cosmic barriers, they hoped to move with ease toward their goal. This essentially slothful approach of eliminating adversity once and for all is countered by images of struggling through. Rather than eliminating the problem of **drooping hands,** the author calls the community to **lift** them up again. Quick and total solutions are to be avoided, so **that what is lame may not be dislocated but rather healed.** The Christian community did not possess magic formulas for solving problems; it was called instead to a life of mutual encouragement that some would call "muddling through." There is an interplay between individual and social engagement in this passage, a sense that the members of the community are running the race together and must see to one another's **lame** limbs.

This exhortation seems particularly cogent for the current state of the American mind. Our dominant religious traditions have tended to erode our willingness to muddle through in face of insoluble problems. By encouraging the expectation that problems will disappear for those who become Christian, and by presenting Christ as a superheroic problem-solver rather than a pilgrim forerunner, the capacity to face adversity is diminished. The millenarian aspects of the civil religion and of popular entertainment tend to lead us in the same direction, expecting that crusades will make the world safe for democracy and that adversity will somehow be eliminated by the destruction of some enemy. We need to recover the sort of Christian realism lying at the root of some of our most cherished institutions. For democracy, as Reinhold Niebuhr loved to recall, is a system of finding proximate solutions to finally insoluble problems of human conflict. To face such problems with courage, knowing full well that they are insoluble, is the highest form of responsibility. It is similar to the kind of pilgrim discipline to which the author of Hebrews called his community.

If pilgrim discipline eschews total solutions, what are the aims that keep it from merely acquiescing in the status quo? The author takes this up in verse 14: **seek after peace with all persons and for the sanctification without which no one shall see the Lord. Peace** and **sanctification** are gifts from God that, as the preceding verses 10 and 11 indicate, are the fruits of the pilgrim discipline. The harmonious sense of health and well-being that comes to the person who accepts adversity as divine discipline is to be sought not just with other members of the church, but **with all persons.** The inclusiveness of this ethic is closely related to a theme that Barbara Ward insists is crucial for developing social and economic guidelines for "planet earth." It is the vision of messianic peace as "an end to social inequalities and injustice and the recovery of primal brotherliness and goodwill." When combined with the idea of "history as the unfolding of a divine purpose, as the progressive revelation of God's will for men which will be realized in the measure of man's free response," these two uniquely Western ideas that are gaining global acceptance can transform "the human experiment" into "a common planetary exercise in dynamic and directed change."

The translation of verse 15a, **taking care that no one fail to keep up with the grace of God,** is clearly demanded by the present participle *husterein.* Yet the theological habit of separating **grace** from its giver, abstracting it from personal relationships by dogmatic guidelines, may obscure the fact that Hebrews envisions the Lord as moving out in front of his pilgrim people, offering himself to them afresh day by day. The danger is not to **keep up,** to substitute yesterday's experience and truth for today's new needs. When adversities and new discoveries undermine the dogmas of the past, the task of pilgrims is to assist one another to receive the love of God anew. The congruence of this thought with 12:5-7 is obvious: it is not a matter of updating God for the current situation, but of hurrying to keep up with **the Lord** who strides through history as the "leader and perfecter of faith," leaving in the wake the shards of yesterday's idols.

The warnings about the **root of bitterness** and **Esau's** sellout probably both relate to the Lycus Valley controversy. The first is cited from Deuteronomy 29:18, in reference to the idolatry of Canaan that threatened corruption for the entire community. The context in Deuteronomy refers to "detestable" behavior that was accepted complacently by the majority. The reference in Hebrews to being **defiled** indicates that the point of comparison was with cultic practices, a crucial area of dispute in the congregation. **Esau's** selling of **his birthright** to his brother in exchange for momentary comfort paralleled the Lycus Valley preference for security gained through manipulation of cosmic forces to the discipline of holding fast to a relationship threatened by adversity. The prospects for anyone believing in this manipulative strategy are just as bleak as they were for **Esau.** To assume that adversity can be controlled by any form of cultic manipulation, whether ancient or modern, is fatal. **Esau** provides a suitable image for what Peter Marin has discerned in current religious consciousness. "We use our spirituality in much the same way we use our technology, as a defense against life. It is no accident that we are drawn to both, for they offer us the same gifts: an end not only to pain, age, and death but also to the complexities of 'personhood.'" The choice is between such an escape into security and comfort, and the pilgrim movement toward the promised birthright and blessing. The author of Hebrews is realistic enough to know that neither his congregation nor Esau could have it both ways.

12:18 For you have not approached what may be touched, a blazing fire and darkness, and gloom, and storm, ¹⁹and the sound of a trumpet and a voice whose words made the hearers entreat that no further word be spoken to them. ²⁰For they could not bear the command that was given, "If even a beast touches the mountain, it shall be stoned." ²¹Indeed, so terrifying was the sight that Moses said, "I am terrified and trembling." ²²But you have approached Mount Zion and the city of the living God, heavenly Jerusalem, to a myriad of angels in the panegyric assembly, ²³and to the church of the first-born enrolled in the heavens, and to the God who is judge of all, and to the spirits of the just persons made perfect, ²⁴and to Jesus the mediator of a new covenant, and to the sprinkled blood that speaks better than the blood of Abel.

The alternative the congregation faces is deepened and rendered more experiential by the stunning contrast the author develops between two mutually exclusive modes of worship. The first is Sinai, which the author assures them has not been what they **have approached**—a technical term for nearing a sanctuary. Selecting certain motifs from the Old Testament accounts of the revelation on Sinai, the author develops a dreadfully negative picture of thwarted dialogue. Friedrich Schröger's analysis of this section reveals the author's effort to eliminate the positive elements of theophany from Sinai, emphasizing the command not to touch the mountain, a motif of secondary importance in Exodus 19. The crucial point for the author is that the experience was so terrible as to make the **hearers entreat that no further word be spoken to them.** The terror of Sinai impeded dialogue.

The criticism of the Sinai type of religion had a direct

relevance for the Lycus Valley congregation, if my reconstruction is sound. They had been interpreting adversity in a
fashion reminiscent of Sinai, assuming its terrors cut them off
from God. They assumed that the way of the soul to its
heavenly homeland was barred by the cosmic powers, similar
to the threats of **fire and darkness, and gloom, and storm.** The
author insists that this assumption was wrong. And by implication, their reverting now to a form of Sinaitic religion like
the Lycus Valley cult would produce the same result. The
polemic is parallel to that in 9:8, that this sort of cult bars
access to God. The appeal to the experience of the Lycus Valley
Christians thus aims at using terror for the sake of comfort;
they had not experienced this kind of terror in their initial
Christian experience and should not now interpret their adversity in such a way.

What they had experienced, at the very moment of difficulty, was dialogue with **heavenly Jerusalem** itself. Here is the
ecstatic climax of the Epistle to the Hebrews. The perfect tense
of the verb **you have approached** makes this one of the most
dramatic and radical statements of realized eschatology in the
New Testament. The access to heaven that the Lycus Valley
cult had sought to attain is pictured here as a reality they had
been experiencing all along. The reference to the **sprinkled
blood** of Jesus **that speaks** to the pilgrim community connects
this theme to the word event as defined in chapters 3 and 4.
God's word encounters the wanderers on their path through
adversity, bringing them before the divine presence, and
opening to them the magnificent celebration. In contrast to
traditional views of pilgrimage, the fulfillment is not postponed
to the end of life. Interpretations of this sort, still argued by
scholars like Spicq, cannot do justice to the perfect tense of the
verb by suggesting Hebrews has in mind a progressive arrival
that will not be finally realized until death. And to suggest as
Hugh Montefiore does, that the author's "readers have not yet
actually arrived at Mount Zion: they have drawn close" is to
miss the technical significance of the verb **approach** as cultic
encounter with God. This passage conveys an unmistakable

transposition of the heavenly city from the "up there" and "over there" to the "here and now" of secular pilgrimage. There is also an unmistakable reference to the adversity theme in the detail about the crying out of the blood of the martyrs in verse 24b. As numerous parallels in ancient Jewish writings make plain, such blood called for vengeance, evoking the terror of Sinai. In contrast, the Lycus Valley Christians are to hear the **sprinkled blood** of **Jesus the mediator of a new covenant that speaks better than the blood of Abel** in the sense that it offers unconditional access for sinners rather than reprisals for their sins.

The dialogical definition of heaven is corroborated by the listing of persons and creatures who participate in the encounter between the pilgrims and God's word. The author pictures a richly peopled **city of the living God,** including the **myriad of angels,** the **first-born** cosmic beings who preceded humankind in Jewish and gnostic speculation, the **just persons made perfect,** as well as **God** and **Jesus** themselves. It is a city whose wealth is the uniqueness of its inhabitants, not the splendor of its streets and buildings. Each person and creature plays a role in the celebrating and speaking, and those who encounter such an assembly could never imagine that they were being absorbed into some impersonal realm of light as in gnostic systems both ancient and modern, indeed included in this vast and varied assembly as the "witnesses" of 12:1 who spur on the pilgrims in the unique paths they follow. The life of pilgrimage takes on its significance from the relation in which it stands to the **panegyric assembly.**

The climax of pilgrimage, according to this passage, is not release from thirst, pain, and insecurity, as in the traditional materials like the Revelation of John. Participation in the **panegyric** celebration is a matter of being caught up in the present by the glory of **the living God.** The transcendence glimpsed and celebrated here is not that of human programming, managing, or moralizing, but rather of divine love. By placing human aspirations in their rightful place of penultimate significance, and by worshiping that which overcomes the fragmentation of life, a valid sense of community emerges. This is what Martin Buber learned from the Jewish mystics, the Hasidim, according to Aubrey Hodes, that "common veneration and common joy are the foundations of real human communion." Victor Turner suggests that a sense of "communitas," of joyful celebration, is essential to pilgrimage: "Pilgrimage devotion, the market, and the fair are all connected . . . with a measure of joyful, 'ludic' communitas. . . . This extends even to the religious activities proper, for comradeship is a feature of pilgrimage travel . . . play and solemnity are equally present." In the last analysis a pilgrim faith must be enlivened by such joyful celebration lest it sink into despair by the very weight of its realism, its serious preoccupation with the condition of the self in a threatening world. This kind of celebration does not eliminate finite threats or release pilgrims from their responsibilities to the world through which they move. Like the word addressing the faithful every time it is called "today" (3:13ff.), the celebration intensifies life in the present moment by celebrating that toward which one moves, the city which is to come.

12:25 **See that you do not refuse him who is speaking. For if they did not escape who refused him addressing them upon the earth, much less shall we (escape) if we reject him (who addresses us) from heaven.** [26]**His voice shook the earth then, but now he has promised, saying, "Yet once more I will shake not only the earth but also the heaven."** [27]**Now this (phrase), "Yet once more," indicates the transformation of what is shaken, that is, the finite, in order that what cannot be shaken might remain.** [28]**Therefore let us give thanks for receiving an unshakable kingdom, and thus offer acceptable worship to God, with reverence and awe;** [29]**for our God is a consuming fire.**

The exhortation that follows the discussion of pilgrimage as celebration is to respond to **him who is speaking,** because the conditions of dialogue are inexorable. If the Sinaitic community could not **escape** the consequences of their covenant even though it was promulgated **upon the earth,** i.e., from the mountain described in 12:18-21, the pilgrim community cannot escape **if we reject him (who addresses us) from heaven.** The celebration of unconditional mercy that centers on the "sprinkled blood" of Jesus serves to heighten the obligations of dialogue. This counters the tendency to understand the gospel of unconditional love as an indication that anything goes, that relationships can be treated with contempt and not be lost: in short, that there are no limits. For Hebrews there is one tremendous limit that remains after all else is shaken and relativized—God, whose **voice shook the earth** and who remains **a consuming fire.** The Transcendent One cannot be toyed with or brought under control even by the most well-intentioned liturgy. For God is the one whose **voice** continues to **shake not only the earth but also the heaven.** By using this citation from Haggai, the author harks back to a theme stated in 1:10-12, that *God* is the author of the flux that makes pilgrimage a mortal necessity. Here it is specifically God's word from Mount Zion that brings on the apocalyptic shaking of the creation, as Otto Michel points out. It is a breathtaking idea, that the dialogue God initiated with humankind in the Christ event shakes and transforms history. The revolutionary process strikes at the entire finite realm, as verse 27 makes plain: **Now this (phrase), "Yet once more," indicates the transformation of what is shaken, that is, the finite, in order that what cannot be shaken might remain.**

To take this conception seriously would mean a revision of typical attitudes toward contemporary history. It would impel the faithful community to examine its experience for signs that the revolutionary message of Christ is shaking up the status quo. Could it be that the message of suffering love provides the ferment that erodes the stability of exploitative systems and regimes? Could the truth about the human condition revealed in the "sprinkled blood" be destroying the facades of virtue and good intentions that disguise the behavior of evil establishments? Could the glory of the truth being celebrated on Mount Zion be exercising its attraction when the Watergates of modern politics come under such relentless scrutiny? Could it be that the ideal of full participation of even the lowliest pilgrim in the cosmic celebration is capable of shaking the dispossessed out of their lethargy and of sensitizing the world to the issues of discrimination and the exploitation of the poor? Is Christ among the subversive forces that military organizations strive so vainly to thwart? If it is God's **voice** that really **shakes the finite** realm, there is no escaping or averting it, and the task of the Christian community becomes one of sharing constructively in the revolutionary process. If this is what ultimately undermines the complacency of the would-be lasting cities, then the pilgrims ought to cease their fretting and **give thanks for receiving an unshakable kingdom.**

The affirmative stance of praising God in the midst of the flux is thus the logical outcome of Hebrews' radical vision. It is important to observe, however, that the pilgrim community is called upon to **give thanks** not for the flux itself or the reactions it provokes, but rather for the **kingdom.** Given the dialogical thrust of Hebrews, there is no choice but to define this in terms of the relationship with God offered day by day in the center of the storm. The **kingdom** is the "city of the living God, heavenly Jerusalem" that the pilgrims have "approached." To give thanks for this relationship is **acceptable worship.** Pilgrimage and **worship** are thus combined; the path through the secular world is the path to God's throne; the sacred pierces the secular by means of the divine word that shakes and transforms the cosmos. Thus the climactic feature of pilgrim existence is the ludic celebration that takes place while the world tumbles in ruins. The thanksgiving does not imply that the pilgrims are untouched by the ruin. Everything **finite** must be transformed, and this is the point of the "discipline" of adversity the pilgrim community is presently experiencing. Ultimately, the pilgrims give thanks because the mercy of God shown forth in the Christ event sustains and enlivens them even when the **earth** is **shak**ing beneath them.

True dialogue with God includes both **reverence and awe.** The suffering love of the great high priest, celebrated so magnificently by the "panegyric assembly," evokes the deepest veneration. The human grasp of that holiness is necessarily so partial, and the power of that creative shaking of the universe is so immense that pilgrims cannot avoid being struck dumb with wonder. The experience of "liminality," to use Turner's term, is the goal and meaning of pilgrimage, and the greatest artistic symbols and the most adequate philosophical definitions fail to measure up to its demands. To encounter a **consuming fire** is to be constantly purged and refined. It is an entirely different matter from believing in a cosmic comforter whose love is predictably soft and who leaves devotees comfortably attached to yesterday's dogmas. With this awesome God who burns and shakes the world, while loving it, the only possible relationship is that of worshipful pilgrims. They are enabled by grace and calling to speak of the Transcendent One as **our God,** to hear and respond to the Living Word, and to **give thanks** while being purified by **fire.**

Chapter Thirteen

A Pilgrim Ethic in the Secular World (13:1-21)

13:1 **L**ET brotherly-love continue. ²Forget not stranger-love, for thereby some have entertained angels unawares. ³Remember those in prison, as though fellow prisoners; and those who are ill-treated, since you also are in the body. ⁴Let marriage be held in honor in all circumstances, and the marriage bed be undefiled; for God will judge the immoral and adulterous. ⁵Keep your life-style free from love of money, and be content with what you have, for he has said, "I will never fail you nor forsake you." ⁶Hence we can confidently say, "The Lord is my helper, I will not fear; what can a human do to me?" ⁷Remember your leaders, those who spoke to you the word of God. Considering the outcome of their lives, imitate the faith.

Although the earlier chapters of Hebrews were marked by the interlacing of theological argument and ethical exhortation, the ethical section proper begins here. The parallels between chapter 13 and the ethical portions of the Pauline letters have frequently been noted, giving rise to various theories about who might have appended this section to the end of Hebrews. Given the language and style of these verses, however, there is little doubt that they are an integral part of the "word of exhortation." This section draws into practical application the implications of faith as pilgrimage through the secular world. Although treated by some commentators as if it consisted merely of random ethical injunctions, chapter 13 is tightly knit and completely congruent with the earlier argument of Hebrews.

The ethic deals with various aspects of bodily relationships experienced by the pilgrim community. The conditions of being a stranger, of being **ill-treated,** of participating in sexual and economic relationships, involve in each instance elements of risk to humans as bodily creatures. The ethical motivation in this passage is therefore grounded in the reality of shared vulnerability. The pilgrim community is to care for **those in prison, as though fellow prisoners;** they are exhorted to care for the persecuted since they all live **in the body.** As pilgrims they are sensitive to their own vulnerability, having been reminded in detail in chapter 12. Just as Jesus' participation in human weakness was redemptive, so the community's daily experience comes to the benefit of others with whom it can sympathize. The ethical guidelines in this situation have to do with the direction of one's affections. The term translated here with **love** in verses 1, 2, and 5 is a form of *philein,* the affection that draws comrades together as participants in a joint undertaking. The term *agapē,* "disinterested love," is not used in Hebrews. The pilgrim guideline is what they are experiencing together as a community: both the alienation as outsiders and the celebration of their membership in the panegyric assembly are used here to give shape to their affections. This accounts for the high value of **brotherly-love** in the pilgrim community itself, with which this section opens and closes; it ensures the openness to outsiders in **stranger-love;** its holiness sustains the covenantal strictness of sexual relations; and its relational fulfillment in the face of threats mitigates against the **love of money,** which, as the argument insists, rests on anxiety.

The nuances in this ethical admonition relate closely to the Lycus Valley situation. That mutual love and support within the community should **continue** reflects the author's reminder in 6:10 that they had exhibited in the past the kind of mutual support that is now in danger of disappearing. **Brotherly-love** is the mark of those who know they cannot eliminate pilgrim risks by cultic manipulations but must instead support one another in facing them. That love for outsiders was something they might well **forget** was a real possibility for a church turning inward to perfect its cultic service for its own benefit. And there may well be a bit of irony in the reference to **entertaining angels unawares** in the manner of Abraham's encounter with the angels of Yahweh in Genesis 18. The proper way to serve the cosmic forces is not to conduct cultic ceremonies, but to welcome strangers. The secularizing thrust of Hebrews' ethic is expressed here with brilliant effect.

To honor marriage **in all circumstances** or respects may speak directly to a loosening of honor for fleshly obligations that marked gnostic movements such as that in the Lycus Valley. The unsettling **circumstances** of adversity may also have heightened the tendency to seek security through sexual liaisons. It is clear that the citations in verses 5 and 6 from the Old Testament strike at the heart of the community's anxiety in face of threatening situations. Rather than treating **money** as an evil aspect of the physical world as gnosticism might, the author seeks to free his congregation from greed by reinforcing the pilgrim faith: **"The Lord is my helper, I will not fear; what can a human do to me?"**

Finally, the curious nuances of **remember**—as if they could actually forget—**your leaders, those who spoke to you the word of God** may reflect a situation of turning away from the original preachers to new and seemingly more sophisticated teachers of esoteric lore. There is an explicit reference to such "teachings" in verse 9 of this chapter. The **outcome of their lives** would have been entirely different from what the new teachers would have promised. Epaphras, for example, was in prison at the time that Paul referred to his exemplary contribution to the congregation, in Colossians 4:12, suffering the typical fate of the great pilgrims through the ages. But their **word** is powerfully sustained by God's spirit, as 2:3-4 has recalled, and their holding fast despite troubles demonstrated what faith was all about. Hence the final admonition to **imitate the faith,** not "their" **faith** as some translations put it, but the pilgrim **faith** itself.

That each person in his or her own way must **imitate the faith** in daily life may seem at first glance all too vague and subjective. It provides no pat answers to social problems and offers no promise of bringing evil forces under control. It is resolutely nonideological. The policies one selects must be decided in pilgrim fashion, with a pragmatic eye for the social reality through which one's community is moving, a decent human sympathy derived from the realization that all humans share the same finite situation, and a vision of the "city which is to come" in whose reconciliation and communication one participates along the way. To imitate the faith is to walk toward that city and in its light to participate with the church, the stranger, the prisoner, the family, and the economic system. It is to live without final answers, to keep the channels of communication open, and to make one's decisions in the full realization that they will never produce a "lasting city" or entirely eliminate the threats that make faith necessary. To live this way is what Hebrews called, in 12:28, "acceptable worship." One does it out of praise, out of the overflowing heart, not to get something out of it or to make the world better. Such conventional motivations break down under the conditions of pilgrimage, but worship continues because it is sustained by the encounter with the heavenly Jerusalem along the way.

13:8 Jesus Christ is the same yesterday and today—also for aeons. ⁹Do not get carried away with manifold and foreign teachings; for it is good to strengthen the heart by grace, not by foods, by which the devotees gained no benefit. ¹⁰We have an altar from which those who serve the tent have no power to eat. ¹¹For the bodies of those animals whose blood is brought into the sanctuary for sin (offerings) are burned outside the camp. ¹²So also Jesus, in order to sanctify the people by his own blood, suffered outside the gate. ¹³Therefore let us go out to him outside the camp, bearing abuse for him. ¹⁴For here we have no lasting city, but we seek the coming one. ¹⁵Through him therefore let us offer up continually a sacrifice of praise to God, that is, the fruit of lips that confess his name. ¹⁶Do not neglect good works and sharing, for such sacrifices are pleasing to God.

l he second paragraph of the ethic opens with what many commentators find a disconcerting doctrinal excursus. Why make a confessional statement, such as verse 8, in the middle of an ethic? Why insert a final warning about procedures of worship? The reason, I would suggest, was intimately related to the congregation's situation. The church was in danger of shifting its form of worship from serving persons along the pilgrim path to saving itself from the necessity of pilgrimage. The shift was provoked by the feeling that current difficulties indicated Christ did not have the cosmic forces under control. Had Christ changed? Was his triumph over the principalities and powers, so powerful a motif in the Pauline churches, now rendered ineffectual? If so, the Lycus Valley cult would be justified and the ethical impulse of the church would properly be focused on the maintenance of appeasing ritual. The faith that **Jesus Christ is the same** thus had a high relevance for ethics for the original audience of this epistle. The curious word order of the Greek would also best be explained from this perspective. Rather than the three temporal designations coming in sequence, they are separated so that the last one receives unusual emphasis: literally "Jesus Christ yesterday and today is the same—also for aeons." In an environment in which **aeons** were both temporal designations and cosmic forces, this formulation eliminated any ambiguity about the continued precedence of Christ. He remains the one who disalienates life by sharing it in the deteriorating world. To follow such a pilgrim leader is to continue as a pilgrim oneself, to live out the pilgrim faith in everyday life.

There is a polemic contrast between **the same** Christ and the **manifold and foreign teachings** in the following verse. His oneness with himself through the aeons contrasts with the contradictory multiplicity of the new **teachings.** And whereas he and his pilgrims belong together, each claiming the other (cf. 2:13; 4:14-16), the new doctrine is **foreign** in the most derogatory sense of the term. The substantive difference is succinctly described in verse 9b. The crucial issue for the author, as noted throughout the epistle, is that **it is good to** strengthen the heart by grace rather than by cultic foods. To live on God's grace alone is true maturity (4:16—6:2), for it gives one the courage to face life squarely and to act responsibly. The heart needs to be strengthened for the tasks of the pilgrim ethic, but some techniques are anything but good. To depend upon foods, which in the context with devotees implies cultic meals, according to F.F. Bruce and Otto Michel, is to be nourished by illusions. A person may derive temporary encouragement from the belief that rituals will make the threats disappear, but it is immature to do so. The reality of the flux will expose the illusion, and the heart will drift toward despair. No matter what they promise, such ceremonies provide in the end no benefit. Grace dispels the alienation by relating the heart positively to its divine covenant partner who, as verse 5 has promised, "will never fail you nor forsake you" no matter how bad conditions may become.

The Christian cult in the real world is located in a series of blessed rests along the pilgrim journey. This revolutionary thesis is developed by contrasting the ministry of Jesus the high priest with that of traditional cultic religion within a sacred enclosure. The Christian altar is outside the camp, outside the sacred realm of the cultic community, for it was there that Jesus . . . suffered outside the gate. The realms of the sacred and the secular are here juxtaposed in unmistakable fashion, with Christ's sacrificial activity concentrated in the latter rather than the former. The exhortation to go out to him outside the camp, bearing abuse for him, makes the daily pilgrimage of the community through a threatening world into an approach to the great high priest. The encounter with Christ is therefore the altar from which those who serve the tent have no power to eat. They cannot participate in this communion, because Christ has departed from the realm where they expect him to be, the realm of the sacred as symbolized by the tent. His death outside the gate of Jerusalem thwarts the ancient human effort to keep God within safe boundaries, confined within a cultic sphere where human religiosity might have its effect, and barred from the rest of life where the divine presence might be obtrusive. Henceforth God can be met only in the realm so resolutely made God's own in the Christ event—where the prisoners, the wanderers, and the outcasts are. To take up one's responsibilities in this realm, **bearing abuse for him,** is the form of worship that results from the ministry of the great high priest.

The central thesis of Hebrews can now be stated, for its comprehension is made possible by everything the author has written up to this point, **for here we have no lasting city, but we seek the coming one.** It was Christ's death outside the sacred boundaries of the presumably **lasting city** that yielded the forthright realism of this statement. It pertains to the illusions, both sacred and secular, that have marked the human endeavor since the beginning of time. It confesses the emptiness of those dreams that have shaped and bloodied history, of eternal Romes, thousand-year-kingdoms, and generations of peace. It acknowledges the surrealism of the newest and most alluring plans to find lasting refuges from the flux. Each person addressed by Hebrews tends to have a private version of this **lasting city,** the comfortable nook or organizational cranny in which to weather the storm and get the most out of life. But the pilgrim knows this is not possible. There is a refreshing frankness and bluntness with which the author includes even himself in the sweeping confession: **for here we have no lasting city.**

The prophetic realism of acknowledging that the city we inhabit is not **lasting** is grounded in the pilgrim's apperception of the city that **is coming.** As Paul Tillich noted in his argument about the faith implicit in honest doubt, one can see the shortcomings of current situations and beliefs only by sensing, however dimly, the reality of a more perfect realm. It is the committed **seek**ing of the "city having foundations, whose builder and craftsman is God" (11:10) that gives the pilgrim community the power to be realistic about the place in which they dwell. In contrast to a generation of social gospel preaching, the author does not claim to be "building" the **lasting city;** the secular service he calls for on the part of his community may not succeed in bringing it any closer; for it comes from God's power and in God's good time. But the pilgrims sense its **coming** as they live in dialogue with it day by day. And in light of the **coming city**, they are not only realistic about the pretensions of their own towns, but effectively set about to share the life of the outcasts thereof. The central thesis of Hebrews thus provides the possibility of a realistic ethic. One does not postpone immediate responsibilities until some satisfactory city emerges or fall into the presumption that the fulfillment of such responsibilities will render life more secure. The pilgrim keeps moving ahead despite all obstacles, drawn by the city she or he believes is coming and sustained by dialogue with it moment for moment along the way. The eschatology of Hebrews, embodied in the expression **the coming** city, preserves both the momentum and the present-mindedness of pilgrimage.

The unity of worship and ethics resulting from the pilgrim perspective is affirmed in verses 15 and 16. The **sacrifice of praise** — an Old Testament expression for the liturgy the rabbis believed would be carried on eternally—is identified here as the daily dialogue of the pilgrim community. To **confess his name** is the technical expression for publicly acknowledging one's faith and holding to it in adverse circumstances. The location and form of such **confess**ion and **praise** differentiate them from traditional cultic forms: they are expressed on the pilgrim path **outside the camp** and they are concretized in the pilgrim ethic. This is driven home by the final verse: **Do not neglect good works and sharing, for such sacrifices are pleasing to God.** Mere praise along the way is not enough. It must be bound up with concrete service to the fellow pilgrims and outsiders that one encounters. **Sharing**—my translation for *koinonia,* or participation—is the crucial means by which dialogue with the heavenly sanctuary is kept from being merely an exercise in superiority. Rather than praising God for making one better than others, one praises God for sharing the journey through the flux and for opening it to the encounter with the panegyric

236

assembly. The ethos of pilgrimage is relational: response to God and responsibility for fellow pilgrims.

13:17 Obey your leaders and yield (to their authority); for they watch over your lives as persons who will have to give account, that they may do this with joy without complaining, which would be unprofitable for you. [18]Continue to pray for us. For we are persuaded that we have a clear conscience, desiring to act honorably toward all persons. [19]I exhort you the more earnestly to do this, in order that I may be restored to you more quickly.
    [20]Now may the God of peace,
    who led again from the dead the great shepherd of
    the sheep, by the blood of a covenant for an aeon,
    even our Lord Jesus,
    [21]equip you in every good thing to do his will,
    working in you what is pleasing before him through Jesus
    Christ; to whom be glory for aeons of aeons. Amen.

The ethic concludes with admonitions intimately related to the congregational situation. With the rise of the Lycus Valley heresy, relations with the congregational leaders and with the Pauline missionary circle had become problematic. Verse 17 deals with the former and verses 18 and 19 with the latter. It is important to interpret these verses in light of that unique situation, lest the position of Hebrews be understood in a purely authoritarian framework. While the author exhorts his congregation to obey . . . and yield to the leadership, this should not in any sense be taken as replacing the earlier stresses on the equality of each member of the congregation. Each member still participates in the mutual exhortation (3:13); each is counted among the "children" Christ brings before the throne of God (2:13); none is exempt from a daily pilgrimage through uncertainty (12:1-17). The problem was that with a rising gnostic sentiment in the congregation, a tendency emerged to oppose communal discipline on principle. Why should one who viewed oneself as a portion of divinity have to submit to the suasion of mere humans? Why should the communal effort to sustain the weak in a fallen world be supported by those committed to an easy way out of this world through esoteric ceremonies? The author appealed in this situation to two factors intrinsic to Christian leadership that differentiated it from mere authoritarianism. The leaders **watch over your lives as persons who will have to give account;** that is, they are not themselves ultimate, but must carry out their calling in obedience. Such exercise of power is humbled and limited by its accountability to God. Also, the spirit of Christian leadership must be consistent with the praise and sharing of the pilgrim ethic. If it is marked **with joy without complaining,** then the entire community will be knit together in the common venture. The alternative of the usual organizational infighting would certainly **be unprofitable** for the Gnostics themselves.

The situation calling forth the request to **continue to pray for us** is sketched in the introduction. Caught in the crossfire of interest groups charging dishonorable conduct, the Pauline circle of missionaries to which the author belongs is facing continued imprisonment and the jeopardizing of the effort to unify the branches of the early church. If my chronology is right, they were gathering to send the offering to Jerusalem at the time the troubles in Greece broke out (cf. 2 Corinthians 1:8). The accusations they faced may have included embezzlement, disloyalty to the Greek-speaking church, and subversion of the Jewish heritage, as well as the more public charges of causing public disorder and spreading propaganda against the Roman gods. That they might keep **a clear conscience** in such a tangled situation would be a worthy object for prayer, but the practical result the author hopes for is not public exoneration, but the freedom to **be restored to you more quickly.** The author appears to have incorporated the pilgrim mentality sufficiently to be able to keep his balance and his sense of commitment to his community even in the most exasperating circumstances. It is a tough, realistic, and resilient disposition that manifests itself in these verses.

A homiletic benediction in the traditional style of the early church closes the Letter to Pilgrims. As I have shown elsewhere, these benedictions were devised to summarize and conclude sermonic exhortations. Although the form remains relatively constant in the various letters in which such benedictions are found, the content varies according to the situation. This particular benediction contains the interlacing of doctrine and ethics that has been typical for the entire letter. The subject is **the God of peace,** which draws together not only the recent guidelines for harmony within the congregation and "peace with all persons," but also the work of reconciliation that was carried out by God's will in the person of the great high priest. In the context of this Letter to Pilgrims, **peace** is the vital, open dialogue that is given by God in the center of the flux. It is not tranquillity or security. Its dynamic quality derives from God who remains "a consuming fire." The long relative clause in verse 20 develops the theme of this **peace** by showing how it was achieved in the Christ event. Christ is proclaimed here as **the great shepherd of the sheep** who became such **by the blood of a covenant for an aeon.** His sharing of human experience even to the point of death broke the alienation so that believers could follow their **shepherd** along the enduring way of pilgrimage. The emphasis on the dynamic quality of pilgrim leadership comes to a suitable climax here.

The reference to the resurrection in verse 20 has puzzled exegetes, because it is the only such reference in the letter. I would suggest that the widely accepted connotation of the resurrection as a triumph over the cosmic powers is presupposed here. Without reverting to an argumentative tone, the author proclaims the **Lord Jesus** as the one whose resurrection, after having submitted to the worst the principalities and powers could inflict, set humankind at **peace.** This reference would thus be an extension of 2:14-15. If so, the lordship of Christ over the hostile cosmic powers is used here to sustain the idea of **peace** for a pilgrim throng following their **great shepherd of the sheep** through a very unpeaceful world.

What the author prays for in this benediction is that God

will both **equip you** . . . and **work** . . . **in you.** The synergism of true faith is in view here, whereby God provides the grace and guidance that humans need for carrying out pilgrim responsibilities. The willful decision of persons is engaged, but only because they have been liberated and drawn into a personal relationship with God. Pilgrims can therefore never point to the accomplishments of their ethic as their own, for if any good comes out of their muddling through, it is God's doing. Ultimately, it is **Jesus Christ** who should receive the **glory.** And as the **sheep** follow **the great shepherd** along the pilgrim path, their praise is mingled with that of the panegyric assembly that dances and celebrates **for aeons of aeons.** The final **amen**—meaning "May it be so!"—thus partakes of the ecstatic affirmation of the entire cosmic order.

Chapter Fourteen

Postscript from No Lasting City (13:22–25)

13:22 **I** exhort you, brethren, bear with the word of exhortation, for I have written to you briefly. ²³You should know that our brother Timothy has been dispatched, with whom I shall see you if he comes more quickly. ²⁴Greet all your leaders and all the saints. Those who come from Italy greet you. ²⁵The grace be with you all.

As Brooke Foss Westcott states, the final verses of Hebrews "come as a postscript after the close of the letter, when the writer has reviewed what he has said." The terminology and style of these verses indicate they were appended by the author of the letter, not some later editor. Perhaps some of the events mentioned here transpired between the completion of Hebrews and its dispatch. The spirit of these final verses, however, is entirely that of pilgrimage, when the unexpected occurs as a matter of course and there is never time to achieve perfect schemes for letters or sermons. The author refers to his manuscript as a **word of exhortation**, thus placing it in the category of the homily or proclamation that played such a key role in the early church. As the author has defined such an exhortation in 3:13, it is the sort of word one utters to one's **brethren** day by day. Despite its length, the author seems conscious of its shortness and inadequacy: **for I have written to you briefly.** He had referred in 5:11 and in 9:5 to other things he might have said if time allowed, but the flux goes on. Conditions have not allowed that he write at greater length or

241

come to speak his message in person. He has done what he could.

Then follow the details about others in the peripatetic company of the saints. That **Timothy has been dispatched**— using the translation favored by Hans Windisch, James Moffatt, and Walter Bauer—may have been unexpected, since the author relates it here, in contrast to verse 19, with his own return to the congregation. The congregation evidently had expected Timothy to visit them, probably in connection with their recent troubles, but he has apparently not yet arrived. Even here the flux of pilgrimage provides an element of uncertainty: **if he comes more quickly.**

The greetings to congregational members are to be inclusive: **all your leaders and all the saints** are to be sought out and included, whether they are temporarily alienated or not, and no matter what the aberrations of the Lycus Valley heresy might have been. That "no one fail to keep up with the grace of God" (12:15) is taken seriously here, so there is no room for discrimination or heretic baiting. The traveling pilgrims **from Italy** add their greetings. It may seem to be an insignificant detail, but it gives the sense of a worldwide community underway, moving with the flux but holding fast to a sense of togetherness along the way.

The blessing of **grace** ends the Letter to Pilgrims. The words are traditional for the early church, being found in one form or another at the close of most New Testament letters. But the content is consistent with Hebrews as a whole, which had earlier proclaimed how Jesus "by the grace of God" (2:9) undertook the pilgrim existence so that he might lead his people to approach "with boldness . . . the throne of grace" (4:16). Blessing one another with that **grace** confirms and keeps alive the enduring joy of those who are met in the midst of their daily journeying by the city which is to come.

Bibliography

The following bibliography includes all items cited in the commentary, including those suggesting modern implications of the text, that otherwise would not be included in listings of exegetical studies. It also includes a selection of historical and exegetical studies not cited in the text but nevertheless influential in forming my judgments.

Anderson, Charles P. "The Epistle to the Hebrews and the Pauline Letter Collection," *HThR*, Vol. LIX (1966), pp. 429–38.

————. "Hebrews among the Letters of Paul," *Studies in Religion*, Vol. V (1975–76), pp. 258–66.

————. "Who Wrote 'The Epistle from Laodicea'?" *JBL*, Vol. LXXXV (1966), pp. 436–40.

Attridge, Harold W. "'Heard Because of His Reverence' (Heb. 5:7)," *JBL*, Vol. XCVIII (1979), pp. 90–93.

Barclay, William. *The Letter to the Hebrews.* Philadelphia: Westminster Press, 1957, 2d. ed.

Barth, Markus. "The Old Testament in Hebrews: An Essay in Biblical Hermeneutics," *Current Issues in New Testament Interpretation: Essays in Honor of Otto A. Piper.* Ed. W. Klassen and G.F. Snyder. New York: Harper & Row, 1962, pp. 53–78, 263–73.

Bauer, Walter. *The Greek-English Lexicon of the New Testament and Early Christian Literature.* Tr. and adapted by W.F. Arndt and F.W. Gingrich. 2d ed. Chicago: University of Chicago Press, 1979.

Beasley-Murray, G.R. *Baptism in the New Testament.* London: Macmillan Co., 1962.

Betz, Hans Dieter. "Zum religionsgeschichtlichen Verständnis der Apokalyptik," *ZThK*, Vol. LXIII (1966), pp. 391–409.

Bleek, Friedrich, *Der Brief an die Hebräer erläutert durch Einleitung, Uebersetzung und fortlaufenden Commentar.* Berlin: Ferdinand Dummier, 1836.

BIBLIOGRAPHY

Bonhoeffer, Dietrich. *The Cost of Discipleship.* Tr. R.H. Fuller. London: SCM Press, 1959, 2d ed.

Bornkamm, Günther. "Die Häresie des Kolosserbriefes," *Das Ende des Gesetzes. Paulusstudien. Gesammelte Aufsätze.* Munich: Kaiser, 1961, Vol. I, pp. 139–56.

Brandenburger, Egon. "Text und Vorlagen von Hebr. V 7–10. Ein Beitrag zur Christologie des Hebräerbriefes," *NovT*, Vol. XI (1969), pp. 190–224.

Brown, Norman O. *Love's Body.* New York: Random House, 1968.

Bruce, F.F. *Commentary on the Epistle to the Hebrews.* Grand Rapids: Eerdmans, 1970.

Buchanan, George Wesley. "The Present State of Scholarship on Hebrews," *Christianity, Judaism and Other Greco-Roman Cults: Studies for Morton Smith at Sixty,* Vol. 1. Ed. J. Neusner. Leiden: Brill, 1975, pp. 299–330.

_____. *To the Hebrews: A New Translation with Introduction and Commentary.* Garden City, N.Y.: Doubleday, 1972.

Cremer, Hermann. *Biblico-theological Lexicon of New Testament Greek.* Tr. from 2d ed. by W. Urwick. Edinburgh: T. & T. Clark, 1954. Reprinted from the 1878 edition.

Dahl, Nils A. "A New and Living Way: The Approach to God According to Hebrews 10:19–25," *Interpretation,* Vol. V (1951), pp. 401–12.

Davies, J.H., ed. *A Letter to the Hebrews.* Cambridge, Mass.: Cambridge University Press, 1967.

Dibelius, Martin. "Der himmlische Kultus nach dem Hebräerbrief," *Botschaft und Geschichte. Gesammelte Aufsätze,* Vol. 2. Tübingen: Mohr-Siebeck, 1956, pp. 160–76.

Dods, Marcus. *The Epistle to the Hebrews: The Expositor's Greek Testament,* Vol. 4. Ed. W.R. Nicoll. Grand Rapids: Eerdmans, 1951.

Erdman, Charles R. *The Epistle to the Hebrews: An Exposition.* Philadelphia: Westminster Press, 1934.

Fackenheim, Emil. L. "Idolatry as a Modern Religious Possibility," *The Religious Situation: 1968.* Ed. D.R. Cutler. Boston: Beacon Press, 1968, pp. 254–87.

Floor, L. "The General Priesthood of Believers in the Epistle to the Hebrews," *Neotestamentica,* Vol. V (1971), pp. 72–82.

Frankl, Viktor E. *Man's Search for Meaning: An Introduction to Logotherapy.* Tr. I. Lasch. Boston: Beacon Press, 1963, 2d ed.

BIBLIOGRAPHY

Grässer, Erich. *Der Glaube im Hebräerbrief.* Marburg: Elwert, 1965.

_____. "Der Hebräerbrief 1938–1963," *ThR,* Vol. XXX (1964), pp. 138–236.

_____. "Rechtfertigung im Hebräerbrief," *Festschrift für Ernst Käsemann.* Ed. J. Friedrich. *Tübingen: Mohr,* 1976, pp. 79–93.

Hering, Jean. *L'Épître aux Hébreux.* Neuchatel/Paris: Delachaux et Niestlé, 1954.

Hermann, Leon. "L'Épître aux Laodiciens," *Cahiers du Cercle Ernst-Renan,* Vol. XV, 58 (1968), pp. 1–16.

Hillmer, H.R. "Priesthood and Pilgrimage: Hebrews in Recent Research," *Theological Bulletin. McMaster Divinity College,* Vol. V (1969), pp. 67–89.

Hodes, Aubrey. *Martin Buber: An Intimate Portrait.* New York: Viking Press, 1971.

Hoppin, Ruth. *Priscilla, Author of the Epistle to the Hebrews.* New York: Exposition Press, 1969.

Horton, Fred L., Jr. *The Melchizedek Tradition: A Critical Examination of the Sources to the Fifth Century A.D. and in the Epistle to the Hebrews.* Cambridge, Mass.: Cambridge University Press, 1976.

Johnsson, William G. "Issues in the Interpretation of Hebrews," *AUSS,* Vol. XV (1977), pp. 169–87.

_____. "The Pilgrimage Motif in the Book of Hebrews," *JBL,* Vol. XCVII (1978), pp. 239–51.

Jonas, Hans. *The Gnostic Religion: The Message of the Alien God and the Beginnings of Christianity.* Boston: Beacon Press, 1963, 2d ed.

Käsemann, Ernst. *Das wandernde Gottesvolk. Eine Untersuchung zum Hebräerbrief.* Göttingen: Vandenhoeck & Ruprecht, 1959, 3d ed.

Kern, W. "Die antizipierte Entideologisierung oder die 'Weltelemente' des Galater- und Kolosserbriefes heute," *Zeitschrift der Katholischen Theologie,* Vol. XCVI (1974), pp. 185–216.

Koester, Helmut, "Die Auslegung der Abraham-Verheissung im Hebräer 6," *Studien zur Theologie der alttestamentlichen Ueberlieferung. Fest-schrift Gerhard von Rad.* Ed. R. Rendtorff and K. Koch. Neukirchen: Neukirchener, 1961, pp. 95–109.

_____. "Outside the Camp: Hebrews 13. 9–14," *HThR,* Vol. LV (1962), pp. 299–315.

Lähnemann, Johannes. *Der Kolosserbrief. Komposition, Situation*

BIBLIOGRAPHY

und Argumentation. Gütersloh: Gütersloher Verlag, 1971.

Lo Bue, Francesco. "The Historical Background of the Epistle to the Hebrews," *JBL*, Vol. LXXV (1956), pp. 52–57.

Luck, Ulrich. "Himmlisches und Irdisches Geschehen im Hebräerbrief: Ein Beitrag zum Problem des historischen Jesus' im Urchristentum," *NovT*, Vol. VI (1963), pp. 192–215.

Manson, T.W. "The Problem of the Epistle to the Hebrews," *BJRL*, Vol. XXXII (1949), pp. 1–17. Reprinted in *Studies in the Gospels and Epistles*. Ed. M. Black. Manchester: University Press, 1962, pp. 242–58.

Manson, William. *The Epistle to the Hebrews: An Historical and Theological Reconsideration.* London: Hodder & Stoughton, 1951.

Marcel, Gabriel. *Man Against Mass Society.* Tr. G.S. Fraser. Chicago: Gateway Press, 1962.

Marin, Peter. "Children of Yearning," *Saturday Review*, May 6, 1972, pp. 58–63.

May, Rollo. *Love and Will.* New York: W.W. Norton, 1969.

Michel, Otto. *Der Brief an die Hebräer.* Göttingen: Vandenhoeck & Ruprecht, 1957, 10th ed.

Moffatt, James. *A Critical and Exegetical Commentary on the Epistle to the Hebrews.* Edinburgh: T. & T. Clark, 1924.

Montefiore, H.W. *The Epistle to the Hebrews.* London: Adam & Charles Black, 1964.

Narborough, F.D.V. *The Epistle to the Hebrews.* Oxford: Clarendon Press, 1948.

Norden, Eduard. *Agnostos Theos. Untersuchungen zur Formgeschichte religiöser Rede.* Leipzig/Berlin: Tuebner, 1913.

Outler, Albert C. *John Wesley.* New York: Oxford University Press, 1964.

Perdelwitz, R. "Das literarische Problem des Hebräerbriefes," *ZNW*, Vol. XI (1910), pp. 59–78.

Purdy, Alexander C. "Epistle to the Hebrews," *Interpreter's Bible.* Nashville: Abingdon Press, 1955. Vol. 11, pp. 577–763.

Renner, Frumentius. *"An die Hebräer"—ein pseudepigraphischer Brief.* Münsterschwarzach: Vier-Türme Verlag, 1970.

Robinson, Theodore H. *The Epistle to the Hebrews.* London: Hodder & Stoughton, 1933.

Sanders, James A. "Dissenting Deities and Philippians 2:1–11," *JBL*, Vol. LXXXVIII (1969), pp. 279–90.

_____. "Outside the Camp," *USQR*, Vol. XXIV (1969), pp. 239–46.

BIBLIOGRAPHY

Schenke, Hans Martin. "Der Widerstreit gnostischer und kirchlicher Christologie im Spiegel des Kolosserbriefes," *ZThK*, Vol. LXI (1964), pp. 391-402.

_____. "Erwägungen zum Rätzel des Hebräerbriefes," *Neues Testament und christliche Existenz. Festschrift für H. Braun.* Tübingen: Mohr-Siebeck, 1973, pp. 421-37.

Schierse, Franz Joseph. *Verheissung und Heilsvollendung. Zur theologischen Grundfrage des Hebräerbriefes.* Munich: Karl Zink, 1955.

Schille, Gottfried. "Erwägungen zur Hohepriesterlehre des Hebräerbriefes," *ZNW*, Vol. LXVII (1955), pp. 81-109.

_____. "Katechese und Taufliturgie. Erwägungen zu Hbr 11," *ZNW*, Vol. LI (1960), pp. 112-31.

Schlier, Heinrich, "*Parrēsia*," *TDNT*, Vol. V, pp. 871-86.

Schmitz, Otto. "*Thronos*," *TDNT*, Vol. III, pp. 160-67.

Schneidau, Herbert. *Sacred Discontent.* Baton Rouge: Louisiana State University Press, 1976.

Scholem, Gershom G. *Major Trends in Jewish Mysticism.* New York: Schocken, 1961, 3d ed.

Schröger, Friedrich. "Der Gottesdienst der Hebräerbrief," *Münchener Theologische Zeitschrift*, Vol. XIX (1968), pp. 161-81.

_____. *Der Verfasser des Hebräerbriefes als Schriftausleger.* Regensburg: Friedrich Pustet, 1968.

Schweizer, Eduard. "Christ in the Letter to the Colossians," *Review and Expositor*, Vol. LXX (1973), pp. 451-67.

_____. *Der Brief an die Kolosser.* Zurich: Benziger, 1976.

_____. "*Sarx, ktl,*" *TDNT*, Vol. VII, pp. 98-151.

Segal, Alan F. *Two Powers in Heaven: Early Rabbinic Reports about Christianity and Gnosticism.* Leiden: Brill, 1977.

Sowers, Sidney G. *The Hermeneutics of Philo and Hebrews. A Comparison of the Interpretation of the Old Testament in Philo Judaeus and the Epistle to the Hebrews.* Atlanta: John Knox Press, 1965.

Spicq, C. *L'Épitre aux Hebreux.* Paris: Gabalda, 1952-53.

_____. *Vie Chrétienne et Pérégrination selon le Nouveau Testament.* Paris: Cerf, 1972.

Theissen, Gerd. *Untersuchungen zum Hebräerbrief.* Gütersloh: Gerd Mohn, 1969.

Thompson, James W. "Hebrews 9 and Hellenistic Concepts of Sacrifice," *JBL*, Vol. XCVIII (1979), pp. 567-78.

BIBLIOGRAPHY

_____. "The Structure and Purpose of the Catena in Heb. 1:5-13," *CBQ*, Vol. XXXVIII (1976), pp. 352-63.

_____. "That Which Cannot Be Shaken: Some Metaphysical Assumptions of Heb. 12:27," *JBL*, Vol. XCIV (1975), pp. 580-87.

Thüsing, Wilhelm. "'Lasst uns hinzutreten. . .' (Hebr. 10,22). Zur Frage nach dem Sinn der Kulttheologie im Hebräerbrief," *BZ*, Vol. IX (1965), pp. 1-17.

_____. "'Milch' und 'Feste Speise' (I Kor 3, 1f. und Hebr 5, 11-6,3). Elementarkatechese und theologische Vertiefung in neutestamentlicher Sicht," *Trier Theologische Zeitschrift*, Vol. LXXVI (1967), pp. 233-46, 261-80.

Tillich, Paul. *The Protestant Era*. Tr. and concluding essay by J.L. Adams. Chicago: University of Chicago Press, 1948.

Turner, Victor W. and Edith Turner. *Image and Pilgrimage in Christian Perspective: Anthropological Perspectives*. New York: Columbia University Press, 1978.

Van der Woude, A.S. "Melchisedek als himmlische Erlösergestalt in den neugefundenen eschatologischen Midraschim aus Qumran Höhle XI," *Oudtestamentliche Studien*, Vol. XIV (1965), pp. 354-73.

Vanhoye, Albert. *A Structured Translation of the Epistle to the Hebrews*. Translated from the Greek and the French by James Swetnam. Rome: Pontifical Biblical Institute, 1964.

Von Rad, Gerhard. "Es ist noch eine Ruhe vorhanden dem Volke Gottes," *Gesammelte Studien zum alten Testament*. Munich: Kaiser, 1961, pp. 101-08.

Weinel, Heinrich. *Biblische Theologie des Neuen Testaments. Die Religion Jesu und des Urchristentums*. Tübingen: Mohr-Siebeck, 1928, 4th ed.

Westcott, Brooke Foss. *The Epistle to the Hebrews: The Greek Text with Notes and Essays*. London: Macmillan & Co., 1892, 2d ed.

Williamson, Ronald. "The Eucharist and the Epistle to the Hebrews," *NTS*, Vol. XXI (1974-75), pp. 300-12.

_____. *Philo and the Epistle to the Hebrews*. Leiden: Brill, 1970.

Windisch, Hans. *Der Hebräerbrief*. Tübingen: Mohr-Siebeck, 1931, 2d ed.

Wuttke, G. *Melchizedek, der Priesterkönig von Salem. Ein Studie zur Geschichte der Exegese*. Giessen: Töpelmann, 1927; *Beiheft ZNW*, Vol. V.